# OUTRAGEOUS FORTUNE

———

# OUTRAGEOUS FORTUNE

———

BOB MASLEN-JONES

**Whittles Publishing**

*Published by*
**Whittles Publishing**,
Dunbeath Mains Cottages,
Dunbeath,
Caithness, KW6 6EY,
Scotland, UK
www.whittlespublishing.com


Copyright © 2006 R G M Maslen-Jones


ISBN 1-904445-23-3

*Lower front cover photograph by Popperfoto,*
*depicting British soldiers of the Gloucestershire*
*Regiment in Korea on 9th May, 1951.*

*Typeset by*
Samantha Barden

*Printed by*
Bell & Bain Ltd., Glasgow

# CONTENTS

———

## PART ONE
## BOAT TO BOMBAY

———

## PART TWO
## PERSIAN MOUNTAINS AND BURMESE JUNGLE

———

## Part Three
## Progress and Development
—

## Part Four
## The Korean War
—

# Chapter 1

## PLATFORM GOODBYE

———

The morning of 3rd February 1941 had been hectic and a slight hangover from my farewell party the night before had done nothing to help. I hated packing at any time; it reminded me of getting ready to go back to boarding school at the end of the holidays. As I put away my treasured possessions I wondered if I would ever come back and unpack them again. This somewhat sentimental nostalgia was tempered by my eagerness to start climbing the next ladder in my life, as a young British officer in the Indian Army.

A hurried lunch had been interrupted by Philip Dumbell, the father of one of my many schoolboy friends, who called with a bunch of carnations for my mother Kitty. "Oh, I'm so sorry," he said when he saw me standing in the doorway. "I thought you'd have left by now and I've brought a few flowers to cheer your mother up a bit". She had joined us at the front door and this kind gesture reduced her once again to tears; it had been that sort of morning for her as the second of her three sons was leaving home for some far-reaching part of the Empire to fight for King and Country. Ted, my elder brother, had been in the Army since the outbreak of war, but he was comparatively safe in Northern Ireland and neither my father nor mother worried too much about him. But I would be travelling to India by sea, and the first part of the journey would be particularly hazardous as our ship faced the dangers of the U-boat wolf packs prowling in wait in the Atlantic.

Philip had put his arm round Mum's shoulder and kissed her gently on the cheek. As he turned to go, I felt a bit choked as I noticed the tears in his eyes that made me realise what a harrowing time it was for parents. We went back into the dining room and quickly finished our lunch just as the taxi arrived to take us to the station in Wolverhampton.

My father was a consultant gynaecologist and he'd had a very full morning in the operating theatre. He had promised to meet us at the station to see me off and as the taxi drew into the forecourt he was waiting for us. We'd cut it pretty fine, and within a few minutes the Liverpool train emerged from the tunnel and drew slowly alongside the platform, hissing steam as it finally came to a stop. "I'll find you a seat," Dad said as he went towards the nearest carriage. "First class, Dad," I reminded him, laughing, "I'm a gent now, remember". But Dad didn't need reminding, he'd finished the last war as a Lieutenant Colonel in the RAMC and knew the ropes. By the time I'd got my luggage into the guard's van and rejoined my parents there was no time left for idle chatter, which was just as well as Mum was clearly fighting a losing battle to keep a stiff upper lip. A whistle blew and at the rear of the train the guard waved a little green flag above his head; more steam escaped from the engine with an explosive hiss. I hugged my father and mother for the last time and jumped aboard the train as it jerked and slowly pulled away. I leaned out of the carriage window, waving to the receding figures on the platform. Dad stood close to Mum, his arm round her shaking shoulders as at last she sobbed her heart out, releasing all her pent-up emotion.

The train clattered over numerous points and wound its way through factory buildings, soon to be replaced by rows of small houses with their tiny garden sheds, many with *Anderson* corrugated metal air-raid shelters. The picture of my parents comforting each other stuck in my mind. But the great adventure had at last begun, and as the train drew clear of the town and the syncopated rhythm of the wheels on the rails accelerated, I sat back in the corner seat Dad had chosen for me. Relaxing after the hustle and bustle of the morning, I closed my eyes and dozed as my thoughts took me back in a kaleidoscopic trail from some of my earliest memories to the last weeks at school, the family holiday in Connemara during the latter half of August 1939, my year as a medical student at Oxford and in spite of being in a reserved occupation my time in the Army until this very special day when, for the first time in my young life, I was going to be out there in the world entirely on my own.

# Chapter 2

## THE LAST NIGHT OF PEACETIME

———

I was a very active young man, and my father, the son of a missionary in India, had instilled in my two brothers and me a very strict Victorian moral code, and with his wide experience as a gynaecologist, one of his most important strictures was always to treat the opposite sex with the utmost respect. It was very early in my life that I had first become aware of the differences between the sexes, and I remembered how as a four-year-old I had become obsessed with the black stockings my nanny wore. Some four years later I was sent away to The Wells House preparatory school on the Malvern Hills and for some reason it had been arranged that I should start there in the summer term of 1929, which began on Wednesday 30th April. The excitement of going to a new school and being shown round by my brother Ted carried me happily through the Thursday and Friday, but Saturday May 3rd was different. It was my eighth birthday, and suddenly I was homesick and miserable. How could they send me away from home just before such an important day I queried, but Ted had no answer. Even a small parcel from Mum — it turned out to be a John Bull printing set — did nothing to lessen my misery, and I spent the whole day in tears. At the end of this miserable day I cried myself to sleep with my head tucked under the blankets so that the other boys in the dormitory might not hear.

The unhappiness of that day meant that I never quite forgave my parents for such a thoughtless decision, but I soon settled down and really enjoyed the next six years there as I grew up and made many good friends. During my first term at the Wells House I became friendly with John Jowett whose home was in Birmingham, a highly intelligent boy. I also soon became a close friend of another new boy called Ken Spray whose parents lived in India and who was destined to spend his school holidays with his granny in Newport, South Wales.

When we first met, Ken and I took an instant dislike to each other and frequently sought to settle the issue, whatever it was, by fighting. He unsurprisingly won these bouts as he had been brought up in a tough environment where he had learnt the art of street fighting down in Newport. During the first summer holidays, my parents arranged a party for Ted and me in our 4-acre garden and amongst several other local friends, they invited John Jowett who, unknown to us, had Ken Spray staying with him for a few days. It turned out to be a really enjoyable afternoon. When it was time to say good-bye Ken shook my hand firmly and at the start of the autumn term he wasted no time in seeking me out. He had so enjoyed the afternoon he spent with us that he rather fancied being a member of the family! We became firm friends, and before the Christmas holiday my father had become Ken's legal guardian, and our lives became closely linked until adulthood. He had, in effect, become another brother.

Great empathy developed between my father and I who was always willing to spend time listening to my questions and problems. He had that wonderful knack of being able to explain what life was all about, and when he wasn't on his beloved golf course on a Sunday afternoon, we would go for long walks in the Shropshire countryside. This afforded him an excellent opportunity to listen to our varied doubts and worries as we grew up, and to put our problems into proper perspective. For me this empathy really began when I was still at prep school. One of my well-meaning missionary aunts who was home on leave from India had given me a book entitled *What Every Young Boy Should Know*. Amongst other things it made dire threats to adolescent boys about the dangers of masturbation, warning them of eternal damnation and that if they persisted in the practice they would contract some foul disease and probably go mad. I was then only 12 years old and had just reached that stage of sexual development, and as I read the book in bed one evening I became absolutely terrified and with tears streaming down my face, I had called to Mum from the landing. Later, sitting on the arm of Dad's chair in the sitting room, I had calmed down as he explained about the 'birds and the bees', and in the process completely refuted the frightening threats contained in the book.

At the Wells House, I became a very keen rifle shot, at first with air rifles and then with .22 bores, and I was also in the rugby fifteen for two seasons. But my lifetime love of mountains and the glorious feeling of freedom that only such wide-open spaces can provide, was born. The freedom provided by the school supplied many memories of the Malvern Hills. On Sunday afternoons we were given a well-known landmark to walk to, and it was up to us to choose whom we were going to walk with, and which way to go. We were free to enjoy all about us and we felt truly sorry for those children who were so regimented that they had to walk in pairs and who looked invariably bored. As long as we reached the target and returned safely in time for tea, all was well, and it was rare for anyone to be late back.

I passed the Common Entrance exam to Oundle School in Northamptonshire without much difficulty and I started there at the beginning of the summer term in 1935. My brother Ted had already been there for 18 months and I looked forward to being shown the ropes by him.

The evening before I started my first term, my father and I sat together in the sitting room of our eight-bedroom country home on the western boundary of

Wolverhampton, and Dad gave me some sound advice that I was never to forget. Life is like a game of Snakes and Ladders, he explained, the ladders represented the many stages in one's life, and as I was starting at a new school the next day, I would be at the bottom of a ladder. "After that there will be a whole series of ladders," he said, "school, university, and then if you still want to be a surgeon, medical school followed by your professional life until you have retired and are growing old. When you reach the top of one ladder you have to start again at the bottom of the next. It is a recurring process throughout your life, and on every ladder, as in the game, there will be individuals ready to send you crashing to the bottom. You must always be watchful for these people, motivated by envy or spite, are treacherous and often attack when you least expect it. So be cautious about whom you choose to be your friends, keep those you do not like very much at arms length, and if you are hurt in any way, take it on the chin, brush the hurt aside and climb back up the ladder."

I spent four very happy years at Oundle, and from an early age I had made up my mind to try to be as good and famous a surgeon as my father. When I left at the end of July 1939, I had achieved much to my credit. I had been awarded my school colours for rifle shooting, boxing, swimming and rugby. I was a house prefect, and secretary of the school Natural History Society. My keenness in rifle shooting soon became noticed, and I had first shot for the school at Bisley during my first summer term when I was only 14 years old. I didn't miss a Bisley Schools meeting during the five summer terms I was at Oundle and I was captain of shooting for my final two years. At boxing I was more brawn than brain and went into the ring intent on a quick knockout of my opponent. I actually hated the sport but had been persuaded, against my better judgement, to box for the house and I had fought so hard that I was selected to box for the school as a middleweight. I won some of my fights and lost some, but I was satisfied that even if I lost in a school match, I gained a point for the school just for getting into the ring. I was soon to learn that my priorities were completely wrong in this respect, but the persuasive powers of Major Butcher, who commanded the OTC and was in charge of boxing, left me with no option but to get into the ring whatever the odds! My boxing career was soon cut short when I was told that Bedford didn't have a middleweight in their team, but that if I went into the ring against their heavyweight, I would gain a point even if knocked out! I did what was expected of me, and early in the first round of a three-round fight I ran into a mighty straight left which shattered the bridge of my nose, leaving it squashed and flattened. Although I could not breathe properly, I survived the next two rounds without being knocked down, and the school got their point. As soon as I got back to Oundle, I reported to the school doctor who did precisely nothing, and the broken bones were allowed to fuse together. At the end of term, Dad noticed that I couldn't breathe properly. When he heard my story he was livid and threatened to sue the school, but eventually he was persuaded by my housemaster not to take such extreme action as it would adversely affect the careers of both Ted and me. I had to undergo a very painful operation in which my nose was re-broken and manipulated into some sort of shape, but it never quite looked the same again.

In the swimming pool I was equally good at the crawl and backstroke, and on the rugby field I played in the second row of the scrum. During the summer of 1938, Dad was playing golf with Major Frank Buckley, the manager of Wolverhampton Wanderers Football Club, and he had been telling the Major that he hoped all three of us would be playing in the Oundle School Rugby XV in the autumn. At the end of their game, Major Buckley told Dad to send the three of us to Molyneux Ground every day, for fitness training, and after our summer holiday we spent five weeks not only getting into top condition, but also learning much about the 'other' game. In this we were joined by Keith James who had been at kindergarten with me and who was at Shrewsbury School where the preferred game was soccer. In fact Ted, Ken and I were all in the XV together when Oundle was unbeaten by any other school for the third successive year, something we were very proud of.

Academically I had done reasonably well and had got a place at New College, Oxford, where I planned to do the first half of my medical training before going on to Middlesex Hospital where Dad had been trained. I had also been interested in the Officer's Training Corps and had become a cadet Regimental Sergeant Major, almost the highest rank a schoolboy soldier could reach.

I tried to show great determination in whatever I undertook, and I had been brought up to work hard and play hard. My main ambition in the short term was to get a 'Blue' for Rugby, and in the long term to be a brilliant surgeon. The fact that a nasty little man called Hitler was making threatening demands for *lebensraum* for the German people had not yet made me contemplate that my carefully charted career might have to be abandoned. After all, Hitler had made the same demands in 1938 and Prime Minister Neville Chamberlain had sorted him out then, so why shouldn't he do the same again?

During the first two weeks of the vacation I spent many carefree days on the golf course or going to tennis parties, and it was not long before I found myself becoming very attracted to a girl I had known and liked since we were at kindergarten together. I had never previously given her a serious thought, although she was always good fun at dances and parties. Now that my libido had developed, my interest in the opposite sex was something I had to reckon with, and I began to 'set my cap at her'.

Joy was the only daughter of very well-to-do parents. Her father was chairman of a big lock-making business and he and her mother adored her, although they were careful not to spoil her. She had been promised her own 'runabout' if she passed her driving test, but only if she passed her School Certificate, which would be at least 18 months ahead.

As the train sped northwards towards Crewe, my thoughts switched to that wonderful family holiday on the west coast of Ireland during the last few weeks of peace. Ted had left Oundle in 1938, and had spent part of the year as an assistant at the Rothamsted Agricultural Research Establishment near Harpenden. The rest of the time he worked on a farm near Pattingham in Shropshire to gain practical experience before going up to Oxford in the autumn of 1939, to read Agriculture. He had matured during that year, and the very close bond between him and me that had developed at school had grown even stronger now we were apart. Our brother, Freddie, was four years younger and had only spent one term with me at Oundle before I left. Because of the difference in our ages we had very little in common and didn't share the same interests. Freddie was far from being a robust boy like Ted and me; he suffered badly from asthma and hayfever, and from his earliest days this condition had called for rather more maternal attention than was good for him. Inevitably he developed into a bit of a 'mother's boy' and usually managed to get almost anything he wanted. It was not surprising that he developed a philosophy of 'there's plenty more where that came from' and he didn't find it difficult to surround himself with friends, albeit not all of the right sort.

The long, hot, sunny days during the latter half of August 1939 had been great fun. My parents knew that this holiday would almost certainly be the last the family would spend together as Ted and I were likely to want to spend our time with fellow undergraduates or perhaps even girlfriends. We were staying as paying guests in a large country house near the village of Moyard in Connemara. Our hosts had moved there from the English-shires during the depression of the early 1930s, and they had two very attractive daughters. Anne, the younger of the two, lived with her parents, looked after the hunters and worked on the home farm when an extra pair of hands was needed. It was an ideal way of life for her, and when they had guests staying, she was available to show them the countryside from the saddle. Phillipa was happily married to Captain Robert Cooper, a career soldier in the Irish Guards, and they were spending a few weeks with her parents before the Regiment sailed for a tour of duty in Egypt. Robert stood a full six feet four inches, had fair hair and blue eyes and was a splendid catch for any girl.

Ted and I enjoyed long rides together, and I remembered how when we were hacking along Cleggan beach Ted had suddenly shouted, "Race you to that cowpat at the end". We had gone off at a mad gallop, and I rode hard right up to the finishing mark to beat Ted by a neck, only to realise that I couldn't stop my hyped-up horse. Anne had not warned us that this particular horse was a retired chaser and that once he was racing he took a hell of a lot of stopping! Two hundred yards was far too short a gallop in any case, and we careered into the rocks, the poor animal grazing his legs on the coral and me ending up on the ground with all the skin scraped off my right forearm. There was no more riding after that, Anne quite rightly deciding that we were too inexperienced and she couldn't risk her valuable horses with us. In future if we wanted to ride, she would go with us. We had lost a lot of face and didn't ride there again.

With only three days of the holiday left, Dad took Ted and me for a day's fishing on Lough Derryclare. He had become uncharacteristically subdued and pensive during the morning and at lunch Ted asked, "What's the matter, Dad, you're very quiet today?" The question gave Dad the opening he wanted. "I've deliberately avoided any talk about what's going on in Europe," he said, "as I wanted this fortnight to be a really happy one right to the end. Something we could all remember for the rest of our lives. But this morning Robert was urgently recalled to his battalion, and I heard on the wireless that things are boiling up over there in Europe and while we have been burying our heads in the sand here, German troops have been massing on the Polish border, and the French have mobilised. Our own reservists have been called to the colours, Robert has left in a hurry and I'm dreadfully afraid we're careering headlong into a war we all know Britain isn't prepared for."

Suddenly the happiness of the holiday was overshadowed by what Dad had said, and we all wanted to get back home to face whatever the future might hold for us. At least young Freddie might be spared having to fight, at any rate for a few years, but Ted and I would be involved. Dad insisted that we should keep a sense of proportion and finish the day's fishing, and that there was nothing to be gained by rushing back to Moyard. There was no cause to panic, and until we knew the final outcome of the ultimatum and messages that were already flying round the world, we should carry on as normal, however difficult that might be.

We had planned to drive up to Belfast and take the ferry from there on the night of Saturday September 2nd, and Dad decided to stick to the schedule. On the Friday morning we drove away from Moyard and headed north past Kylemore Abbey, then through Westport, Charlestown and Sligo to the Ulster border at Blacklion-Belcoo. For some extraordinary reason the early morning Irish news bulletins made no mention of the situation on the Polish border, and whenever we stopped for coffee or petrol the locals assured us with unfounded optimism, "There'll be no war, you'll see". Even at Blacklion customs post the news had not reached them, but only a few yards over the border at Belcoo the story was quite different. "Didn't you know?" they said, "the Germans invaded Poland early this morning and they've been dive-bombing Warsaw and other cities continuously all day". Dad suddenly felt sick in the pit of his stomach; his worst fears were realised and quietly we drove on to Portrush, barely aware of the lovely countryside through which we were passing.

Dad had booked rooms in a hotel overlooking the Giant's Causeway, and at dinner he quipped 'eat, drink and be merry, for tomorrow – who knows?' He had stopped himself before uttering the fatal words 'ye die', for experience told him that many a true word is spoken in jest. Next morning we drove to Belfast and after dinner on board the ferry, we listened to the 9 o'clock news. The attacks on Poland had continued with unabated ferocity both from the air and on the ground where the Polish horsed cavalry's naked courage was no match for the German panzers which continued to drive deep into their territory showing mercy to no one, military and civilian alike. Long streams of slow-moving refugees constantly came under air attack from Stuka dive-bombers creating chaos and panic. By now there was little left standing in the centre of Warsaw and other cities, and only the magnificent bravery of the Polish army did anything to slow the relentless German advance. At home the British government had been in constant consultation with the French, Dutch and Belgians, and had issued a final ultimatum to Hitler to cease hostilities by 11:00 on Sunday September 3rd.

Sleep did not come easily that night. The bunks were narrow and uncomfortable, and the vibration of the turbines added to the difficulty. Well into the small hours of the night my thoughts were of the future and how our family might be affected. The way ahead was full of doubts and uncertainties, and Dad worried throughout the hours of darkness for his two elder sons, and how Britain could possibly survive another war. Of one thing he was certain, that life would never be the same again.

We were all glad to see dawn breaking and after an early breakfast we were soon on our way out of Liverpool through the Mersey tunnel, heading for the Midlands and home. We knew that the Prime Minister, Neville Chamberlain, was going to broadcast to the Nation at 11 o'clock that morning, and Dad decided to drive as far as Newport in Shropshire, where we would stop for coffee and listen to the broadcast.

I remembered the Prime Minister's sombre tone and his last few words as though it had been only yesterday. "I have to tell you that no such undertaking has been received and that this country is now at war with Germany." There followed the National Anthem, and everyone in the crowded room stood, some of the older ones who had seen it all before were overcome by emotion and silently wept. There was a strained silence as we all tried to absorb what we had just heard, those of Dad's age appearing suddenly older as they re-lived August 14th 1914. That had been within a few weeks of Dad qualifying at Middlesex Hospital, and he had enlisted immediately in the RAMC.

"Come on, chaps," Dad had said, struggling to hide the turmoil in his mind, "let's get home and sort things out". As we left the hotel lounge an elderly man stood up and clasped first Ted's hands and then mine, wishing us good luck and a safe journey. We both knew what he meant. Meanwhile Mum went out to the car, her arm round young Freddy's shoulders, a gesture of maternal protection for her third son. When pregnant with him she had been convinced he was going to be the daughter she had so longed for. The rest of the journey home was quiet and gloomy, the gravity of the situation matched by the weather.

I sat back in the corner of the back seat, and thought about whether I should join up immediately or carry on with my planned career at Oxford. "We'll need plenty of doctors, son," Dad replied when I suggested the former, "and I think you'll find that as a registered medical student you'll be in a reserved occupation which means they won't accept you in the forces so the question will be answered for you". I thought how disappointed I might be if most of my peers went off to fight, leaving me behind to carry on with my studies. It even occurred to me that I might be given a white feather by some over-zealous patriot, and I almost gnashed my teeth at the thought of such a gratuitous insult. I felt deeply that I couldn't let Ted go off to war whilst I stayed behind, possibly working alongside a 'conchy'. Dad calmed some of my fears by saying that he doubted very much whether the Army could possibly cope with everyone who wanted to join up at once and anyway I would probably find that there would be a minimum age limit to enlist.

Ted had already made up his mind what he would do. He was certain to be called up anyway, and as he was over 19, there would be no question of any age limit for him. The next day he would go to the local TA centre and enlist in the Field Regiment, Royal Artillery in which several of his friends were already serving and he reckoned that with his Certificate A from the school Officers Training Corps, he should be able to get himself earmarked early on as a potential officer. I remembered how excited Ted had been when he came home for lunch after enlisting as a gunner, and it had been only two days later that the Regiment had mobilised under canvas on Cannock Chase. Early in October they moved to Northern Ireland, and Ted had been sent to an Officer Cadet training unit in Yorkshire. Six months later he came home on leave, proudly wearing his second lieutenant's pips on his shoulders. It was quite a coincidence that he rejoined his regiment at Limavaddy some 20 miles from Londonderry and Portrush, where the family had spent the last night of peacetime together at the end of our Irish holiday. It was ironic that a year later I was on my way to embark for India while Ted was still training in Britain.

# Chapter 3

## FROM STUDENT TO OFFICER

———

I put aside all thoughts of joining up and I went to Oxford as planned. I joined the University Senior Training Corps to keep my hand in, but my hope of getting a Rugby blue, even a wartime one, had been forgotten in the general excitement of starting a new life and making new friends. I had been particularly pleased when I discovered that Ian Beddows, one of my earliest childhood friends, was also going up to Oxford having been advised to undertake a short degree course before enlisting.

Ian's father had managed to 'acquire' sufficient petrol coupons to drive the two of us to Oxford. He was a retired Royal Artillery colonel who sported a monocle and was kind. He took us to lunch at the Mitre Hotel, an old coaching establishment in The High, and then left us to settle into our respective colleges before driving the 90 miles home.

It took me a few days to find my feet in my new surroundings. I knew only one other fresher in New College whom I had met when I came up to be interviewed and take the college entrance exam. He had a triple-barrelled, aristocratic name and had been at Eton. So for me it was a matter of gradually forming a new circle of friends. During my first week, I had been summoned to meet the warden, my academic tutor, and my moral tutor who would be responsible for my general well-being and guidance. I had entered the latter's study to see a rather podgy middle-aged little man peering at me through incredibly thick steel-rimmed spectacles. He held out his limp, fleshy hand, and as I recall, it felt like a warm, wet fish. The reverend doctor of divinity spoke in a lilting, effeminate manner and I took an immediate dislike to him. The hand-shaking over, he squeezed my biceps and said, "You *are* a strong young man, aren't you?" The interview was as short as I could make it, and when I turned to leave, he suggested that I should have a glass of sherry with him sometime. I decided that 'moral tutor' was a possible misnomer and that I would give him as wide a berth as possible.

Ian's college, Exeter, was quite close to New College, and during that year we saw a great deal of each other and became very close friends. Sunday afternoon tea was a permanent event when the two of us always had hot toasted crumpets with any butter we'd managed to save from our meagre ration during the week. By careful budgeting, we could afford to have a good lunch together every now and then at either the Mitre or the Randolph, but these were rare treats. During one of our Sunday afternoon teas in Ian's room I suddenly noticed thick smoke seeping into the room under the door. The room was at the top of a very narrow, steep wooden staircase, and the dormer windows opened on to a stone parapet that was covered with frozen snow. I had opened the door to see how bad the smoke was, but the whole stairway was full of thick, pungent blackness, and I quickly shut it again. I tied a wet towel over my mouth and nose, and once again opened the door to try to escape down the stairs. It was a stupid and futile thing to do, and after a few steps I was forced back coughing and spluttering, into the comparative sanctuary of Ian's room. In the meantime Ian had opened the windows and leaning out over the parapet was shouting "FIRE!" at the people in the street below. Thinking that no one had taken us seriously, we climbed out and leaning backwards onto the snow-covered roof with our feet against the icy parapet, we started edging our way along as far from the window as we could. The fire brigade soon arrived and dealt with the outbreak, reduced by then to the smouldering remains of a sofa on the ground floor. As soon as the smoke had cleared, a fireman had come up to check that everyone on the staircase was all right, and he helped Ian and me back into the room where we finished our crumpets, now cold and clammy and completely spoiled. It could so easily have been a very different story and we were thankful that we had avoided the effects of the poisonous smoke.

Apart from rationing and the blackout, life went on as usual. However, daily reports of merchant ship losses in the Atlantic reminded us that someone, somewhere, was paying a high price for our continued relatively peaceful existence. The land battle in Western Europe had not yet been joined and this strange situation had already been dubbed 'The Phoney War'.

In 1940, Ian and I had both joined our respective college Conservative Associations and become active organisers of our college programmes. Communism, or anything politically left wing, was complete anathema to us, and when the Oxford City Labour Party announced its intention to stage a May Day rally and march through the streets, no one objected very much. But when the University Labour and Communist Associations made it clear that they were going to join in, the Conservatives decided to do all they could to prevent them. After all, at that time Russia had entered the war alongside Germany, and to us the Red Flag was as bad as the Nazi swastika. The City Labour Party was warned not to allow the Communists to join their march, otherwise the Conservatives would physically oppose them along the whole route. Sadly the Labour Party took no notice, and when they proudly marched over Magdalen Bridge, the Conservatives were out in force to try to remove any Red banners being paraded. The decision to allow the University Communists to take part was astonishing, especially considering the recent duplicity of the Russians in siding with the Germans.

A group of skirmishers armed with over-ripe fruit and vegetables and far from fresh eggs, all of which had been given by local trades people, stood in wait outside Magdalen College and as the marchers came across the bridge a barrage of unpleasant missiles was hurled at them. My friends and I were in the front rank and I was greatly surprised to see some from my college whom I had previously regarded as being a bit 'wet' and rather prissy throwing themselves wholeheartedly into the battle. I spotted a big red-headed Scot from New College called Archie Bell who was always creating strife in the junior common room with his extreme left-wing opinions, and I took immense delight in seeing a rather overripe orange score a direct hit on his face. His look of rage was frightening, but I don't believe that Archie ever knew who threw it.

As the rally, which heavily outnumbered the anti-communist demonstrators, pressed onwards up The High to Carfax, they were subjected to continuing attacks in the street, and missiles of all sorts were thrown from windows on both sides. The intention of the Conservatives was to get at the Reds and as far as possible to avoid involving the real workers whose march it was and whose work in the factories was so vital to the war effort. This ploy seemed to be fairly successful and many of the Labour Party marchers coming along behind rather enjoyed their immunity.

A few days later the phoney war came to an end and fighting suddenly burst into life in western Europe, as soldiers and civilians alike took the brunt of the massive onslaught by the Germans into France, Belgium, Holland, Denmark and Norway. Cities came under terrible air attack, and the allied armies were hurled back in the face of the unrelenting blitzkrieg. Now that Germany and Russia were fighting on the same side, and Italy had allied herself to Germany to form the 'axis' right across Europe, things looked almost beyond hope. My friends and I became very restless, weighed down by a feeling of utter helplessness and fear for the future. When the Local Defence Volunteers was formed, we all joined, but it seemed that word had gone out that preference should be given to older men rather than undergraduates, and in any case there were no weapons available. The force had been set up in great haste and it took a long time to settle down and get itself properly organised, eventually being renamed The Home Guard.

America was morally on Britain's side and was generous with all sorts of help, notably the 'lend/lease' arrangement. An act of congress was passed in 1941 allowing the President to order any defence article for any country whose defence was deemed vital to the USA. One of the early land/lease agreements was the loan of 50 destroyers used in the Battle of the Atlantic. However, there was still a strong isolationist element in the United States that had to be persuaded that the ideology of taking sides was mistaken. Only then could any of their armed forces be committed to battle. Notwithstanding that, many fine young Americans saw it as their duty to protect freedom and democracy, and join the fight as volunteers. Quite soon an Eagle fighter squadron was formed to take its part alongside the RAF against the Luftwaffe when the time came.

The end of the phoney war and the desperate rescue from the beaches of Dunkirk introduced anxiety into the even tenor of university life. Whilst the miracle rescue of so many of our troops was taking place, word got round that the first batch of the BEF was to be accommodated in Cowley Barracks, on the outskirts of Oxford, and I stood aghast as a column of tired, dirty and dejected soldiers, some with blood-stained bandages covering their wounds, shuffled its way from Oxford railway station and down the High towards Cowley Barracks, for there was no transport to carry them. The same evening Ian and I took a punt and polled slowly up the river Cherwell to one of our favourite pubs. We had both been very shocked at what we had seen that morning – the remnants of a once proud professional army, our own army, coming home as if it were a rabble. As we sipped our pints, we clearly understood that Britain was on her own, with her back against the wall.

In the beer garden on that fine, peaceful summer evening, there were other soldiers who claimed that they too had been snatched from the jaws of captivity or death at Dunkirk, and they were full of bravado and boasting how they were ready to go back and have another go at Adolf. Ian and I had been impressed by the spirit of those men that had obviously been raised by more than a few pints of English ale, and as we punted homewards down the placid river we felt that all was not yet lost. Spurred on by Churchill's fighting call to the nation, offering nothing less than blood, toil, sweat and tears, we decided like hundreds of other undergraduates that the time had come to join up. Ahead of us was a long vacation, and it seemed that the need for our services was now. Notwithstanding my reserved occupation status, I joined a group of my closest chums, many of them medical students like me, and went to London with them to enlist as a potential officer in the Brigade of Guards. Ian had been persuaded to stay on for another year, and enlist when he had taken his short wartime degree. Those of us who went to London were all accepted but were then told that the minimum age for enlistment was still nineteen and a half, and as I had only just passed my nineteenth birthday it would be another five months before I would be called to the colours. When I returned to college, I did as much revision as I could for my exams, but otherwise I tried to carry on as normal for my last week or two at University.

I only just scraped through my exams, and after taking the last paper, I formally 'signed out' and went down. The warden had been very understanding, and said that in my position he would have done the same, but he very much regretted that the academic studies of all those who had made the same decision would be so disrupted. He promised me that my place in college would be waiting for me when the war was over.

My arrival home for what my father and mother naturally thought would be the long vacation was going to be traumatic. "Dad," I said, "I've joined the Guards and I will be reporting for duty at Caterham towards the end of the year". Dad just stared at me, not wanting to believe what he had just heard. He had hoped so much that I would be able to finish my medical studies and follow in his footsteps, and with his memories of what happened in war, he didn't believe that, as I had put it, it would only be a short break in my studies. He remembered so many of his contemporaries who had done the same thing but, because the war had dragged on for so long, had given up the idea of going back to read medicine long before the war had ended. Dad realised that the way things were going, if Britain managed to survive at all it would be years before we could possibly turn the tide and eventually secure victory. We could only do that if America came in on our side with the full might of their armed forces. Dad knew it would be no good arguing with me; the die was cast and disappointed as he was, he and Mum accepted my decision and gave me all the love, affection and encouragement they could. But first he had said, "I think you have made a mistake, son. We're going to need doctors, and this war isn't going to be over, as you seem to think, within a year or two. It may drag on for years or more and you'd be qualified long before that." I explained how I felt about being left behind at university when my friends had gone off to fight, and I told him how I had felt when I saw the troops come back from Dunkirk. I looked my father straight in the eye and asked him, "What would you have done, Dad?" After a few moments he replied, "A good question, son. I'd almost certainly have done the same." And I remembered the warm embrace of father and son as he added, "We're very proud of you". Ian was not too happy to have been persuaded to remain at the University to complete his degree, and sadly we said a warm and sincere farewell to each other. We had become the closest of friends and I wondered whether our paths would ever cross again.

The call came much sooner than I had expected. It didn't take those in the War Office long to realise that the task they faced in rapidly rebuilding and expanding the shattered Army was going to demand a much larger number of young officers than they had originally planned. By July, letters were going out calling forward those who had volunteered and were on the waiting list, and I was instructed to report at the end of the month to Caterham Barracks, the Guards depot on the southern outskirts of London and only a few miles from Kenley RAF fighter station. I joined my friends in the brigade squad where, although we were potential officers, we were treated every bit as severely as other trainees, and my first impressions were something of a culture shock. The platoon sergeant was a Welsh Guards reservist who had been recalled to the colours from his second career in the Metropolitan Police, and our 'trained soldier', guardsman Birchenall, was responsible for 'nursemaiding' the squad to show us the ropes. His was a daunting responsibility, although most of his recruits were excellent officer material and gave him their full support. There were one or two, however, for whom I had little or no time and who seemed to have no initiative. The more senior ranks such as the Company Sergeant Major and the Company Commander had all been medically downgraded, but the young subalterns were only recently commissioned into the Brigade and they regarded a posting to Caterham as a welcome stepping stone before joining one of the front line battalions.

It was made clear at the outset that no recruit would be allowed out of barracks until the squad had passed the Commanding Officer's inspection which normally took place after five weeks of hard, unremitting square-bashing, and the only recreation the squaddies could look forward to was an evening visit to the NAAFI canteen where Tolly ale was always particularly drinkable. One member of the squad, David Thorpe, a man in his mid-thirties, who had already 'gone to seed' through his self-indulgent lifestyle in London had enjoyed a privileged life. He had joined up to avoid his inevitable call-up as a conscript where there would be no possible chance of him pulling any strings. He had found the going terribly hard, particularly on the square, with his fat, flabby body pouring out pints of evil-smelling sweat as the drill sergeants did their best to make or break him. At times he sobbed with sheer exhaustion as he was kept at it up and down the parade ground until he got a particular movement right. His sheer courage in keeping going evoked a great deal of genuine sympathy amongst the rest of us until his first private hamper from Fortnum and Mason arrived, delivered in his own Rolls Royce. Never once did David offer any of his luxurious fare to anyone in the barrack room, not even the one or two who fawned on him in the vain hope of getting a few crumbs from the rich man's hamper, and sympathy for him soon evaporated. In the end it had been to no avail and when the training period was over he failed to pass out, was medically downgraded, and became a clerk. I had been one of those who had sympathised to some extent with David, and although I had been a bit envious, jealous almost, that someone like him should inherit and enjoy so much wealth, it was obvious that most felt that his meanness had been well rewarded.

After Dunkirk and Churchill's rallying cry to the people, an invasion attempt was thought to be imminent and as reports of massive concentrations of German troops, equipment and barges in and around the French channel ports were confirmed by aerial reconnaissance, the likelihood of an attack increased daily even though the Luftwaffe had not yet made any effort to soften up the defences. At the depot, where there were some 5000 recruits and staff, rumour had it that there was only one serviceable Bren gun, and there were certainly not enough rifles to go round. By mid-August, shipments of P14 (1914 pattern) rifles started to arrive from Canada, and gradually the weapons needed to defend the country became more readily available and broomsticks were relegated to their cupboards.

On August 15th 1940, I had my first taste of what war was like. During the morning the squad was on the short range a quarter of a mile away on waste ground at the rear of the depot when air-raid sirens began to wail somewhere away to the south. The alarm was soon taken up by local sirens and then those to the north *en route* to London joined the cacophony of undulating sounds. The duty bugler inside the depot could now be heard sounding the alert (a repetitive sound to which the words 'there's a bomber overhead' were quickly coined). We were ordered to double back to our slit trenches behind the barrack block, but this seemed completely illogical as the range was well away from any possible target. We had a grandstand view of the air battle that had been joined right above us as the young RAF pilots went tearing into the fifteen German bombers which were heading straight for Croydon aerodrome. Suddenly one of the escorting Messerschmidts that had broken off its engagement with a Spitfire belched smoke from its engine and the pilot ejected before the plane crashed a short distance beyond the range. The pilot hit the ground rather hard and as we raced over to where he was struggling to stand up, he feebly raised his arms in surrender. It was apparent that he had broken his leg, and with a hastily bodged up stretcher made with rifles and capes, we carried him to the depot hospital. I was still present when the medical officer examined the young pilot, and although he was at pains to treat him as one of our own, all he got from the arrogant young German was filthy abuse and the declaration that the war was almost over and he would soon get expert treatment back home. The MO, to my surprise and admiration, kept his cool, although the German got a good deal of abuse in turn from the medical sergeant and his staff.

My colleagues and I left the hospital to go to the trenches, but by now the battle was all but over. The bombers never reached their target, as one after another they were shot out of the sky. It was a tremendous start to what came to be known as The Battle of Britain, and it did much to raise the morale of the whole nation.

The Germans, however, were undeterred by the failure of their first daylight raid on London and for the next three weeks they continued to use the same strategy day after day, trying to knock out airfields and industry. They scored some spectacular successes and I remember one particular fine, sunny day when I was number two on a Bren gun manned by a trained guardsman, and the two of us watched from our sand-bagged emplacement as a huge formation of bombers with escorting fighters flew right above us heading for the Vickers factory at Weybridge. The RAF fighters soon joined battle, but the number of escorting Messerschmits was so great that they were able to prevent the Spitfires and Hurricanes getting at the bombers. The pilot of a burning Spitfire had to bale out, and as he parachuted down, his assailant followed him and circling round and round the helpless man, riddled him with machine-gun fire. We heard later that the bombers struck their target as shifts were changing over and inflicted a large number of casualties in addition to severely damaging the factory itself. Night raids soon took over as the main tactic in the pre-invasion softening up process, and blackout precautions assumed the greatest importance and demanded the utmost vigilance, whilst ARP wardens ceased to be figures of fun and were at last taken seriously.

Kenley aerodrome, one of the main fighter bases in the defence of the capital, was only four miles from Caterham and came in for a great deal of attention from the Luftwaffe whose planes time and again swept in low over the Guards depot as they headed for their target. Every time this happened, whether at night or during the day, the bugler sounded the alarm and those inside the depot found themselves spending much of their time crouching in the bottom of air-raid trenches. The training programme was disrupted to some extent and most of us felt that we were sitting ducks with no means of hitting back; unsurprisingly morale was not at all good. On a night in early September we had been in our trenches for over an hour when the all clear sounded. It was then about 10:30 pm, and I remarked to the man next to me, "That's bloody silly, I can still hear that bomber up there." But the order had been given to return to the barrack room and I sat on my bed, still wearing my steel helmet, listening for the bomber that I thought was still around. The silence was suddenly shattered by a bellow, "Put that bloody light out!" but it was too late. Within seconds violent explosions followed the screech of falling bombs, shaking the building and filling the air with dust and acrid fumes. I had dived under my bed where I stayed for some minutes, listening to the mayhem outside the block as rescue squads rushed to the scene. We were ordered outside to help in the rescue work and were told that Victoria block had received a direct hit and at least half the two storey block had simply disappeared leaving a 15 foot crater in the ground. There was little to be done as everyone in the building had been blown to eternity, and as there was no doubt that there would be some unexploded bombs in the area, we were ordered back to the trenches where we spent a very uncomfortable night. Soon after dawn we were allowed back into the barrack room where we waited, tired and frightened, until the breakfast call was sounded. As we made our way to the mess hut we saw the full horror of what had happened; there were mattresses, severed limbs, bodies and other horrors hanging in the trees and no one had any appetite for greasy bacon and eggs.

It soon became known that the squad in Victoria block had been on their 'passing-out' weekend leave and had arrived back at the depot while the original alert was still on and they had sheltered in trenches near the main gate. When the all clear sounded they made their way back to their barrack room and switched on the lights. As the room had been unoccupied until that moment, the blackout had not been fixed and a vast flash of light suddenly shone out of all the windows. It was then that a vigilant sergeant major had to douse the light, but it was too late. The stalking bomber suddenly saw an unmissable target, let go his bombs and the whole squad of 24 men was annihilated.

Two days later was Sunday and as usual the choice was either to go on church parade or do fatigues. I found religion a great source of strength and comfort and I always chose church parade as did most of my fellow squaddies. As I filed into the chapel the one Sergeant Major I simply couldn't abide was standing just inside the door, and as I walked to a vacant pew near the front of the chapel I felt his eyes following me. I sat down next to a young soldier who was clearly a new recruit, said my prayers and sat up. I put my peaked cap under my seat and glanced round to see the Sergeant Major's eyes still glaring at me and wondered what on earth I might have done wrong. I quickly faced the front again as the steady tread of measured steps coming up the aisle told me that my name and number were about to 'go in the book'. The footsteps stopped right beside me, and I sat motionless, not daring to move and waited for the worst to happen. An arm reached round in front of me and firmly tapped the young recruit sitting next to me on the shoulder. "Don't you know you're in the 'ouse of the Lord," hissed the Sergeant Major, "take yer bloody 'at orf, ****", the last venomous hiss spitting out a much used but very unattractive four-letter word. I relaxed and silently prayed for tolerance towards the ignorant and for a happy issue out of all my afflictions.

As church-parade ended, the alarm sounded yet again and I raced back to the barrack room to get my rifle and equipment, for by now the squad was considered to be sufficiently well-trained to man a roadblock on the perimeter of the depot covering the road junction towards Kenley. This time it proved to be a false alarm and after twenty minutes we were stood down. The all clear was short-lived, however, and no sooner had I taken off my equipment and started towards the mess hut for lunch, this time carrying my kit with me, than the bugler was sounding the alarm once again. I turned towards the roadblock trying to get my equipment on as I ran, and raced across the parade ground with others making for their various action stations. I was right in the middle of the square when the first bomber roared over immediately above our heads at little more than roof-top height and the tail gunner sprayed bullets at random across the parade ground. My attention was distracted for a moment, and still running forward I tripped and went sprawling; as I fell forward I heard the soldier next to me utter one convulsive gasping cry as he pitched forward to lie alongside me. I turned to look at him and to my horror I saw a slow trickle of blood coming from a neat hole in the middle of his forehead. His eyes were still open, but he was clearly dead and I picked myself up again and made all speed to the roadblock. I was sick to the pit of my stomach, but it wasn't the sight of the blood that bothered me, for apart from seeing a man killed by lightning on the beach at Paignton when I was a very small child, this was my first encounter with death, and its suddenness shocked and sickened me. "Perhaps", I thought as I ran on, "if I hadn't fallen, the next bullet might have got me too". It was a sobering thought and worth a short prayer of thanks which I duly uttered.

The following week the squad passed the Colonel's inspection, and accompanied by trained soldier Birchenall, most of us went out on the town in nearby Purley where the evening ended with Birchenall, with far too much beer under his belt, doing a war dance round his peaked cap in the middle of the road. He had trained and mothered his recruits well, and we escorted him safely back to the depot undetected by the Military Police. Shortly after this episode, Ossie Wall, one of my closer chums in the squad, and I went out to enjoy dinner together at the Surrey Hills Hotel in Caterham, and as usual the sirens started wailing soon after dusk. As wave after wave of enemy bombers with their menacing, undulating drone made their way northwards, it was clear that their deadly loads were destined for London. By now we had become used to such an event, and realising that there was nothing we could do about it anyway, we enjoyed our meal and afterwards went into the basement for a game of billiards.

All too soon it was time to return to barracks and as we approached the depot gates the raid increased in intensity and shrapnel, mainly from exploding anti-aircraft shells, could be heard coming back to earth all around us. Ossie suddenly suggested that we should walk out on to the Surrey hills to see what was happening, we could always say we'd been caught in the raid and stayed in the shelter if there was any trouble with the guard. It did not take us long to get clear of the houses and out on the high ground we saw an awesome and truly fantastic scene. It was like a picture from Dante's inferno; the whole length of the distant horizon was a burning holocaust, and we were spellbound by the horrible panorama. As we wandered slowly along the footpath, now completely forgetful of time, we were suddenly brought back to life when we were challenged by the harsh words, "Halt; who goes there". "Friend", I answered. "Advance and be recognised, friend", came the reassuring voice of a Canadian soldier. The guard had automatically turned out, and we were escorted back to the guard tent where we were told that we had wandered into a Canadian battalion camp. We had no idea there were any troops in the area, but then why should we after being virtual prisoners inside the Guards depot for six weeks! After establishing our identity and explaining how we came to be out on the Downs after midnight, we were given hot tea and spent an hour talking to our hosts about the war and the blitz.

It was then time to make our way back to the depot and as the raid seemed to be almost over we were able to enjoy a more peaceful walk whilst London still blazed away to the north. The depot gates had long since been locked, and never lost for a brilliant idea, I suggested to Ossie that we should get in by climbing through the roadblock position which would by then be unmanned. I'd had plenty of practice at climbing back into College in the small hours of the night without being caught – despite the sharp spikes that were cemented along the top of the walls. Ossie was not too happy at first, but I persuaded him that it would be all right. "We'll climb in over the road block and then pretend we're officers if anyone challenges us; you know, gas mask slung over the right shoulder and speak with a distinctly Oxford accent, old boy." We made a detour round the gates, successfully negotiated the road block, and were making our way towards our barrack block in the semi-darkness when out of the corner of my eye, I spotted a familiar figure standing in the doorway of one of the warrant officers' billets – it was the RSM, no less! Without a moment's hesitation Ossie and I slung our respirators over our right shoulders, a style restricted to officers in the Brigade, adjusted our peaked caps and walked slowly and outwardly unconcerned but with our hearts pounding towards the barrack block. As we passed about 30 yards from the by-now curious RSM he barked "Hey, you two people", and before he could say more I interjected in my most polished Oxford accent, "It's all right RSM, just checking up". "Very good, Sir. Good night, Sir", came the reply with the unmistakeable stamping of the foot as the RSM came to attention and saluted into the darkness. A few paces more and we were round the corner of a building out of sight of the RSM, and immediately we took off like hunted hares. Inside the door of Codrington block we paused to listen and recover our breath before creeping to bed. "You know, Ossie" I said the next morning, "we could easily have been a couple of enemy infiltrators last night. This discipline is all very well, but when it comes to the RSM taking us for granted without even checking us out, it really makes you wonder, doesn't it?" But from our point of view it was just as well that we got away with it.

After two months at Caterham the squad had their passing-out parade. With one or two exceptions we were all going on to Sandhurst Officer Cadet Training Unit (OCTU) for what I expected to be a four-month course before being commissioned into the Brigade. I was looking forward to it enormously as I had heard that the OCTU was still being run very much on peacetime lines and little had changed. I would be able to play some rugger, and I had heard on the grapevine that there was still a pack of beagles there. And above all, it was far enough from London so that with any luck life should be much more peaceful than it had been at Caterham.

At about midday on the day we left the Guards Depot, we were waiting on Purley station for the train to Camberley. It was all very peaceful for a change, a bright sunny day with hardly a cloud to be seen. Apparently there had been an air raid warning which we hadn't heard as we had been in transit when it had sounded. There were no shelters nearby so we all sat around on the platform shortly to be treated to a grandstand view of the last of the epic daytime air battles. Away to the south we could see the battle in full swing as the massed formations of German bombers pressed on relentlessly towards the centre while their escorting fighters did their utmost to ward off the defending Spitfires and Hurricanes. As interlaced vapour trails crisscrossed the blue sky, it seemed that the RAF were wreaking terrible damage on the bombers and fighters alike as one after the other they were sent hurtling down to crash and explode in vast balls of fire. It was an inspiring sight that brought great cheers from the squad as each enemy plane screeched down out of control. The young RAF pilots simply tore into the battle intent on just one thing, to win at all costs.

The battle had moved away to the north and the squad, still savouring what they had just witnessed, had safely entrained for Camberley where we arrived during the afternoon. Although the early evening radio news bulletins spoke of 185 German planes being destroyed during the day, the final tally proved to be significantly less than that, but nevertheless it had been a remarkable and stimulating victory for 'The Few' as Churchill had so aptly called them. Thankfully the Germans paused to lick their wounds after which they switched their tactics to night-time bombing. Had they known how sorely stretched the RAF had become, they might well have pressed home their daylight attacks and the course of the war could well have been very different. We did not play a part in the opening phase of the Battle of Britain although we'd been under fire in a target area for several weeks and had seen death and destruction at close hand for the first time in our young lives. Needless to say we did not much care for it.

# Chapter 4

## SS *MULBERA* FROM LIVERPOOL

———

Soon after arriving at Caterham, I received a letter from my Uncle Eric who was a senior officer in the Indian Police in Delhi where he had many friends in GHQ. It went,

> "I've just heard from your Dad that you've joined the Welsh Guards. Splendid show, Bob, and what I would have expected of you. Of course, Sam was very disappointed at first but I'm glad to say that he is now giving you his full support, and he and your mother are very proud of you. Now, a word of advice. The Indian Army is expanding fast and British Officers will be needed in increasing numbers. Those who get in first will stand the best chance of rapid promotion, and as I expect you know Indian Army pay is a lot better than the British Army rates! If I were you, I would ask for a transfer as soon as you can, and if you decide to do so, let me know which regiment you would like to join and I will do a bit of string-pulling for you."

I read and re-read those words several times, and the more I thought about it the more the idea of going out to India where my grandfather and uncles and aunts had been missionaries over the last half century appealed to me. However, I had made the decision to join the Brigade of Guards fully intending to give them my total support and at the end of the war to go back to medicine. Mindful that I was already filling a potential officer's slot in the Brigade squad, it seemed to be an act of betrayal to rat on my chosen regiment so soon after joining. But the thought of rapid promotion, and the higher rates of pay and life in India won the day and I decided to apply. I realised that there was no guarantee that my application would be granted unless there was a very good reason for it. Since I didn't have one, I told a little white lie that I intended to make the Indian Army my career after the war ended. My company commander, Major 'Duffy' Rice, had not questioned me too closely and my application was forwarded to the War Office. Weeks had passed and I had moved to Sandhurst. Since there was still no reply, I had no option but to assume that it had been put into some junior Staff Officer's 'too difficult' tray, and I decided to carry on as though I had never applied.

The lifestyle was very different to that at the Depot where to all intents and purposes we had been treated as ordinary recruits. Here the peacetime permanent staff had been largely retained although the role of the RMA had been changed to cater for much shorter courses, thus providing a greatly increased throughput of young officers. Habits die hard though, and the OCTU cadets, especially those in the Brigade squad intakes, were treated very much like the Gentlemen cadets of yesteryear.

The first thing that struck me as we were driven through the grounds was the neat and tidy appearance of the place. I felt that I was living a dream as the lorry pulled up outside the main building that was more like a stately home than a college. We were taken to D block in the new building which was to be our home for the next four months, and each cadet was given a single room of his own. The furniture was bare but adequate and would probably not have been out of place in a monastery. The servants, whose job was to look after and valet several cadets on the same landing, were introduced and I found myself comparing the somewhat dour and melancholy Dickens with my old scout, Green, at Oxford. A conducted tour of the amenities boosted my spirits even more as it became clear that the standard of living was going to be on a par with what I had been used to at New College.

I found the wooded surroundings and relative peacefulness very relaxing after the daily air raids at the depot, but then came the night of the Coventry Blitz. It was a still, clear night and the countryside was bathed in bright moonlight. Soon after dark, wave after wave of German bombers with their characteristic undulating drone flew northwards directly over Sandhurst. After an early air raid alert the all clear was sounded as it soon became obvious that their target was somewhere up in the Midlands and there was no imminent danger to those in the flight path unless the pilot of a damaged aircraft indiscriminately jettisoned his bomb load. As I lay in bed, listening to the incessant drone of the marauding bombers, I worried about my parents somewhere up there in Wolverhampton and I prayed that they would come to no harm. I got out of bed and went down the passage to see if Ossie Wall was awake and for a while we talked about the course and what a change it was from Caterham; suddenly the intensity of the raid seemed to increase and we discussed why the bombers seemed to alter course directly above the college. "I know," I said, "It's the lake! It must be shining like a beacon in the moonlight." Then came the realisation that if the Luftwaffe pilots were in fact using the lake as a landmark, it put us right in the firing line as a worthwhile alternative target. And as we talked about this possibility the familiar shriek of a huge bomb coming uncomfortably close sent us both diving under the bed. There was an almighty explosion and the building shook as the 1000 lb bomb hit midway between the old and new buildings. Damage was slight except for a vast crater in the connecting roadway. After a few minutes, while we waited to see if there were any more bombs, we somewhat shamefacedly emerged from our hiding place.

The far distant rumble of gunfire and heavy explosions could be heard far into the night as the Germans systematically destroyed their chosen target, the city of Coventry, leaving the cathedral a ghostly ruin. No more bombs fell within many miles of Camberley and the one that had fallen during the early part of the night turned out to be the only one which I was to hear during the remainder of my time at Sandhurst. The lake just inside the main gate was drained the very next day to deny the Luftwaffe the use of what was an obvious landmark, especially on moonlight nights.

I found the training and life in general at Sandhurst full of fun and interest. Early in October I tried desperately to find a second-hand motor bike so that I could drive the 90 miles home for my brother Ted's 21st birthday party. I spent a whole weekend searching within a 20-mile radius of Camberley and only gave up when someone told me that the Army had requisitioned every machine they could lay their hands on. However, they had not taken a small two-seater Morris Minor coupe that I spotted in a dealer's yard just down the road in York. At first sight it looked a sad and forlorn little car with four flat tyres – a picture of utter dejection. But on further inspection I noticed that it had an almost new hood and both the bodywork and upholstery were in excellent condition. The dealer assured me that the engine was sound, and making a characteristically quick decision I bought it for £20 on the understanding that he would have it ready for the road, licensed, insured and with all the tyres checked, within 48 hours. That would be on Thursday afternoon and would give me just enough time to test the car and get any minor adjustments done before I set out on my marathon 90-mile journey on Friday lunchtime.

As I happily drove the little car home on a weekend pass, at no time exceeding 60 mph (its maximum speed), I revelled in the ownership of my first car, small as it might be. I arrived in time for Ted's party in Wolverhampton and drove back to Camberley on the Sunday afternoon without incident. I was pleased with my purchase, and the little car served me well during the rest of my time at Sandhurst. It stood up valiantly to the somewhat rough treatment it was occasionally subjected to, often being overloaded when some friends and I went out for the evening to the Ely Hotel up on the Hartford Bridge Flats just outside Camberley. The little car put up well with the many indignities I inflicted on her. The day before I left home on my way to India, I sold her to a local doctor for £25 as a run-about for his wife, having enjoyed a little over 1500 miles of trouble-free motoring thanks to some buckshee petrol coupons whenever and wherever I managed to get them.

The Sandhurst Beagles had been disbanded for the duration of the war, but I was surprised and delighted to find that my old friend and mentor from the previous season at Oxford, Ronnie Wallace, was a cadet in the Old Building. He'd managed to get together a small private pack which he hunted two days a week with his usual consummate skill until he was commissioned and posted to his new regiment. I had greatly enjoyed beagling during my short time at Sandhurst, and I had also played rugger for the OCTU XV although the standard was not all that good.

Early in December I found myself on Company Commander's Orders to be told that my application to transfer to the Indian Army had been approved. Contrary to my expectations, my Company Commander wished me the very best of luck and showed no irritation that I had taken up an officer cadet vacancy on the course. My platoon commander, Lord John Hope, told me that I would enjoy soldiering in India, his knowledge of the subject obtained from his father, Lord Linlithgow, who was the Viceroy of India just before the war. I was overjoyed and immediately wrote to Uncle Eric in Delhi to tell him the good news and ask him to do all he could to get me posted to the Indian Army equivalent of the Brigade of Guards. This was Queen Victoria's Own Corps of Guides, whose Regimental Centre was at Mardan 40 miles north of Peshawar on the road to the famous Khyber Pass. The Guides consisted of a Cavalry regiment and an Infantry battalion, both of which had superb records of service both on the northwest frontier of India and in other wars elsewhere. I hoped dearly that Uncle Eric would be successful in getting me posted to the Guides Infantry.

By the middle of December our company was told that because of the acute shortage of junior officers the four month course was to be cut to three months and we would all be commissioned on 23rd December. I just hoped that my letter to Uncle Eric would reach him in time for him to pull a few strings in the right places. But apart from anything else, this news meant that I would be able to spend Christmas at home as a 2nd Lieutenant, and I began to look forward to impressing the 'fillies', especially Joy. In the meantime there was a great deal to be done urgently, and all the usual military tailors were summoned to attend at the Academy to rush through the production of around two hundred uniforms. A few cadets had already had the foresight to be measured for Brigade uniforms, but I had not done so as I had been uncertain which pattern of uniform I would require. It would not be possible for me to get the Guides uniform in time, and I had to make do with a standard Service Dress with Indian Army unattached list badges and buttons. The tailors and their seamstresses had worked around the clock to have everyone's uniform ready by 22nd December, and the next day I was proudly dressed as an officer for the first time. As I made my way to the Mess for breakfast I passed a cadet who threw up a punctilious salute that caught me completely by surprise. By the time I realised that the salute was for me and I should have responded to it, the cadet had disappeared down the passage and it was too late. I was furious, but could do no more than give myself a good ticking-off! After breakfast I packed all my gear into the little car and for the last time drove home from Sandhurst. It had been an enjoyable three months that I wouldn't have missed for anything. And now, with a shiny new pip on each shoulder, the next chapter had begun and as the miles went by my excitement grew as I planned how I would spend my embarkation leave.

The few weeks from my arrival home for Christmas and until I left from Wolverhampton railway station had rushed by and not a second had been wasted. Ted had come over on a week's leave from his regiment in Limavaddy, and of course young Freddie was home for the school holidays. Christmas was spent in the usual way, and after breakfast and the opening of presents, we had all gone to church and then visited the hospital where Dad was required to practise his skill as a surgeon on a number of enormous turkeys! Mince pies and a glass of sherry in Matron's room brought the morning to a late close, and we had all gone home for a light lunch before settling down to listen to the King's wireless broadcast to his people all round the world. It was a whole year since King George VIth, with the war still less than four months old, had finished his message with the words, "Put your hand into the hand of God, that shall be to you better than a light and safer than a known way". Generally life had not changed much; the phoney war had slowed things down until the German blitzkrieg on France and the Low Countries made the Nation aware of the imminent threat to its very existence, but cinemas and dances in the Civic Hall were still well attended. To me the most noticeable change was that so many of my friends had gone away, some already never to return, but there had been several parties to go to which were great fun. Ian's father, who had been appointed to command the local 22nd battalion of the Home Guard, had persuaded me to give a talk to his officers on street fighting, a subject about which I felt the audience, most of whom had fought in the Great War, could have taught me a great deal more than I could teach them. However, I accepted and the evening went extremely well, boosting my self-confidence enormously.

Joy and I became closer to each other during the short time we were able to spend together. She was still a schoolgirl, but was growing up quickly and was already quite a beautiful and sophisticated young lady. She would be leaving school at the end of the summer term, and said that she planned to be a nurse, "Probably in the Red Cross to begin with and then I'd like to join the RAF as a nurse". "Splendid idea", I had replied, but secretly thought to myself that some gallant young pilot would certainly sweep her off her feet. There's no point thinking like that, I told myself, as I'll probably be away for years. When Joy went back to school during the second week of January, we promised to write to each other and she gave me a small silver locket containing her photograph which I vowed to keep with me.

A week before I was due to report at Liverpool, I became involved in a rather unpleasant incident that I later regretted. I had met one of my contemporaries, Brian Parsons, whose father was the chairman of a large steel company. Brian and I had been at Prep school together but we had never been particularly close friends. We met each other at the many dances and parties the parents of our circle of friends arranged for us during school holidays, and whilst my father was comfortably off and we were generally regarded as a good upper-middle class family, many of our friends came from a much wealthier circle. Their fathers were successful industrialists whose wives had been Dad's patients at one time or another, and whilst it was inevitable that although most of them accepted and treated Ted and me as equals, a few of them knew that we could not match their lifestyle and from a rather snobbish viewpoint we felt that they tended to look down on us. Brian Parsons was one of those people who never really wanted to know me due to his higher spending power and newer car.

I had gone into the bar of the Victoria Hotel for a quick half while I waited for my mother to finish her shopping and saw Brian standing at the bar with two other young men, all smartly dressed in dark business suits. "Hullo Brian," I said, patting him lightly on the shoulder, "what a nice surprise".

Brian looked round, saw my uniform and pip and looked a bit embarrassed. "So you've joined up," he said rather blandly, and proceeded to introduce his two companions.

That done, I told him that I was sailing for India in a week's time to join the Indian Army, and the obvious excitement and pride in my voice clearly nettled Brian and his friends. I went on, "What service are you going to join, Brian – Army, Navy or Air Force?"

"None", he replied, "Dad reckoned that I am essential in the business and he's made me a Director. So I'm afraid I've got to sweat it out at home while you blokes enjoy yourselves abroad." Brian's companions sniggered into their drinks and I felt my hackles rising.

"Tough luck" I retorted, "and tell me, Brian, what experience have you got of running a company? You are only 20 years old, and you must be really stupid if you seriously think you're essential to a business that you scarcely know anything about." There was an embarrassed silence as the three young men looked into their half empty glasses as if they hoped to find a way out of the awkward situation.

"Have a drink, Bob," invited Brian, "Someone's got to keep industry going, and if the Government in its wisdom has decided that directors of companies vital to the war effort are to be exempt from military service, who are you to argue?"

I knew that Brian had made a telling point, and I quickly replied, "I'm not arguing about that, Brian. Of course industry must be kept going, but you! Why are you a Director?"

"Because my father made me one", he replied.

That little streak of envy had for a brief moment thrown me off balance, and I knew that I hadn't come out of the altercation at all well. But I was still extremely angry and was disgusted at what I conceived to be a lack of moral fibre shown by Brian.

When Dad came home later that evening, he noticed that I seemed to be preoccupied about something, and asked what was worrying me. So I told him what had happened in the hotel at lunchtime and said, "How many of our so-called friends are as yellow as Brian, Dad? I suppose they'll all become fat cats and their fathers will get titles like Sir John Williams did in the last war, and their sons will bask in reflected glory. I'm mad about it, Dad, but at least I know that I'm doing my bit for the country, even though my plans to follow in your footsteps have had to be put on hold until the war is over, and God knows how far into the future that will be".

Dad was very understanding and fully appreciated how I felt. "They're not worth bothering about, old son," he said, "and anyway, there are very few I know of who are doing that sort of thing round here. The fathers of your real friends all fought in the last war and wouldn't dream of allowing their sons to chicken out of this one. Just think of poor old Freddy Steward, he did his bit, was wounded three times and has already lost his two boys this time round. Go to it, son. You'll do your best and when it's all over and you come home you'll be able to hold your head up high and command the high moral ground. You know how proud we are of you, Bob, but there'll always be people around who have little or no moral fibre and given half a chance they look for the easy and cowardly way out. It is so much more galling when those who do that are not only gutless, but are also happy to let others do the hard graft while they themselves grow rich. But don't give way to envy, old son. It is a cardinal sin, and there is no honour in it. Ignore these people and in the end you will always come out the winner." I felt a lot better for this piece of fatherly advice, and turned my thoughts once again to the great adventure I would soon be embarking upon. The next few days were very hectic, and time simply rushed by until the great day arrived and I boarded the train to Liverpool.

The train arrived at Lime Street station, I took my suitcase down from the luggage rack and joined the crowds making their way to the station exit. I followed the signs to the RTO's office in the station forecourt where I was told to get a taxi to the Adelphi Hotel where a room had been reserved for me. The Embarkation Officer would meet me later in the evening to brief my fellow travellers and I for the following day.

In the hotel, the draft of 50 newly commissioned subalterns, all sporting bright new pips on their shoulders, were gathering together from all parts of the country and after dinner they were told to report in the vestibule at 9:00 am the next morning ready to be taken to Prince's Dock. Their heavy baggage had already been taken care of and was waiting on the dockside to be identified when the draft arrived.

The ship, the SS *Mulbera*, was a British-India Line vessel of some 10 000 tons and she was still plying between her home port, Liverpool, and Bombay though she now had to use the long route via Cape Town. Her master, Captain Cooke, was a seasoned mariner with a face to match, and his dour weather-beaten features gave us confidence that we would be in safe hands for the next ten weeks or so – the estimated duration of our journey.

The ship's officers were all British, the crew were Lascars, and the passenger list included mainly Indian Nationals returning home. There were doctors, teachers, and several missionaries going back to continue spreading the Gospel after leave in the UK. The remainder were either military officers or diplomats returning to India to rejoin their units or take up Government posts. In case the *Mulbera* was unlucky enough to be intercepted by the German Navy, all the military personnel on board had to travel as civilians, and they were instructed to pack every item of uniform in their heavy baggage until they arrived in Bombay. Amongst the military personnel there were two Indian Army majors, Bamfield and Armstrong, on their way to take up staff appointments after completing the Staff College course at Camberley, and they were detailed to be in command of the draft of subalterns.

Embarkation was quickly completed, and the SS *Mulbera* slipped away and moved downstream where she hove-to and dropped anchor to await the convoy we were to join. During the night Liverpool and Birkenhead were heavily bombed in one of the worst air attacks they had yet experienced, and those on board the *Mulbera* watched from the comparative safety of the middle of the Mersey estuary.

At 3 o'clock the next afternoon, 4th February 1941, instructions were given that all passengers must carry their life jackets with them at all times as the danger of being spotted and torpedoed by a marauding U-boat was very real. The SS *Mulbera* sailed out of Liverpool Bay and in the fading light of a cold, clear winter's day, I watched the snow-covered peaks of Snowdonia slowly disappear into the distance behind us. I silently bade farewell to my beloved mountains where as a young boy Dad had taught me the basic skills of mountaineering, and leaving the darkness behind me I went below to enjoy a cup of tea. All the excitement of the journey, embarkation, and the grandstand view of the blitz into the small hours had been somewhat exhausting and now began to catch up with me. I experienced something of an anti-climax, and until dinner I settled myself in the bar and began to get to know some of my fellow passengers with whom I would have to live in very close quarters until sometime in April when, God willing, we would arrive safely in Bombay. When I got into my bunk that night, I was conscious that life on board might become tiresome living so closely with some people I'd already decided I would probably not like. I prayed for tolerance and patience, and reminded myself that my college motto had been 'Manners Makyth Man'. As my father had often told me, courtesy costs nothing, yet it is beyond price.

# Chapter 5

## THE LONGEST TRIP

———

The following morning dawned overcast, dismal and grey. During the night the SS *Mulbera* had sailed northwards, and many other ships of all shapes and sizes joined her to make up the convoy. Soon after breakfast the First Officer announced on the ship's tannoy system that we were already passing the Clyde and that by early afternoon we would be approaching Cape Wrath, the most northwesterly point of Scotland. We were, of course, out of sight of land, and during the morning Majors Bamfield and Armstrong called a meeting of the subalterns and set out a daily routine which would include Urdu instruction and essential keep-fit. It was vital that although we were travelling as civilians, we should be under some degree of military and self-discipline. Some of the Indian nationals were invited to assist with the Urdu lessons, and one of the subalterns who happened to be a Cambridge University Rugby Blue had volunteered to organise the Physical Training programme. I was relieved that the time on board, with all its inherent boredom, was not to be left entirely to us to spend as we wished. There would be something to do to which we could all apply ourselves, and at the end of the voyage we would arrive reasonably fit and ready to join our regiments.

At 4 o'clock in the afternoon most of the passengers went into the lounge to have afternoon tea, when a sudden change of course 90 degrees to port would have sent tea cups sliding off the side tables if the 'fiddles' had not been fitted. Shortly afterwards another announcement over the tannoy told us that the convoy had left UK waters and was now heading out into the Atlantic Ocean. The route would take us to a point about 80 miles south of Iceland, and it was a bit puzzling why the SS *Mulbera* should have to go half way to America in order to reach Cape Town. The ship's officers explained that until the convoy was reasonably clear of the U-Boat packs which were operating mainly in the northern area of the Atlantic, it was essential that every ship, whatever its destination, should as far as was practicable stay under the protection of the Royal Navy escorts.

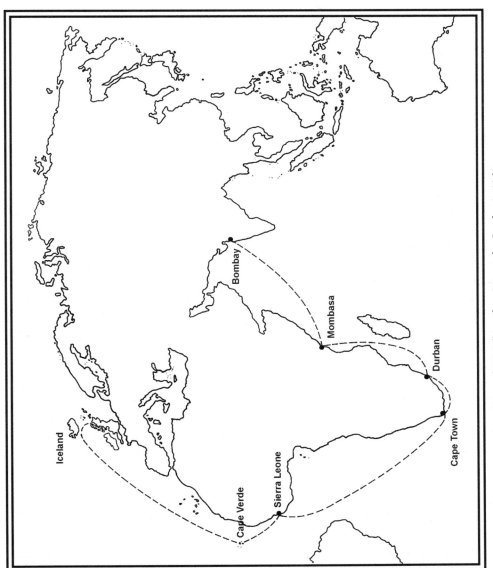

*Route of SS Mulbera from Liverpool to Bombay in 1941*

I soon found my sea legs, but I much preferred to be out on deck in the fresh air where I could see what was going on around the convoy, than below deck where I soon started to feel queasy in the stuffy atmosphere. The Urdu lessons had to be shelved for the present as the instructors and the students were too seasick. By midday the wind had begun to strengthen, and the ships, now sailing directly into the rising gale, were soon pitching into the huge waves and 'shipping it green' as their bows ploughed into the base of the mountains of seething water. I found a kindred spirit, Bill Waters, and together we watched for the next massive wave for the old ship to pit her strength against. Even on the top deck we could not avoid getting drenched as the sea cascaded over the bows and sent masses of spray over the bridge. Looking around us, it was a fantastic sight as ships buried their bows into the green ocean, exposing their screws that screamed defiance as they thrashed the air with no resistance from the water to slow them down. Every time the *Mulbera's* propellers thrashed the air, the whole ship shuddered and vibrated until once again she regained a level keel for a few seconds.

The fierce wind increased to a Force 10-11 gale, and almost all the passengers stayed in their cabins. No one managed to turn up for meals in the dining saloon except for a handful of hardy souls including Bill and me. We quickly made friends with the ship's officers who were a cheerful and chatty lot. The youngest was a young Scot from Greenock called Rory Campbell, who was always smiling and had a word of reassurance for anyone whom he thought looked a bit apprehensive. Then there was the wireless officer David Sims, inevitably called Sparks, who came from Liverpool, and the Second Mate, David Watts, from Southampton. These three were on the same watch and were therefore always in the Dining Saloon together, including the few stalwarts who never missed a meal, and we all became very friendly.

We were allowed to visit the bridge and the wireless room, which helped to pass the time and reduce the boredom. At the height of the storm, on the fourth day out from Liverpool, the *Mulbera* started to roll as the wind backed into the southwest. The usual crowd were having lunch when the ship gave a sudden and violent lurch, almost sending us all hurtling across the saloon. Simultaneously there was a tremendous bang that shook the old ship from stem to stern. Bill and I were first on our feet, grabbing our life jackets and making for the main stairway. I suddenly realised that we were alone, and turning round I saw the three ship's officers sitting there laughing at us. "Think we'd been torpedoed, Bob?" quipped David Sims, "We knew that would probably happen as we're just about 80 miles south of Iceland and this is where we leave the convoy and sail on our own right down the middle of the Atlantic, next stop the Cape Verde Islands. As we changed course, we turned across the waves and caught a huge one on our starboard bulwark, hence the bang. But don't worry, we are soon going to leave this storm behind and from then on, for want of a better term, it will be 'plain sailing' and we'll be able to make better speed. Before long we should be in warmer and sunnier climes." Bill and I naturally felt rather stupid as we went up on deck to watch the convoy slowly disappear as it continued on its way to Canada and America, whilst the SS *Mulbera* sailed bravely southwards on her own across the main Atlantic shipping lanes. Instructions were issued that from now on everyone on board must carry their life jackets with them at all times due to the risk of being intercepted by German U-boats on the prowl. The ship's officers were working overtime keeping a keen watch for tell-tale periscopes, and the Royal Artillery subalterns in the draft formed gun crews to man the rather archaic artillery piece mounted on the poop deck. The wind eased and the sea became calmer, passengers began to feel better and emerged from their 'sick beds' to enjoy the warmer air.

Soon the two Majors restarted the Urdu lessons, and some of the doctors, solicitors and of course the white missionaries helped out by taking on small groups to teach the young officers the basics of the language. We all took this very seriously so that we would be able to communicate with our Indian soldiers. Even the cabin stewards became involved when we tried to make ourselves understood in Urdu. Two or three hours each day were spent on Urdu lessons, and table games such as Bridge, Poker, and even Snap with the missionary ladies, soon became the normal way of passing the time. Walking round and round the deck was a useful addition to the keep fit programme, but as the weather stoked up and temperatures reached levels that very few of the draft had ever previously experienced, limited sun bathing was the preferred occupation until the cool of the evening made walking more acceptable, albeit at a much slower pace. As expected, it had become a very idle and boring existence, and there was great excitement when a rocky coastline appeared out of the hot hazy horizon. David Watts, second mate, had told me that we would be stopping at St Vincent on the Cape Verde Islands to take on water and fuel, and had also warned me that it was a favourite area for U-boats to lie in wait for an unsuspecting ship like the SS *Mulbera*. As the old ship drew nearer, the shoreline cleared and revealed an arid and uninviting land. There was no question of any of the passengers going ashore anyway, as we would be in harbour only for a few hours. I wondered where they got the water from, and was told that there were considerable storage facilities, sufficient to last through prolonged periods of little or no rain.

Without the movement of the ship to provide a welcome and cooling breeze, the afternoon was spent in sweltering heat and most of the passengers stayed in their cabins which were probably the least unbearable places to be. At dinner that evening it was announced that the ship would sail at 10 o'clock the next morning, but at about midnight there was surreptitious activity amongst the crew who were creeping around making as little noise as possible. I wandered round on deck and suddenly bumped into David Watts who told me that the skipper had filed his sailing plan with the Port Authority to up anchor, as announced, next morning. We knew that as soon as this information was passed to the PA, there would be a leak to the Germans, and in all probability a U-boat would be out there waiting for us. The skipper had decided therefore to run the gauntlet at midnight hoping to be well clear of St Vincent many hours before a U-boat was on station to intercept his ship. It was incredible how quietly the ship was made ready and slipped her moorings to head, ever so slowly, for the open sea. As the moon rose, those out on deck could see the zigzag pattern of her phosphorescent wash as the skipper put on full speed and constantly changed direction to make it as difficult as possible for a U-boat to intercept the ship. When she was well clear of the islands, the *Mulbera* was set on course for Cape Town but after about twelve hours sailing the engines lost nearly all their power and the old ship was reduced to only a few knots. In the warmer waters of the tropics, a school of dolphins appeared and were to provide a welcome distraction as they played around the bow of the ship, keeping pace. Flying fish would suddenly leap out of the water and skim gracefully over the surface of the dead-calm sea. They were pretty, colourful fish, and it was sad when Bill found one of them had come in through the open porthole and landed on my bunk.

There was much excitement as we unexpectedly made landfall and sailed up the estuary to dock in Freetown, Sierra Leone for repairs to the engines. It was then late in the afternoon, but there was no question of anyone being allowed ashore until it was certain how long the repairs might take. At dinner that evening the First Officer announced that some major work was necessary and this would probably take at least two or three days. We would then have to wait until a convoy, sailing direct from Southampton, arrived off the estuary that we would join *en route* for Cape Town. It looked as though we would be in Freetown for the better part of a week and passengers would be allowed to go ashore each day until further notice. For those who wanted to enjoy bathing from a splendid silver-sand beach, there was a private club some ten miles from the town itself, and arrangements were made for passengers to become honorary members. The Royal Navy shore establishment would organise transport for those who wanted to use the club.

"Before I do that", said John Bradburn, who had been commissioned into the Indian Army with his younger brother Chris, "I've got some private business to see to in Freetown". He smirked as he said it, but it was completely lost on me as I was interested only in having a few days swimming and sunbathing. Others who heard his remark knew exactly what he meant, and were not particularly impressed. Certainly no one offered to keep him company, and next morning when the rest of us all trooped ashore, Big John, as he was nicknamed, went off alone to see to his 'private business'.

After a really enjoyable day on the silver-sand beach, we came back on board to enjoy a good dinner. Big John sat at our table, but it was not until someone asked him if his business meeting had been a success that he told us what he had been doing. "Well," he said, "it didn't take me long to find what I wanted. She was big and buxom, and on the game".

"You don't mean…." I exclaimed.

"Oh yes I do", answered Big John, "and before you ask and look too shocked, she was a coal black mammy".

"But what on earth would your father say?" I asked.

"I thought you told us he's a vicar, didn't you?"

"Yes, he is a vicar, and that's exactly why I had to go off on my own and get rid of some inhibitions which have been etched into me right through my adolescence."

"But you've probably gone and got yourself a filthy dose of clap or something," chipped in Bill.

"No, I haven't. I took the proper precautions, so you needn't worry on my behalf. Now let's change the subject. What have you lot been doing?"

"We've been swimming on the beach", someone said. "Want to join us tomorrow John?" The best thing we could do was to keep relationships on a friendly basis.

"Yes, I'll come with you," said Big John. "We'll meet up at breakfast, OK?"

The meal over, we went out on deck to watch the sun dip down over the end of the estuary, and feeling relaxed after such a change in our daily routine, we all turned in early. And so the days went by in Freetown with little change until news came through at the end of the week that the convoy we were to join was only a few hours sailing from the rendezvous. It wasn't going to stop at Freetown, and the *Mulbera* sailed out on her own to make contact with what turned out to be a huge collection of ships of every kind, with frigates and destroyers circling round them as a mother duck would guard her brood on a village pond. There were two much larger warships, both cruisers, and the sight of this strong naval presence shepherding its charges southwards towards Cape Town and into the Indian Ocean gave all those on board a sense of reassurance.

SS *Mulbera* took up her station at the rear of the convoy, but after some six hours steaming, she suddenly went dead in the water and the other ships steamed away from her. "Afraid it's the same old trouble," said David Watts as he dashed down to the engine room. A destroyer came back to us but when there was no sign of the trouble having been repaired a couple of hours later, she signalled that she had been ordered to rejoin the convoy and that the *Mulbera* had to fend for herself. "Good luck and *bon voyage*", she made with her Aldis lamp, and a feeling of anxiety settled on all of us aboard the stricken ship. This was a pretty desperate situation, for she had no power and was right in the main shipping lane, a sitting duck for any alert U-boat captain. Life jackets were at the ready and secretly those on board prayed, especially the missionaries. The *Mulbera* drifted powerless for eleven hours, but eventually the engineers managed to get her going on half power and we dawdled towards Cape Town at a few knots. During the third night on her own, I met David Watts out on deck at around midnight. It was a dark night, the sea was as calm as a millpond and all was peaceful. As we stood enjoying the cooling breeze, chatting about this and that, I suddenly noticed what looked like the dark shape and the phosphorescence of a ship's bow wave. "God, yes," agreed David. "Crippen, look at that, and that! We're in the middle of a convoy going north," and with that he dashed up the gangway to the bridge. They had everything under control and although they were operating under radio silence, the alert lookout had spotted the oncoming ships in time for the skipper to steer straight between two lines of approaching ships. There was no real danger as it turned out, but it was a shock I could have done without. A few days later we made landfall and knew that Cape Town was only a few hours sailing away. It was after dark when the old ship limped the last few miles into Cape Town, which was in March 1941. There was no blackout and every one on board lined the deck rails to see a blaze of lights we had almost forgotten existed. There was a lot of excited speculation as to how long the ship would be under repair, but word came down from the bridge that no one should make plans for more than one day at a time as we would put to sea as soon as the repairs were completed, as we were already very much behind schedule.

Next morning the passengers all went ashore as early as possible. We were eagerly looking forward to stretching our legs after being cooped up on board for so long, and to be relieved from the boredom of the daily routine which had been our lot now for almost eight weeks. Bill and I had decided to have a look around the town before it got too hot, and then perhaps take a taxi to one of the beaches before having a slap-up dinner somewhere. But we hadn't taken into account the remarkable hospitality of the South Africans; as we approached the exit from the dock area we were confronted by a long row of cars parked by the roadside. The drivers were standing by their vehicles, and as each pair or group of officers approached them, they offered to look after them for the rest of the day and drive them around the countryside. Bill and I realised what was happening long before we reached the cars, and we began guessing which driver we would get. Just before our turn arrived, the pair in front of us was whisked away by a gorgeous blonde, leaving us a youngish man who turned out to be a South African Army dentist who was home on leave. He had a Cadillac, and as we accepted his hospitality he swung round and grabbed the next two subalterns as well. "Pity to waste a big car," he said, "my folks asked me to find four of you so that we can show you something of our country and hopefully give you a good day out."

"That's very nice of you," we all murmured together.

"OK then. I'm John Baxter, and as you can see I'm in the Army. A dentist actually, and I'm home for a few days before I go back up country to my station. I'll take you home first to meet my parents, then we can take off on a round tour which will include lunch at a nice country club about forty miles out of town, and possibly an afternoon on the beach at Muisenberg. Any of you ever done any surfing?"

I was the only one who admitted that I had played about in the surf at Newquay in Cornwall, but of course the rollers there were nothing like those in South Africa. By the time we reached John's home, we'd all relaxed and were all looking forward to the day ahead. The two other officers John had grabbed on the dockside were not particular friends of ours; in fact we hardly knew them at all. It was impossible to know everyone on board the ship and the pattern of life had been somewhat cliquey. One of the two, Bert Simmonds, was rather too coarse for my liking, and I hoped I would be able to get through the day without becoming abrupt with him.

It was a great day, and to crown it all John and his parents took the four of us out to dinner in a very expensive hotel near Table Mountain. The menu was fantastic without a hint of rationing, the four of us agreed it was the best meal we'd had for months. We talked of many things during the evening, and when we were taken back to the dockside we could not thank John and his parents enough.

Back on board I met one of the Indian doctors I had made friends with and told him about the tremendous welcome the four of us had received. "What have you done in Cape Town?" I asked.

"You really are a naive young man," the doctor said. "Haven't you heard about apartheid?"

"Well, yes, but surely that only applies to the local black Africans, doesn't it?"

"No, certainly not," the doctor replied, "it applies to any and everyone who has a dark skin". And then he talked about how Ghandi had first encountered the hatred of the white South Africans against coloured people wherever they came from. "So you see, there is no place ashore here for the likes of me, even for a few hours. It is most unpleasant to feel that there is enmity all around you. No, all of us Indians stayed on board. There is nothing for us in Cape Town." I felt ashamed we had been so well received while my fellow travellers were so unfairly treated.

The following day, Bill and I planned to have a good look around the town on our own. We certainly didn't think there would be a repetition of the hospitality shown to us on the previous day. Soon after breakfast the two of us set out with instructions to be back on board by dusk. There was no firm news about how long the ship repairs might take, and the captain was taking no chances of being held up once she was ready to sail. He certainly didn't want to have to send out search parties to round up his passengers at short notice, so to play safe he had ordered everyone to be back on board for dinner. As Bill and I rounded the large warehouse at the end of the dock area, there was the same sight that had greeted us the day before – a long row of cars waiting to pick up British servicemen and take them out for the day. We were at the front of the queue of young officers making their way out of the docks, and the first car in the column was a smart cabriolet, the epitome of luxury. The owner, a youngish man in his mid-thirties, greeted us warmly and asked us to join him and his family for the day. He hadn't been able to look after any of the passengers the day before as his wife had not been well, but she was fine today and they invited us to their palatial house in Rondebosch for the day. He introduced himself as Tim Jameson, "The same name as on the dock-side". I had noticed the large signs all round the docks that announced the Jamesons were the 'number one' marine engineers, but I thought that our host was just spelling out the name for us. In the car, pretending to be the driver, was a tubby young boy of about ten years old who had come with his Dad to collect a couple of guests for the day. Introductions completed, we got into the car and Tim Jameson set off in the direction of Rondebosch. Soon he swung the car into a wide sweeping drive with exotic shrubs along one side and a large open lawn with a tennis court on the other. The drive opened into a large semi-circular forecourt in front of a most palatial mansion. "OK chaps," said Tim, "this is where we get off. Come inside and meet the wife." As we entered the open doorway, his wife was coming across the hall to greet us.

"Welcome" she chirped, "my name's Cherry. What have you got in mind for us, dear?" she asked Tim.

"Well, we did Muisenburg and the Country Club the day before yesterday, so I thought we'd drive up Table Mountain for a start, and then do a tour round to the south side out to the Cape and round to the naval base at Simonstown. Then we can come home for a late lunch, perhaps play a little tennis and have a swim in the afternoon. I thought we'd have dinner here at home and introduce Bob and Bill to our excellent wines.

"That sounds great", I said. "We'd like that very much indeed." It was a great afternoon and both Bill and I soon felt very much at home with Tim and Cherry and their children.

Late in the afternoon Tim said he had to go down to the office, and when he came back he had a few words with Cherry alone before we all went out on to the terrace for drinks before dinner. "I've got news for you two," Tim said. "We've discovered that the damage to your old ship is going to take at least another three days to repair. So how about you staying here with us for a couple of nights so you can relax and see some more of the town and countryside?" We were initially a bit wary of accepting such an attractive invitation, but our hosts soon put us at ease. "Don't worry about missing your ship when she sails," he said, correctly diagnosing the reasons for our hesitation. "I own the whole shooting match down there in the docks, and I know exactly when every ship comes in or goes out. I will have advance information about your sailing time and I promise I will have you back on board in plenty of time." We gratefully accepted the hospitality offered by Tim and Cherry. It seemed too good to be true. "I will take you down to the ship after dinner," said Tim, "so that you can tell them on board where you are staying, and can collect your overnight things."

Our stay with the Jamesons was full of fun and interest, and when, four days later, Tim told us that it was time to rejoin the ship, we were sorry to say goodbye. I hoped that provided I survived the war, however long it might take to beat the Germans, one day I would try to return to Rondebosch and thank Tim and Cherry more eloquently than I could at that time.

Back on board all was bustle amongst the crew, and the ship's purser busied himself checking the passenger list to find that second lieutenant Teddy Younger, one of the officer draft, had not been seen for a couple of days. There was nothing we could do about it, as no one had any idea where he might be. However just as the

*Mulbera* pulled away from the quayside, a taxi drew up. Out jumped Teddy who exclaimed loudly, "Oh shit!" He shouted to those lining the rails on the upper deck that he would fly to *Durban* and wait to rejoin the ship there. The message was passed on to the captain who puckered his weather-beaten face and simply said, "Silly young bugger." It was also passed to the two majors in charge of the draft who gave the impression that they were outraged, declaring that it was a "Damned bad show". They were, however, secretly rather amused that Teddy's amorous adventures (for that's undoubtedly what they were) had caused him to miss the ship. It was going to cost him quite a packet to fly to Durban.

Excitement over, life resumed its humdrum routine as we made our way, still unescorted, to Durban where Teddy was on the dockside waiting to greet his friends. The majors had to go through the routine of having him on the mat, but there was nothing they could do about his exploits, and he got away with a good 'bollocking'. The stop in Durban was just long enough to take on board a few more passengers to replace those who had left the ship in Cape Town, and then the *Mulbera* made for Mombasa. The stay here lasted two whole days, and Bill and I hired a car and drove along a dusty road into the jungle. Our nerve failed us when we began to run out of metalled road and found ourselves almost enmeshed by the trees and undergrowth closing in on us on both sides. Suddenly we caught sight of some lions that had been warned of our approach by monkeys screeching from the treetops. Time to go back, we thought, particularly as we did not have too much faith in our somewhat elderly vehicle. It had been a bit of an adventure and a nice change from shipboard routine. But equally it was nice to get back on board and relate our jungle adventure to those who had preferred to stay on the ship.

It seemed surprising to me that after being cooped up for so long in such confined surroundings, most of those on board still managed to be civil to each other. This was especially so amongst the young officers, but it was beginning to be a bit of a strain and by now everyone was eagerly looking forward to our arrival in Bombay and being told which regiments we were to be posted to. I had urged my uncle to do his best to get me into the Guides Infantry, 12th Frontier Force Regiment, a splendid infantry regiment with a fantastic reputation as one of the crack fighting units on the North West Frontier. I prayed that I would be lucky, but until we docked in Bombay none of us would know our fate. Once again we settled down to the same familiar routine, only this time it was more tedious. The weather continued hot and calm, the dolphins still played around the bows, and the flying fish sporting their vivid colours flew across the calm water before dropping into the sea.

With only a few days to go before we were due to arrive at the end of our marathon journey, some of the officers started bragging about what they were going to do in Bombay. "I've got it all planned out," said Big John, and it didn't take much imagination to guess what he intended to do. I had received a very strict warning about promiscuity by my father before I joined the Army, and I fully intended to stick to his advice. "96 Grant Road is the place to go," he continued, but I didn't want to know. Even the hot weather had not affected me as it had my colleagues, and I had no intention of visiting Grant Road.

# Chapter 6

## A Captain for the Guides

————

The longed-for day dawned and soon after lunch the Indian shoreline rose up through the heat haze and within a couple of hours the old ship that had been our home for the past eleven weeks was safely docked. It was April 1941. Various officials came on board amongst who was a Lieutenant Colonel from the Military Secretary's department. All the officers were ordered to assemble in the main lounge, and the colonel started reading out from his list of postings. With baited breath I heard that my wish had been granted and I was to join the Guides Infantry; I was delighted. The regiment had recently left its home station in Mardan between Peshawar and the Khyber Pass on the North West Frontier, and was now stationed in Bowenpalli, near Secunderabad (also known as Hyderabad) in the state of Andra Pradesh where it was being mobilised in the newly formed 6th Indian Division. This division was destined for Malaya, but nobody knew then that before the end of the year the whole of South East Asia would be a major war zone. I guessed it would be as hot there in central southern India as anywhere else in the country and it was not long before I was proved correct.

As soon as we had been told which regiments we were to join, an officer and several senior British NCOs who had set up their stalls at tables round the lounge, issued instructions and rail warrants for our journeys the following morning. We were then told that we would all spend the night on board, but we could go ashore until midnight. "Just the job", said Big John. "Who wants to be initiated into the wonderful ways of the Orient? I'm heading for number 96, so who's coming with me?"

"You're a sex maniac, John," I told him. "You're bound to get what you deserve before much longer." No one seemed too anxious to go along with Big John, and Bill and I decided to spend our last evening together having a stroll round the great city before having a reasonably early night. We were both tired after the excitement of the day, but elated that we were both going to the regiments we wanted to serve with and of which we could be proud.

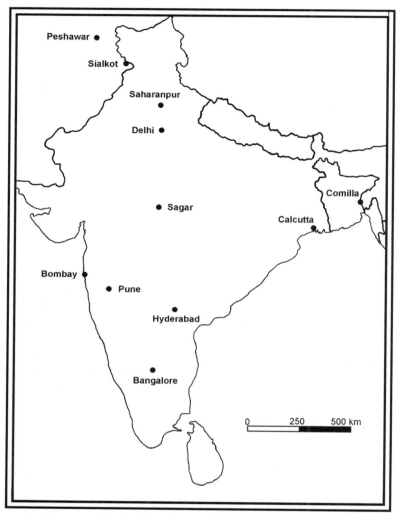

*Map of India showing the location of Hyderabad, the capital of the state of Andhra Pradesh*

Just as we were about to go ashore, Sparks Sims bumped into us and said he had been invited to a drinks party just outside the dock area where there were bound to be some attractive 'birds'. "Why not come along?" he said, "It's open house and if you don't like it you can always leave." We decided to string along for a short while and then have the quick look at Bombay we had earlier planned. At the bottom of the gangway Big John, still on his own, was haggling with a taxi driver, and I urged him to be careful, and make sure he had a 'Frenchie' with him.

"You tell your grandmother to suck eggs", retorted John, "you haven't a clue what it's about or you'd come with me".

"We're going to spend the evening with some decent birds, John, and there's no way I'd set foot in your famous brothel."

When we got to the party, it was already in full swing, and it was not long before we were approached by some extremely attractive girls in their early twenties. With the help of a drink or two, I relaxed but when I realised what was expected of me, I cooled off. Thoughts of the girl I'd left behind in England crowded into my tiring mind and as I fingered her locket, I remembered my father's health warning. "I suppose I'm just as likely to catch a dose from this girl, who probably meets most of the drafts arriving in Bombay, as Big John is in his filthy brothels," I told myself. My attitude towards the girl changed, but I could see no sign of Bill and I didn't want to leave the party without him, partly because I was not sure whether either of us would be able to find our way back to the ship. My initial enthusiasm had now deteriorated into complete disinterest, and when I spurned a direct invitation to go into the girl's bedroom, she drawled, "You might have spared me the effort". It wasn't long before she was snogging a Merchant Navy officer from another ship who had clearly had more than enough to drink. "Poor sod", I thought

I didn't want another drink, so I sat and waited until Bill made a very bedraggled appearance from the direction of the bedrooms. "God," I thought, "this is a brothel, even if it is a bit up-market." Bill confirmed my thoughts and I asked him whether he had protected himself. "Of course, old man," Bill replied. "She had a supply in her room, and oh boy, was she just great." I had a twinge of that old jealousy, but I was disappointed that my close friend had, in my estimation, sunk to the level of sex-mad Big John. But I vowed that I would stick to my principles and if any others wanted to put themselves at risk, then so be it.

It was too late now to go walking round Bombay, so we made our way back to the ship. Back on board we went straight to our cabin and I hurriedly washed and got into my bunk. Bill took longer over his ablutions and from my top bunk I looked on as he carefully washed himself. "Poor fool," I thought, "it's rather like shutting the stable door after the horse has bolted".

We both found it difficult to sleep that night. The excitement for what lay ahead of us kept the adrenalin coursing through our bodies into the small hours. Eventually sleep came, but all too soon it was day again and the moment we had awaited for so long had arrived. As we went down on to the dockside I looked one last time at the old ship that had been our home for 11 weeks, and turning away I wondered how many more such journeys she would be able to make. She was old and clearly nearing the end of her life, but four and a half years later I was surprised and overjoyed to see her in the bustling port of Calcutta. Against all odds, she had survived the war.

We were taken to the main railway station in an open lorry, all our heavy baggage following close behind in a second vehicle. My train to Secunderabad was due to leave an hour before Bill's, and after a few emotional words we grasped each other's hands in a firm grip. Then I turned on my heel and walked towards my carriage. Further down the train I saw that the third-class carriages were already full, and locals were swarming all over the roofs where they proceeded to make themselves as secure and comfortable as possible until they arrived at their various destinations. It all seemed very incongruous to us, but no one else even turned to look at the strange sight. It was part of the national scene, as we would very soon find out. I stepped up into the coach and closing the door behind me, I turned and leaned out to have a few last words with Bill. I had a feeling of *déjà vu* and for a brief moment I imagined myself in the train in which this great adventure had started – but there were no parents supporting each other and I saw only my friend Bill. We were on our way to fight a war, wherever it might lead us. Even if we both survived perhaps we might never see each other again. A whistle blew from the rear of the train, the same little green flag was waved aloft by the guard, a cloud of steam was released, and the Madras Express slowly pulled away and was soon speeding across open plains heading for the first stop, Pune. Here I saw a number of my colleagues from the SS *Mulbera* get off the train to be met by subalterns from their new regiments. "Thank God we're not expected to find our own way when we arrive," I thought, and I began to relish the thought of my arrival in Secunderabad in 24 hours time. The night came and went, and one of the English passengers in the same coach very kindly brought me a cup of tea soon after daybreak.

It was about mid-day when the train steamed into Secunderabad station. Like Bombay and Pune, everything was bustle and noise. An unintelligible cacophony of strange languages assaulted my ears and the hot smell that pervaded everything was even stronger there than it had been in Bombay. I gathered my belongings together and prepared to step down on to the platform, wondering who might be there to greet me.

For a few moments it seemed that no one had come to meet me, and I began to panic. But I need not have worried, for suddenly I saw a smartly dressed subaltern run on to the platform. I picked up my gear and made my way through the milling crowd to meet the subaltern who introduced himself as Michael Lord. He was a tall willowy young man with fair hair and the suggestion of a moustache. "I'm to be your guardian for a few days while you get used to things," he said, "so if there is anything you want to know or you're not clear about, just ask me". Michael had been with the regiment for only two weeks himself and his fair complexion showed signs of slight sunburn. Not time enough yet to have acquired a tan, but then he seemed unconcerned. "I always burn badly," he said, "so I try to keep out of the sun as much as I can. If you are wise, you'll always wear your *topee*, and take things slowly." I warmed to him, and was glad to have a companion to get me through the first strange days in a new regiment with soldiers whose language I could barely understand. Although I had learned the basics of Urdu during the long, tedious sea journey, it was a different thing to be able to speak it colloquially and fluently. Michael told me that the most important thing I would have to do would be to learn the language as quickly

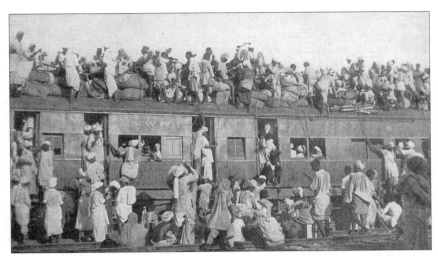

*Locals securing themselves and their goods in preparation for a train journey to Pakistan*

as possible, and to that end I would be supplied with a *munshi* (teacher) whom I would have to pay for myself. The colonel would expect me to pass the elementary standard within a few weeks. "It won't be easy, as we are starting field training in a couple of weeks' time," he said, "so any ideas you might have about swimming and poodle-faking in the club can be forgotten!" I hadn't given much thought to what I might get up to when off duty, so I was not too upset by Michael's remark.

We arrived at the mess in time for lunch, and Michael introduced me to some of the officers who were either unmarried or who had left their wives in quarters in Peshawar. After lunch I was taken to the British Officers' lines where I was allocated a 'bungalow'. This was in fact just a single room with no mod cons and very sparse furnishings that included a *charpoy* (bed), a *kursi* (chair), and a coir mat on the otherwise bare concrete floor. An old fashioned wash stand and a commode (known as the thunder box), stood on one side of the room, and Michael explained that there was a *bhisti* (water-carrier) allocated to the row of bungalows, and a *bhangi* ('untouchable', of the sweeper class) whose unpleasant job it was to be responsible for clearing away night soil from the thunder-box. The *bhisti* would be around at all times to bring washing water whenever the *sahib* wanted it. Michael then explained that from 2:00 pm until 4:00 pm, it was siesta time, and every one in the regiment went to their beds to sleep during the heat of the day. "But I have to warn you," he went on "that you'll be expected to spend an hour after lunch with your *munshi* once you start your Urdu lessons, and if you're anything like me you'll be hard put to keep awake. Anyway, have a siesta now, and I will bring your new bearer along to meet you at 4:00 pm with a cup of *char* (tea). Then the Commanding Officer — we never refer to him as the CO in this regiment — will see you in his office at 5:00 pm".

"Fine," I said, "any particular hints?"

"No, not really. His name is Ted Rich, usually known as Colonel Ted. He's been a great polo player in his time, used to hunt with the Peshawar Vale when the regiment was on the Frontier, but is a very professional soldier and demands very high standards. He is married to Gwyneth and has two children, a daughter, Nancy, and a baby son, James. Second to soldiering, his family is what matters most to him. You'll find him very understanding, and if you have any problems that cannot be dealt with at a lower level, he'll sort them out for you. The second in command, Mike Bailey, has sent his wife home to England for the duration of the war as his two boys are at prep school near Newbury and are due to go on to Eton in the next year or so. He has been fighting in Norway as an expert in mountain warfare, and covered himself with considerable glory up at Trondheim where he took over command of a British battalion after they lost their colonel and senior major. He was awarded an immediate DSO for what he did over there, and we are all very proud of him. He's not used to living the life of a bachelor, misses his wife a lot, and you'll find him a bit 'off' first thing in the morning. The only other officer I should mention at the moment is the adjutant, and you'll meet him this afternoon when you see Colonel Ted. His name is Goff Hamilton and members of his family have served in the Guides continuously since the regiment was formed. His forebears have won VCs and DSOs – the lot, and although he is not given to bragging about his family's tremendous service, he is nevertheless very proud of them. In fact he himself was awarded a DSO as a young captain on Hill 4080 on the Frontier in 1936. I'll tell you the story when we've got a bit more time".

It was all very exciting to me, and I listened intently to all Michael told me. My interview with the Colonel went well I thought, and I liked the attitude of the three senior officers to whom I was introduced. If I devoted myself to my new profession as though I was going to stay with the regiment after the war ended, I couldn't really go wrong. Colonel Ted told me that although the regiment was mobilising for war, there would be at least four months of hard training ahead of us. In order that company commanders could run their field training more efficiently, they would be given chargers.

Did I ride? "Well, yes, Sir", I replied, "but not sufficiently well to ride in point-to-point races, although I have been out hunting occasionally."

"Well, starting next Monday there will be stables for all newly joined officers. Have you got any breeches or jodhpurs? If not, get Michael to take you to the *darzi* (tailor) who will knock a pair up for you very quickly. Finally you will be commanding D Company. I know you have only a smattering of Urdu and I expect you to learn it as fast as you can. Practice with your Indian platoon commanders and your company second-in-command. He will be more help to you than your *munshi* who will teach you the basics of the language and you can build on that. You are only a second lieutenant so far, but in the Indian Army company commanders all have to be

Captains. Your second-in-command is a *Subedar*, the equivalent of a lieutenant, and your platoon commanders are *Jemadars*, second-lieutenants. Your first job now is to change your badges of rank and put up three pips. Your promotion to acting-Captain will appear in ACIs (Army Council Instructions) in due course, but your pay will be effective as from today."

I couldn't believe what I was hearing; only four months ago I was still a cadet at Sandhurst, and here I was, carrying the rank of Captain in command of a company of Indian soldiers to whom I couldn't yet make myself understood. Of course this was what Uncle Eric had meant when he urged me to transfer to the Indian Army, and I was agog with the thrill of everything that was happening to me. Twenty years old, and a Captain with the responsibility of 130 soldiers: unbelievable. I must write to Joy and tell her. Every day brought new surprises. I was able to take the stables in my stride; I had in fact had a reasonably good grounding in horsemanship, and riding bareback round a dusty ring was no strange thing to me. But some of the young officers had never ridden a horse in their lives and found it very difficult to stay aboard. The Colonel had borrowed a *risaldar*-major from the Pune Horses who were stationed nearby, and he put the officers through the routine which every *sowar* (cavalryman) had to endure, and we found it very tough indeed.

By the end of the first week, I was beginning to get the hang of things. So far I had spent little time with my soldiers, but I was already gaining the respect of my *subedar*, Rolu Ram, who was doing all he could to help me with the language problem. So far I had enjoyed my new lifestyle and those things I didn't like quite so much I took in my stride as part of the settling-in process.

Saturday was party night in the Secunderabad Club, and I was whisked off by some of my fellow officers to relax and enjoy a bit of social life, which meant an evening of fairly serious drinking. The club was full of officers and their families who were dining and dancing, as well as parties of unaccompanied officers from the regiments being mobilised into the newly formed division. The evening passed all too quickly and I had little time to take much notice of the diners and dancers – although one of them had apparently seen me. The evening drew to its close with Mike Bailey missing the top step on the way out and somersaulting all the way to the bottom of the stairs. Peals of laughter greeted this extraordinary sight, and even I, slightly the worse for wear, saw the funny side. There was some concern to begin with, but Mike immediately got to his feet, brushed himself down, spluttering "my goodness me" through a cloud of scotch, and walked on as though nothing had happened.

A day or so later, I remembered the advice I had been given by Michael Lord when I first arrived in the mess, that Mike Bailey was always a 'bit off' first thing in the morning. I had come down to breakfast early, and the only other officer in the mess was Mike. He had the Times of India propped up in front of him and was reading the latest war news. I picked up a paper and walked to a seat on the opposite side of the table. As I did so, I said *sotto voce* "Good morning, Sir". I didn't expect a reply, and I didn't get one. A few minutes later a newly joined subaltern, an Irishman named Ian Maclachlan, came into the mess. He saw Mike and came to attention bringing his heels together unnecessarily loudly. "Good morning, Sir", he said with exaggerated cheerfulness. He obviously expected a reply, but didn't get one. I glanced at Mike and saw a distinct grimace at this unwarranted intrusion into his privacy. Ian picked up a paper, and walked to a seat right opposite Mike, but before he sat down he said once again, but this time even more robustly and in a tone of even greater cheerfulness, "GOOD morning, Sir." Mike Bailey could contain himself no longer. He gripped his newspaper firmly in both hands, brought it down on the table in front of him, turned several deepening shades of red, and between splutters said, "Good morning, good morning, good morning, good morning, and may that do for the rest of your bloody service." He then picked up the Times of India again and resumed his reading.

Ian had in the meantime turned very white and muttered a quiet, "Sorry, sir." No more was said, but the damage had been done and a few days later Ian disappeared from the Regiment when a request was received for a Staff Captain at Brigade Headquarters. It seems that he had not had the same detailed briefing as I had, but his ebullient manner fitted in well at Brigade, and he became an efficient staff officer, reaching Brigade Major within two years.

Company training now started in earnest, and in the intense heat we quickly discovered the meaning of real thirst. Apart from our individual water bottles, we had no means of slaking our thirst until we returned to our bungalows in the late afternoon. On one exercise my company was under instruction by Captain Gerry Lynch who was a pre-war officer and a hard taskmaster. He kept my men and me on the go the whole time with barely a pause to rest. It was probably the hottest day I had yet experienced and by midday my thirst was insufferable. I found myself near a small village and surreptitiously sneaked across to the village well where some of the inhabitants were glad to let me have a drink. A loud bellow from Captain Lynch pulled me up in my tracks, but not before I had taken a large draft of the cold water. I hurriedly thanked the villagers and went over to see the Captain who was angrily and impatiently hitting his leg with his stick. "Haven't you ever heard of water discipline, Captain Maslen-Jones," he snapped.

"Well, yes Sir," I replied.

"Then what the hell are you doing drinking untreated water from a village well, eh? And furthermore a good officer never looks after his own needs until he has made sure that his own men are all OK. All your men know the rule about drinking village water, but all you have done is to show them that you put your needs before theirs."

I thought for a few moments and then replied, "I am sorry, Sir, but no one has explained the rule about drinking untreated water, and I will never do it again. And I was wrong to drink when my men were probably thirsty, and I have learned that lesson as well."

"Good for you, Bob. A good officer will always take advice. Go on like that and you will soon make the grade. Well done."

For a short time I came to be known amongst my men as the *pani wallah* (the water man), but as we got to know each other better, the nickname was soon forgotten and was replaced by the more respectful title of *sahib*.

It was on a day-long exercise that I took my charger with me, and I very nearly made a similar mistake as I did not think of the welfare of my horse. I should have known that as I myself became hotter and thirstier, my horse must have been suffering in the same way, especially with my twelve stones of dead weight on his back. In the end he taught me a most salutary lesson, for as we crested a small knoll, there was a small lake nestling in a hollow just over the ridge. It was more than the animal could do to resist racing into the water in spite of all my efforts to keep it under control, and having slaked its thirst with me still in the saddle, the horse suddenly rolled over to have a refreshing, cool bath – and so did I! By the time I got back to Bowenpalli I was completely dry and none of my colleagues ever heard about it. It was a lesson I was to remember.

When we were not out on field exercises, Wednesday afternoons were free and during the few weeks that followed some of us went to the club swimming pool, foregoing our siesta. On the Wednesday following my first Saturday night out in the club when Mike had done his famous acrobatic stunt down the stairs, I was aware of a lovely looking girl who couldn't take her eyes off me. She sat on the side of the pool, her shapely legs dangling lazily in the water, while trying to give me the impression that she wasn't interested. Eventually she got bored and slipped quietly into the pool, surfacing alongside me in just a few short underwater strokes.

"Hullo", she said, "I'm Penny Somerset, and I think I saw you in the club last Saturday evening, didn't I?"

"Well, yes, I was in the club with some of my friends. But it was all so new I didn't have much of a chance to look around. I only joined my regiment two weeks ago, and I was being shown the ropes, so to speak. By the way, my name is Bob. Bob Maslen-Jones, and I'm with the Guides Infantry down in Bowenpalli."

"Yes, I know," replied Penny. "My father in Major Somerset, Garrison Engineer, and he knows exactly which regiments are here, and which lines they are in. You are not very far from my parent's bungalow actually, so perhaps you would like to come over and meet Daddy and Mummy sometime."

"Fast worker, this girl," I thought, "but I reckoned I could do a lot worse; she had a gorgeous figure and my first impressions of her were most promising. "That would be fun," I said, "but I have no transport, although I suppose I could get a taxi".

"Never mind about that," she replied, "I'm sure one or other of my parents will come over to pick you up. We've got three cars altogether – two of our own, and one which Daddy has from the Army."

And so the afternoon went on with me never sparing a thought for Joy, whose locket I was wearing round my neck and which, as far as I could see, Penny had not noticed. I knew I must accept the invitation to see her again, and felt reasonably safe in the knowledge that my stay in Secunderabad would not be for very much longer, perhaps four months at the most, and I might as well enjoy myself as much as I could. It all began to look very promising. "I must be going back to the Mess now," I said. "Our transport has arrived, and I mustn't miss it. Also I haven't booked out of the mess for dinner tonight and if I don't catch this truck, I won't get any dinner."

"I understand, Bob," she purred, "It has been such fun with you this afternoon and I'll see when Mummy can have you over for a meal". As we said good-bye, Penny turned and walked over to the ladies changing rooms, and I watched her graceful movements, admiring every curve of her body. It never occurred to me that such beauty might be only transient.

The invitation to meet Major and Mrs Somerset arrived the next day, and I excitedly accepted. The major, accompanied by Penny, collected me from my bungalow in Bowenpalli and drove us to their palatial residence in the more select part of the garrison. Mrs Somerset came out to meet us, an attractive middle-aged woman, with black hair and dark features, clearly an Anglo-Indian.

The evening went well and I had made the required impression on Penny's parents. When the major took me back to my bungalow, I sat in the back of the car, hand in hand with Penny, and I felt myself falling in love with her. The affair, still within the bounds of my strict upbringing, proceeded at a breathtaking pace, and we were soon the talk of the town. Within a week, I had been to dinner or to the club with Penny every night, and her parents had given me every encouragement, including the permanent use of one of their cars. It all made it so easy for me to dash over to be with her every time I had a spare moment. Inevitably, news of this whirlwind love affair reached the ears of the Adjutant, Goff Hamilton, who immediately informed Colonel Ted. I was summoned to his office, and for the first time I came face to face with what I considered to be unacceptable ethnic discrimination against Anglo-Indians, or chi-chi's as they were derisively called.

Colonel Ted looked very stern as he sat at his desk when I marched in to see him. Goff, proudly wearing the ribbon of the DSO he'd won as a subaltern in 1936, stood with an expression of stone, slightly behind and to one side of the Colonel. "Captain Hamilton tells me that you are behaving in a manner which is bringing no credit to this regiment, which I understand you asked to join of your own choice," he began. "There are so many things you will obviously have to learn about the way in which a British Officer is required to behave, and to be fair, it is difficult for a newcomer like yourself to be expected to know it all straight away. But you have certainly beaten the pistol, and from what I hear, you are getting very close to the point of no return. What have you to say about it?"

"I presume you are referring to my relationship with Penny Somerset, sir?" I replied.

"Well, if that is the young lady's name, yes I am" said Colonel Ted. "I don't mind what you do during your off-duty time providing it does not affect firstly your duty as a company commander and your responsibilities towards your soldiers, and secondly the reputation of this regiment. You see, Bob, in India there are strict class barriers, not only between various levels of society amongst the Indians themselves, but between the whites and what we rather insultingly call the off-whites, or Anglo-Indians – chi-chi's for short. Whatever you may think about it is immaterial. You have come to the Indian Army, and you have to accept the rules of the game whether you like them or not. You will appreciate that for a chi-chi girl to marry a British Officer would be a prize worth doing anything for, and I have to warn you that your young lady is, in fact, a chi-chi, sad as it may be. I am not going to beat about the bush, and I have to say straightaway that as long as you are in my regiment, I have to look on you as someone placed in my care. In other words I am in *loco parentis*, and have to take the place of your father. But further than that, I am responsible for the reputation of the regiment and I have to say straight away that unless you stop this affair without further ado, I will have you transferred to the Frontier Militia, probably the *Tochi* Scouts, and you can then look forward to a celibate existence for the length of your posting. That's all I wish to say, but I think you should talk to Goff and let him know what you intend to do."

The bottom fell out of my world. I was suddenly faced with leaving the one regiment I would have given anything to join, or giving up the girl I had fallen in love with and whom I was already planning to marry. If I went ahead and married her, I would be virtually drummed out of the regiment and posted to the North West Frontier, probably for the duration of the war, and if that happened there was no point anyway in going ahead with my plans to marry Penny. I thought about all the kindness Penny's parents had showered upon me, and suddenly I realised how blind I had been, and why they had pushed hard to make it so easy for me and Penny to spend so much time together. It was not lost on me that probably their ultimate purpose had been to get me into an uncompromising situation where I would have to marry their daughter. There seemed no way out, and there was certainly no point in arguing.

I had a long chat with Goff a couple of evenings later, and well primed with Scotch, I asked him to tell the colonel that I accepted his ruling but that it would be difficult for me to suddenly break the affair off. Goff agreed and said that he thought he could see a way out of the problem. He said, "There is a vacancy on a supporting weapons course at the Small Arms School at Saugor which begins in a week's time, and I think we will send you on it. It lasts for three weeks, and apart from the fact that it will be useful training for you and important for the regiment, it will give you the chance to make a clean break from your entanglement with Miss Somerset. And although it is still not confirmed, it is likely that we will be off to Malaya soon after you get back. Is that all right, Bob?"

"Yes, thank you, Sir," I replied, relieved that the complication was to be so simply solved.

When I visited the Somersets the following evening, I said nothing about the interview I had had with the Colonel, nor about my rather bibulous talk with the Adjutant. All I told them was that I was going to be away for at least three weeks on a course and that I was leaving the next day for Saugor in Central Provinces. I also said that after the course I proposed to see my uncle in Delhi and tell him about Penny. This was of course subterfuge, as I knew from what Colonel Ted had said that Uncle Eric would take the same line if there were any suggestion that I was intending to marry a chi-chi. The reaction of Penny's father was anything but enthusiastic at my plan to involve Uncle Eric. I could see that this development had put a spanner in the works as far as Penny's parents were concerned, but so far my relationship with Penny herself had gone on much as usual. The next morning, I took the car back to Major Somerset's office and bade him farewell, and I came away sure that my would-be father-in-law had realised exactly what was going on.

When I returned to the battalion some three and a half weeks later, all was hustle and bustle. No longer was the Brigade going to Malaya; something was afoot in the Middle East, and all the vehicles were being rapidly repainted in desert sand colour. Every officer and man in the Brigade worked flat out to meet the tight deadline in the most terrific heat, until one afternoon the long threatened monsoon finally burst upon us. There was no violent thunderstorm; the clouds simply opened and spilled out torrential rain. Junior officers and men stripped down to their underwear and everyone stood wallowing in the downpour, faces turned upwards, whilst as if by magic the parched vegetation took on a fresh greenness and gave off the most delicious smell. After the rain came a welcome drop in temperature, making life so much more pleasant.

The two other Brigades were still earmarked for Malaya, but Divisional HQ and 27th Indian Brigade were needed elsewhere in a hurry. Things were not going at all well in the Western Desert, but it seemed extraordinary to think that one Brigade would make any worthwhile difference. It would not be long before we were to know our destination and only two days after I rejoined the regiment after my course, we spent our last Saturday night in the club with our lips tightly sealed. I had not made any effort to get in touch with Penny, and I was not in the least surprised to see her dancing cheek to cheek with a young officer in the Royal Indian Army Service Corps, commonly known as the 'Rice Corps'. "I suppose any white officer will do," I thought.

# Chapter 7

## LESSONS IN BOMBING

———

It was September 1941 when the battalion entrained for Bombay; most of the transport had already gone ahead by road leaving only a rear party to tidy up. At Bombay we embarked on a troopship that had seen better days, and as soon as the rest of the Brigade and Divisional HQ had embarked in their respective ships, the convoy, escorted by two destroyers, set sail for the Persian Gulf. It was now known that we were to take part in an invasion of Persia, and that we would disembark at Basra at the head of the Gulf. On 31st May of that year Iraq was safely back in British hands following the battle of Habbaniyah and capture of Baghdad when General Wavell's forces had attacked across the 600-mile-wide desert from Palestine making short work of the rebel leader Rashid Ali who had seized power only one month before. Under the terms of the surrender agreement and setting up of a new government, Britain would have access to all road and rail communications and would guarantee to preserve Iraq's independence. This would secure a strategically important region and deny control of it to the Nazis who had a non-aggression pact with Turkey.

The invasion of Persia began on 25th August with British and Indian troops crossing the border from Iraq at a number of points while the Russians invaded from the north between the Caspian Sea and Turkish border. It was all over in four days.

It was not for me as a junior officer to worry about the political implications of campaigns, but I was concerned about what long-term effect, if any, there would be if the communists became firmly established in Persia. This concern was reduced by the fact that for the time being the Germans were approaching the gates of Moscow and Kiev, and the Russians were fighting with their backs to the wall along the whole of their front. But if Persia could be 'taken out', and an incursion by the Germans through Turkey prevented, a strong line of communication could be opened up from the Persian Gulf ports into southern USSR, and this, it was hoped, would turn the balance in favour of the hard-pressed Russians. In the meantime, the little convoy made its way through the Strait of Hormuz, and soon the outline of the vast oil installations and docks at Abadan and Khorramshah were seen through the shimmering heat haze to the east. Shortly afterwards we arrived at Basra with its torrid smells and teeming thousands of curious inhabitants. Some wag said that the Persian Gulf was the arse-hole of Asia and Basra was an ulcer 400 miles up it. I entirely agreed with that description.

The Brigade disembarked and met up with its transport which had arrived earlier, and a twenty-mile journey brought us to a tented camp in the flat, featureless desert to the north of Basra. The intention was that we would stay here just long enough to become acclimatised to the heat, dust and flies, whilst the Division would be made up to full strength with battle-hardened troops brought over from Eighth Army reserves in Egypt. Training in the desert began immediately and it was during a night attack exercise involving a ten-mile approach march that I changed my attitude to soldiering, albeit temporarily. I had an overwhelming wish to be out of that filthy, smelly place, and be somewhere that I could eat my food without flies and dust. As I led my company across the bleak desert through the darkness, I couldn't understand why the stars kept disappearing over the horizon, and as the night wore on, hallucinations of self-inflicted injuries that would get me back to England clouded my vision.

The company arrived at the forming-up place for the dawn attack and having secured the objective I lay down and took no further part in what was going on. As soon as Colonel Ted drove up in his station wagon to see how the exercise had gone, he asked me where my outposts where. I tried to be enthusiastic, but my slurred and completely disinterested speech left the Colonel in no doubt that I was far from well. One look into my eyes told him that I had jaundice, and he despatched me immediately to the field ambulance. By this time the illness was fully established, and I found myself vomiting frequently until it became an extremely painful process of retching concentrated bile. I was thankful when I eventually arrived in the Combined General Hospital that had been set up not far from the battalion camp, where I could sleep in a proper bed. The tents had been half dug-in which was perhaps not a bad thing; it made us cooler, but since the dust storms started blowing each morning at around eight o'clock, the patients found themselves lying level with the ground outside and unprotected from the full blast of the blown sand. This purgatory lasted throughout the day until five o'clock every afternoon, when it stopped as suddenly as it had started.

For the next two days I was joined in my misery by four other officers from the battalion, and we all lay there in the vile conditions which even for fit active men were pretty intolerable. Looking at the world through jaundiced eyes, death could not come soon enough. It was not surprising that the medical specialist prescribed the one thing which everyone knew was the worst possible infliction on a troubled liver – whisky, albeit only one medicinal tot of Scotch each evening! His reasoning was that the morale of his patients was so low that any damage a tiny measure may have done would have been more than offset by the uplifting effect of the drink. It was of course quite true and my colleagues and I found our spirits rising as the day wore on with the anticipation of the 'treatment' as soon as the wind, dust and flies disappeared at dusk. The Guides had been left behind when 6 Division, otherwise at full strength, had moved north into Persia. After forming up near Khanaqin, ninety miles northeast of

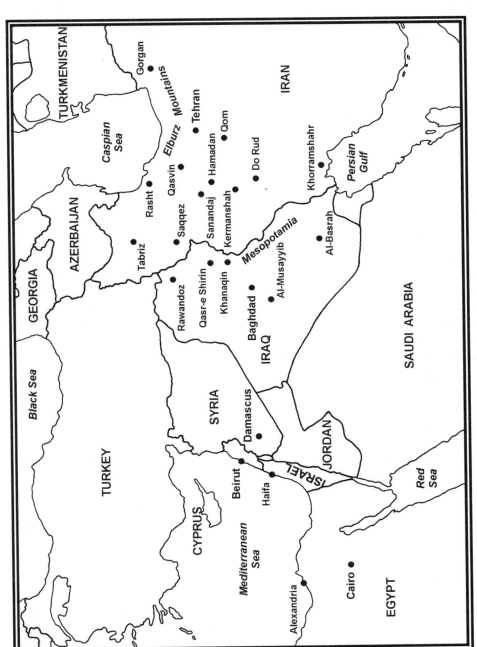

The Middle East

Baghdad on the road to Tehran, the attacking troops eventually passed through the border village of Qasr-i-Shirin, only to be held up by spirited resistance in the 4000-foot Pai Tak Pass. With only a single-track road winding upwards, this feature was an almost impregnable fortress. But after a bitter battle, Indian troops were able to perform an outflanking movement, and roll up the defences from the rear. From then on resistance, in the form of horsed cavalry units and an occasional Chevrolet armoured car was spasmodic. It was notional, and the morale of these ill-clad, ill-equipped Persian soldiers was very low.

*Pay parade. The Guides' Dogra company inside requisitioned Persian army barracks*

By the time the Division had reached the market town of Kermanshah, we had been discharged from hospital and had rejoined the battalion that had in turn rejoined the division. We were despatched northwards towards the small hill town of Senandaj, or Sennah for short, with orders to get there before the Russians who were already reported to be closing in having made a headlong rush south from Tabriz, 250 miles to the north. It was not in the Allied plans to have Russian troops sitting astride the main line of communication from Baghdad to Tehran, and so deep into Persian territory. By then I was back in command of D Company, and leading the battalion drive northwards to Sennah, 90 miles north of Kermanshah as fast as the rough and rutted road would allow. We saw telltale dust streamers from vehicles approaching from the opposite side of the valley. Feet pressed down harder on accelerators, and I reported the situation to Colonel Ted who responded by tagging on to the rear vehicle of D Company. As we raced through Sennah, chickens and dogs were sent scuttling out of the way to the intense bewilderment and anger of the local inhabitants. About a mile beyond the town, we drew up facing north to await the arrival of the Russians, who were not long delayed. Their consternation at having been thwarted was intense and no doubt they probably had visions of a long sojourn in Siberia for having failed the fatherland, but a show of camaraderie by our British officers and the Indian soldiers soon had both sides shaking hands. A party was quickly arranged for the officers of both sides, the Russians brought out a plentiful supply of vodka and it was not long before the British learnt how to toast Stalin, Roosevelt, Churchill and others by knocking back a glassful of the neat spirit in one burning gulp!

My letter home after that race carried a cryptic clue: "the place where the pods come from". My father quickly put Sennah and pods together, having the advantage of medical knowledge!

It was now October, and the climate up in the mountains was extremely pleasant after the purgatory of the desert some four hundred miles to the south. Sennah itself was on a plateau four thousand feet above sea level, whilst the surrounding mountains rose to almost ten thousand feet. They were rugged, challenging ranges and I looked forward to tackling some of the nearer peaks when I got the chance. My hopes of that were given a boost when the battalion was told it would remain in Sennah as garrison troops at least until the spring. Preparations were made to ensure that when the winter arrived, the soldiers would be in warm and comfortable quarters, and the Persian Army barracks, which had been built quite recently, were requisitioned.

Colonel Ted was most concerned that the Indian soldiers were protected as far as possible against contracting venereal diseases from the local women, and he took the initiative of setting up the battalion's own brothel. It fell to the medical officer to carry out an examination of all the selected girls once a week, and the scheme kept the incidence of disease to an absolute minimum throughout the winter months when the only entertainment for the *jawans* was in the 'red light' house. The colonel made it clear that if any soldier contracted VD he would assume that he had caught it from a woman outside the battalion brothel, and he would be punished severely.

Local intelligence revealed that the River Diyala on which Sennah stood, opened out into some huge *jhils* (lakes) only a few miles south of the town. Through the medium of 'John Simon', the self-given name of the interpreter employed by the battalion, it was also revealed that these *jhils* abounded with every kind of wildfowl, with blackcock for good measure. Shotguns arrived from India as if by magic, and a large supply of cartridges was bought in Baghdad. The evening flighting against the setting sun was a sight beyond description, and those of us who enjoyed shooting spent as much time as we could down there. The others merely enjoyed a welcome and rich addition to their diet.

One of my *Jemadars* had suggested that if we could get some dynamite, perhaps we could 'bomb' some smaller tributaries of the Diyala. The *jawans* in my company had seen large numbers of marcia (a type of fresh-water fish) in these streams, and the *Jemadar* assured me that although the fish were rather bony, the meat was very tasty and the men liked it. On my next visit to Kermanshah, I managed to persuade the local Royal Engineers to let me have a supply of ICI dynamite, with sufficient length of fuse and detonators. To cover themselves they gave us careful and explicit instructions on how to use the material, and told me that if anything untoward happened, they would deny all knowledge.

Several fish-bombing expeditions took place, and there was sometimes enough fish left over to supply the officers' mess whose menu seemed to improve as the winter grew harsher. Wildfowl, blackgame, and fresh fish were augmented by wild boar as these bear-like creatures came down from the hills to find food nearer the town.

On a cold but fine day in December, I took a party once again to do a bit of fish-bombing. A number of successful bombs had been thrown, and we had taken almost enough to supply the whole company. I was sitting on a bank a short distance away from the pool, and as I watched three *jawans* preparing the bomb, I thought I saw a wisp of smoke coming from the fuse. I immediately shouted "Phenko, phenko" (throw it, throw it) but the *jawans* did not react as they did not think it was lit. They struck another match and applied it to the fuse which I now saw clearly had already been lit. I yelled "Phenko!" again, but it was too late and almost immediately the dynamite exploded. There was a stunned silence followed by screams of pain. The three men were my orderly who was a bright and very intelligent young soldier, a *naik* (corporal), and the company *havildar*-major (sergeant-major). My orderly had been holding the stick of dynamite in his right hand, the *naik* shielding the end of the fuse with both his hands cupped, and the *havildar*-major holding the match. All the men lost their hands and my orderly lost his arm below the elbow.

My initial reaction was to be sick, but I pulled myself together and organised the NCOs in the party to give the injured men first aid. Having been a medical student, the sight of blood did not come strangely to me, and in a state of shock I attempted to cope with the tragic situation. When we had done all we could, the soldiers threw all the fish they had caught back into the river, for none of them could face eating it when their friends had paid such a high price. We returned to the barracks in silence, and after seeing to the needs of the injured men and leaving them in the regimental-aid-post with the medical officer doing all he could with his limited resources, I went to my room to try and compose myself.

Word of what had happened quickly reached the mess, where Colonel Ted was entertaining the Divisional Commander, Major-General 'Tiger' Thomson, for lunch. The General was making a quick visit to the Guides to see how things were going, and until that point he had been impressed with all he had seen and heard. Bertie Berdoe, a recently joined brother officer, came to my room and did his best to comfort me. Bertie had been the vicar of an English church in Madras but had decided to join the army as a combatant; he felt this was a more positive way of playing his part in a war that he believed was just. "Will it help if we pray together?" he said, and I knelt down at my bedside as Bertie asked God for strength to meet the tragic situation which had so suddenly come upon us. While we were kneeling down by my bed, my Hindu orderly came into the room, and my immediate reaction was to get off my knees. I had never prayed like this except in church and my immediate reaction was to think I shouldn't be seen praying by one of my soldiers. I looked at Bertie, and he was oblivious to the fact that I was no longer on my knees or that *sepoy* Raja Ram was in the room. I knelt down again, ashamed at my reaction, but Bertie never mentioned the incident to me afterwards. It was something of a turning point in my life and I felt that my faith had in some way been strengthened by Bertie's example.

Fortified by Bertie's support and encouragement, I went to the mess and asked the Adjutant if I could see Colonel Ted alone for a moment or two. The Adjutant already knew what had happened, and excusing himself to the General, he drew the Colonel to one side. A severe glower came across his face as he heard the news, and he came across to me. "I don't want any excuses, Bob," he began, "Just write out a full report before you do anything else, and that includes lunch". I had not expected such an abrupt reaction, and I returned to my room feeling very unhappy indeed.

Back in the mess, Colonel Ted told the General what had happened and added that he had sent me to write a report. "I think you are being a bit harsh, aren't you, Ted?" said the General. "From what I could see the lad is shattered and needs a bit of moral support. Give him time to get his thoughts together, and then we can see how it happened. From what you tell me he is a very promising young officer, and it is hardly likely that this is anything but a very unfortunate accident."

"You're probably right, General," said Colonel Ted. "If you'll excuse me, I'll go and see him in his room, and have a chat with him. In fact I'll take him a gin to bolster him up."

When he came into my room with a gin and angostura, Colonel Ted found me lying on my bed actually crying. It had all been too much, and the Colonel realised that his own severe reaction had been the last straw. With this fatherly encouragement I quickly recovered and after a friendly talk together, the two of us went back to the mess where I had my lunch sitting next to the General who talked to me about everything except what had happened by the river. "Well, Ted," said the General when he got up to drive back to Kermanshah, "about this morning's accident. When I get your report I will have to forward it to the Army Commander in Baghdad as the three men will clearly be discharged as a result of their injuries, and the high-ups will want to know where to place the blame." Then he turned to me and said, "Don't worry too much. Just carry on soldiering and we'll see what can be done."

The incident was duly played down by Colonel Ted and the General, both of whom gave the opinion that there had been a very unfortunate accident and that I could not be held entirely to blame. But the Army Commander, General Quinan, considered that I had been most irresponsible in allowing myself to get involved in such pranks as bombing fish in the first place, and even more so by not exercising proper control of the bombing operation. I felt it was a harsh decision, but I had no alternative but to accept the Army Commander's severe reprimand and try to forget all about the unhappy affair. Colonel Ted himself did not get off without an Army Commander's reprimand either, not for condoning the bombing expeditions, but for not knowing that they were taking place!

As far as my *jawans* were concerned, they felt that I was not to blame and their respect for me was in no way impaired. I was a popular and respected company commander and the men knew that I had gone along with the idea of bombing fish to introduce a bit of entertainment as well as putting a bit of variety into their menu.

During the second week in December, a detachment of two companies was sent down to the Pai Tak pass area to work on the defences. The situation in the Western Desert had taken a serious turn for the worse, and it seemed likely that if Rommel managed to break through into Egypt, the Germans would quickly reinforce whatever resistance there might remain from the Red Sea, through Jordan and Palestine and across 600 miles of desert, to Iraq and Persia. They would then attempt to sweep northwards and attack the soft underbelly of Russia through the Caucasus. The Pai Tak Pass was the one place where the Allied forces might stop them, and it was with this in mind that the General ordered his troops to repair and improve the positions that had been so valiantly held on to by the Persians during the invasion.

At the time, the detachment moved down to Kermanshah and then westwards to the Pai Tak Pass, and I was sent on a fortnight's camouflage course near Khanaqin. The course ended on Christmas Eve, and I travelled to the detachment position at the top of the pass where I had been 'invited' to stay over Christmas before rejoining the battalion in Sennah on Boxing Day. That Christmas dinner was one party I would never forget; as we drove up the snow-covered pass, I savoured the thought of the evening ahead but by the time we arrived I was chilled to the marrow. I was amazed at the warmth inside the officers' mess. This was a so-called 'Wana Hut', which consisted of the top of a square marquee supported on walls made of sand-filled ghee tins, half the height of the wall being dug into the ground to afford extra height, and in one corner the battalion pioneers had built a fire place that was roaring away as it consumed large logs of sisal oak.

The party was in full swing with some rather irresponsible drinking already underway. I wasted no time in warming myself with Pink Gins, forgetting that I had an empty stomach, and so I didn't get beyond the stage of sitting down to dinner before the sight and smell of greasy soup sent me rushing outside where the snow lay several inches deep. After taking deep breaths of the cold air for ten minutes or so to clear my head, I ventured back inside and for a time I thought I was going to make it. But a plateful of greasy roast goose finally settled the issue and after dashing outside I collapsed in the snow and lay there semi-conscious for a considerable time. With my core temperature plummeting, I found my way to the bath tent where, having despatched numerous cackling chickens from their night perches, I passed out on a *charpoy* (bed) with my feet dangling in icy water. Why I did not die of hypothermia during that night I never understood, but if there was ever any truth in the old adage that the Good Lord looks after drunkards, it was proven to me beyond any doubt that night. Next morning, feeling like nothing on earth, I bade my fellow officers farewell, and was driven back to Sennah in an open 15 cwt Chevrolet truck. I was never more grateful for the warmth and comfort of the battalion mess and after a good hot meal I went straight to bed to sleep it off. It was not until I got my mess bill at the end of the month that I realised I had consumed seven large pink gins by the time we had sat down for the first course. It was a lesson well learned and one I took to heart. As my father told me – one is enjoyable, two are even better and a third is one too many!

# Chapter 8

# AVOIDING BILL HARRIS

———

Throughout January and February 1942, the winter remained hard and bitterly cold. The town of Sennah was virtually cut off although bulldozers managed to keep the line of communication to Kermanshah open. As March arrived there were signs of a let-up, and soon the weather turned far more clement. The snows started to melt and the roads once more became passable. Orders were sent from Divisional HQ that the battalion was to start regular patrols deep into Kurdistan where the local tribesmen were reported to be preparing a spring offensive against what remained of the Persian Army. The detachment was recalled from the Pai Tak Pass, and Colonel Ted planned a series of expeditions at company strength to cover large areas of both northern Persia and northern Iraq taking in towns such as Bijar, Saqqez and Rawandoz. On the first of these operations Colonel Ted decided to escort my company. I travelled in relative comfort in the station wagon with the colonel and it was my job to keep a detailed diary and record of all meetings with Persian, Iraqi or Kurdish leaders. The interpreter, John Simon, travelled in a truck behind and would be present at all these discussions. He was not a young man, and did not find travelling in an open vehicle particularly enjoyable.

These patrols lasted three or four days and were, strangely enough, highly entertaining. Colonel Ted put on the air of the great British Raj coming to lay down the law, and the Kurdish tribesmen, festooned with bandoliers of cartridges slung across each shoulder, were very impressive to behold. Their rifles were old, but there could be no doubt that these men were first class shots. This fact was sadly proven when the *Subedar* of the Punjabi Musulman company was picked off by a sniper when he stood up in his truck as his patrol made its way through a rocky defile.

On the second expedition I made with Colonel Ted, I witnessed an extraordinary scene that gave me a little more insight into his character. The convoy had stopped for a brief rest, when a heavily laden donkey came along the unmetalled road. It was being urged to go faster by its owner who kept jabbing a sharp stick into the poor animal's backside, causing it obvious distress. In a flash Colonel Ted jumped from the station wagon and rushed at the donkey-*wallah*, shouting to him in what little *Farsi* (Persian) he knew, to stop ill-treating his beast. "You swine of Hell," he roared as he proceeded to lay about the man. He grabbed the stick, in the end of which there was a very sharp nail, and took it away from him. I was at first inclined to be amused at this extraordinary scene, but I soon realised that Colonel Ted had completely lost control by what he saw as downright cruelty. To me, still an inexperienced young officer, it seemed to be a simple case of the man knowing no better. He had probably always prodded his donkey to keep it moving, and however cruel other people might think it to be, no amount of beating and shouting was going to change the habits of a lifetime. I kept silent, tacitly agreeing with whatever remarks the colonel might make about these "ignorant and cruel bastards".

*Armed Kurdish horseman, 1942*

The following day the patrol had passed through Saqqez and reached a spot about twenty miles northwest of the town when we unexpectedly came across a newly constructed road. It was wide enough to take four lanes of traffic and ran dead straight as far as the eye could see in both directions. From the west it appeared to come from the nearest point on the Turkish border, and then followed a southeasterly line across Persia towards India. There was no sign that the road had ever been used, and Colonel Ted thought that it had been made under the supervision of the Germans in preparation for a new *drang nach osten* (drive to the east) that would take them across the North West Frontier into India. I agreed, and realised that this was obviously one of the factors that had brought about the invasion of Persia a few months earlier. The discovery of this new *autobahn* triggered a discussion between the colonel and me about world politics, and I was horrified when he said he would be quite happy to see the Russians sitting along the English Channel. I presumed that he meant to imply that the number one priority was for the Russians to defeat the

Germans and replace them as far as France, Belgium and the Netherlands. "What then, Colonel?" I asked.

"We'll have to wait and see, Bob, but for my part as things are at present, I think the West will have to learn to live alongside the Russians."

"But they will still be Communists, Colonel, and surely you cannot be serious that their next conquest would not be directed against Britain ?"

At last it seemed to me that I had made a telling point, for the only response my last question had evoked was just one word, "Perhaps".

During the early spring, there was good news for me and my fellow company commanders in an Army Council Instruction which stated quite simply that with immediate effect all company commanders in Infantry battalions were to be promoted to the rank of Major. There were four rifle companies and a headquarters company in a battalion, and all of them in the Guides were still commanded by captains. This was cause for celebration, and the corks duly popped. I was not quite twenty-one when I became a major, and it made a great deal of difference to my pay and allowances. I planned to save as much as I could, and certainly in Persia there was little to spend my money on other than my mess bill.

Soon after this welcome announcement, I sat my Urdu higher standard examination and passed with ease. This, too, meant an extra allowance, and I began to learn Pushtu, the language of the Pathans, while tackling reading and writing the Arabic script.

Spring had arrived by mid-March, and wildfowling came to an end as the masses of duck and geese paired off to breed. I took to the crags, and soon enthused another young officer named Ronnie Noyce whose elder brother was already an experienced climber. The two of us would take a foot patrol with us for local security, and spend all day tackling routes that we had selected with the aid of maps and binoculars.

By mid-April, the Army Commander had got wind of the regimental brothel which Colonel Ted had set up to protect his soldiers. Although the number of men in the Guides who had contracted VD was by far the lowest percentage of the posted strength of all other units in the theatre, the General chose to ignore this. It was said he was a very straight-laced, clean-living man, who never drank or was unfaithful to his beloved wife. He couldn't accept Colonel Ted's defence of the brothel, and could only see that it encouraged the soldiers to live sordid and depraved lives. It was beyond him to understand that without the Regimental red-light house with its weekly health inspections, the soldiers would go into the town brothels and an even higher number would contract VD. This would reduce the fighting efficiency of the battalion, and it was Colonel Ted's aim to prevent that happening at all costs. But the Army Commander was not to be moved, and in punishment he ordered the Guides to be withdrawn from their pleasant mountain station to do a stint of six months on guard duties in and around Baghdad, including the vast Command Ordnance Depot at Musaiyib some forty miles to the south.

The move down to the desert was not at all to my liking. I was enjoying my climbing, and a training programme had already been started when the bad news was announced. By this time I was probably as fit as I had ever been, even in the halcyon days when my brother Ted and I were in the school Rugger XV. I used to race up and down steep mountain slopes, and learned a great deal of mountain lore from my *jawans* who were Pathans from the North West Frontier. Not for nothing was I nicknamed *Bakra*, the Urdu name for goat, and the thought of spending the next six months in the heat, dust and flies, losing much of my fitness, distressed me greatly.

The battalion packed everything up within a very short time and moved down to Baghdad where we were encamped about four miles to the west of the city at Quetta. There was nothing to be said to commend it; it was dead flat but at least an effort had been made to keep the dust down to a minimum by spraying waste oil along all the roads and paths within the camp area. Unfortunately, I was riding a 350 cc AJS motorcycle along one of those oily roads soon after we arrived in the camp, and came off with the motorbike on top of my legs. The exhaust pipe caused a very sore lesion that took many weeks to heal properly. The Officers Mess had been well prepared in a dug-in double EP/IP tent, and there was no shortage of gin and whisky. Several other units, including a General Hospital, were stationed within the square mile, forming a sizeable garrison, large enough to justify occasional entertainment by courtesy of ENSA as well as Indian films for the *jawans*.

Soon after arriving at Quetta, my company was detailed to do the first spell of guard duties in and around the city. Special responsibilities included the British Embassy, the Alwiyah Club, Army HQ and vital bridges. It was a sizeable list, and it was the company commander's job to inspect all his guard posts at least once a day, usually in the morning before it got too hot. On one of those inspections, I recall being excessively warm and completely dehydrated long before I had completed the round. My uniform had turned white, the salt from my sweat having dried on the cloth. I pressed on with my inspections, buoying myself up with the thought that I would drop into a hotel and have a beer as soon as the job was finished. And so I came gasping into the Semiramis Hotel on the bank of the River Tigris, which I had already visited on one or two previous occasions and was the only bar in Baghdad with an air-conditioner. Walking into the bar was like entering a cold store. The cool air made me feel much better and I ordered a pint of Allsop's Export Ale. The barman, whose name was Jesus, produced a bottle covered with condensation which he poured into a pint glass. I seized it and almost without tasting it, gulped it down. My uniform turned black in seconds as the liquid coursed through my body, replacing much of the liquid I had sweated out. "That was superb, Jesus," I said, "I'll have another please".

"Yes, sahib, but please pay for that one first", replied Jesus, "It is ninety rials."

I nearly had apoplexy! Ninety rials was the equivalent of eighteen shillings in 1942. I paid, and had another for good measure.

*Street scene in Baghdad, October 1942*

In between guard duties, a training programme was carried out, and whenever possible my fellow company commanders and I chose an area of desert as near to the RAF base at Habbaniyah as possible. This was simply so that after the morning exercise, the *jawans* could spend the rest of the day swimming and relaxing on the shore of the big Habbaniyah lake. It was something we all looked forward to and it certainly helped to maintain morale in the scorching heat of the summer when the daily routine was very boring to say the least. As a side show Sunderland flying boats would quite frequently come in low over the 'beach' and land on the lake.

After three months in Quetta Camp, the battalion was moved to Musaiyib, a small town on the river Euphrates about forty miles south of Baghdad. The ordnance depot was far bigger than I had imagined and covered a huge acreage, which made raids by organised gangs of Arabs relatively easy. Those raids had become so serious that reinforcements were rushed down there to stop the wholesale plundering of stores. Those were non-perishable items, such as small-arms ammunition, as well as certain dry foodstuffs like rice and dahl.

As soon as the battalion had settled in, the magnitude of the task we had been given became clearer. Whilst some of the officers were sent away on courses, and one or two managed to hitch a lift on planes going to India for a few days leave, it had already been decided that our time in Musaiyib would be used to carry out a refit of the battalion's transport. Unfortunately one of those who had seized the chance to get a bit of leave in India was the MTO, Wyon Stansfield, and I had been given the job of supervising the refitting programme in his absence. This meant that not only would I have to carry out my normal work of commanding my company, but every afternoon when the senior officers were taking their siesta, I would be checking up on the progress of the refit.

It was soon apparent that the nightly ambush patrols the soldiers had to carry out and which for the most part lasted from soon after dusk until dawn, were beginning to affect our efficiency and morale. Tiredness began to show, and when one night, in spite of what was thought to be adequate coverage of the depot, camels and donkeys were brought from miles around to carry away amongst other items more than half a million rounds of ammunition, I decided that I myself must take my turn, along with my Indian Officers, in a spell of ambush duty. By now I was extremely fatigued, and I found the evening mess routine boring and infuriating. My morale began to sink as evening after evening the other young officers and I had to wait for our meal while the pre-war regular officers, including Colonel Ted, who was probably the chief offender, told the same old stories about life in India before "this bloody show started", usually to the accompaniment of near hysterical laughter depending on how many pink gins they had drunk. The mess table was always laid out on the open desert and without this lengthy 'entertainment' each night it would have been a very pleasant sort of life.

It was not long before Mike Baily hit on the brilliant idea of having his Bren gun carrier, a small tracked armoured vehicle, brought round to his tent every afternoon at 4 o'clock, after his siesta and cup of *cha*. He had named his carrier after his hunter, Kylemore, which he had left behind in Mardan, and he played a little game of make believe, "To keep myself sane, don't you know", he said. He had laid out a course taking in all sorts of difficult, but imaginary hazards to drive over, matching a point-to-point course somewhere in the shires! Probably the idea was a good one if, in the end, Mike became a really competent driver. (The story of Lt Colonel Cummings, the commanding officer of another battalion of the Frontier Force Regiment who had driven his carrier through the Japanese lines during the disastrous campaign in Malaya, and had then escaped to Java earning himself the Victoria Cross in the process, is well known throughout the world.) Unfortunately, everyone had to listen to a commentary every evening about how Kylemore had taken the various 'fences' during the afternoon.

The strain under which the junior officers were working had to give sooner or later. This eventually happened one evening when the mess *havildar* came across to Colonel Ted for the second time to announce *"Khana Taiyar hai, hazur"* (Dinner is ready, sir), only to be dismissed with the order *"Ek aur Pink Gin lao, mehrbani se"*. (Bring me another Pink Gin, please). The stories went on until Colonel Ted had finished his drink then he told the *havildar* to bring the meal in. After dessert the mess waiters served the coffee, and the stories began again. There was a mess rule that no officers were allowed to leave the table until the commanding officer permitted them to do so. I was longing to go to bed, and was finding it extremely difficult to keep my eyes open as the voices and ribald laughter went on and on. I happened to be sitting directly opposite Colonel Ted that evening, and again and again I pinched myself to keep awake. In the end I could fight it no more, and I slumped across the table, momentarily fast asleep. The reaction was immediate. "For the love of God, Bob, wake up or go to bed," roared Colonel Ted.

"Thank you, Sir," I replied, "I'll go to bed. Good night, Sir". I left the mess to be followed by others after the colonel had given them permission to go.

The next day I was summoned to see the Adjutant to give an explanation for what was seen to be atrocious behaviour. Goff Hamilton had left the battalion to take up a staff appointment, and Archie Pugh, who had been working for Burma-Shell before volunteering to join the Indian Army was now firmly in the Adjutant's driving seat. I didn't pull any punches and spelt out exactly what sort of workload my colleagues and I were under. "Good God" said Archie, "I hadn't realised that any of you were actually taking a stint on ambushes. We can't have that. Wait here while I go and see Colonel Ted." After what seemed a long time, I was asked to go in and tell the colonel what I had already told Archie, with the result that the mess rule was immediately waived and as from that evening any officer who so wished was allowed to go to bed as soon as the coffee had been served. Furthermore, as a result of representations to Command HQ, another battalion was brought down to share the guard duties of the depot.

The situation changed for the better, the *jawans* found a bit of time to relax, and I took my soldiers to bathe in the vast barrage across the River Euphrates at Hindiya, until the medical officer got to hear of it and nearly went berserk. "Haven't you ever heard of 'Bill Harris', Bob?" He asked impatiently. "Its proper name is Bilharzia, and is an *extremely* unpleasant and dangerous disease which results in the swelling of various organs. Yes, you may grin – those too. It is commonly known as Elephantiasis." I had of course heard of it, but there had never been any warning about it, or how it was caught, and as far as I was concerned it was one of those diseases that you did not catch as long as 'you kept your nose clean'. The MO went on to explain that the barrage was an ideal place for a certain snail, which acted as an intermediate host, to thrive. With immediate effect the swimming had to stop, but happily there were no cases of 'Bill Harris' in the battalion.

Soon the summer had passed its peak, and the extensive *jhils* between the rivers Tigris and Euphrates provided blackgame shooting as good as we had enjoyed near Sennah. But this did not last long, and in September the battalion was ordered back to Kermanshah to do a line of communication duties and to carry out extensive training in mountain warfare. Over in the Western Desert things were at last going our way, and plans were already being made for an assault on the Italian mainland followed by a very tough mountain warfare campaign in the Appenines, the mountainous spine of Italy. An adequate reserve of properly trained mountain divisions would therefore be required. The battalion set up camp near the main supply route to Tehran just outside the town, and we were to stay there until the following May. I very soon became mountain-fit again, and until deep snow more or less confined our training to the immediate neighbourhood for a few weeks, I thoroughly enjoyed taking my company on extended exercises into the higher mountains to the north. It was not difficult for me to imagine that I was back in my beloved Welsh hills, for there was a great similarity in the scenery, and I loved every minute of it.

# Chapter 9

## BAGHDAD SICK LEAVE

———

Quite soon after Christmas, 1942, I was sent to Hamadan on a short explosives course and I learnt all I could about the subject of laying mines and handling explosives. There was no doubt a connection between my presence on that course and the tragic fish-bombing incident in *Sennah* a year earlier. If the truth be known, I was not all that keen to be the battalion's explosives officer.

At lunch one day during the course, I had noticed how dirty the plate was on which my meal had been dished up, but I was very hungry after an energetic morning in the cold air, and I let it pass, eating the food with relish. It was a few days later that I was to remember the dirty plate with regret. There was no pain as such, just a feeling of discomfort, and I put it down to a bad stomach upset. I had gone to the 'Kitchener' – the officers' latrine tent – and experienced diarrhoea that I likened to 'turning on a tap'. To my dismay, I had to repeat the process another three times in fairly rapid succession before I could get dressed. By this time I felt perfectly normal and I went to have breakfast, but for safety's sake I did not eat much so as to give my digestion a chance to right itself. The following morning and every subsequent morning the same thing happened. I was able to carry on with my training programme, but when there was no change in my condition after a week and I was beginning to feel weaker and less inclined to run up and down steep slopes, I decided to consult the MO. There was no doubt whatsoever in the doctor's mind. I had dysentery, not the straightforward, comparatively easily cured variety, but he suspected it was amoebic. Being a medical student I was quick to understand when the MO explained that amoebic dysentery was caused by a simple single-cell organism which, as I well knew, was capable of rapid development by sub-division of the nucleus; these organisms also had the ability to encyst themselves inside the wall of the intestine, and were therefore very resistant to almost every type of treatment. As a final *coup-de-grace*, he told me that treatment would be long, tedious and very unpleasant probably with daily enema bowel washes. There was no alternative but getting me into proper medical care as quickly as possible and I was sent at once to the Casualty Clearing Station

(CCS) where I was admitted for tests; within a few days Amoebic dysentery was confirmed.

My world had fallen apart. The treatment was exactly as my MO had described, and it went on for week after week. There seemed to be no improvement in my condition, and I quickly lost a lot of weight. There could be no question of my return to the battalion, and I knew from visiting brother officers that Pat Phelps, whom I did not like very much, had been appointed acting company commander in my place, although I was still nominally in command so that I did not lose my rank. This could not go on for very much longer, and at the end of March I was sent down to Khanaqin and admitted to a British General Hospital for further treatment. Soon the summer with its unbearable heat, dust and flies had begun again, and I spent my days lying on my bed in between treatments, clad in pyjama trousers or sometimes only underpants.

Two events happened during the ten weeks that followed, one of which brought me up with a jolt. Two officers who had been on a course in Palestine, and who had celebrated the end of the course far too well, were admitted to my ward in a state of collapse after a six-day journey across the desert in the back of an open lorry! Both were diagnosed as suffering from DT's; they were completely dolali (service slang for mad), and spent their time screaming at imaginary pink elephants or green rats climbing up the walls. Sadly both those young officers died in the ward, in full view of all the other patients, in spite of the efforts of the doctors to cool them down by covering them with a wet sheet and blowing a fan across it to reproduce the effect of a refrigerator. At that time I was still intending to return to my medical studies after the war ended, and unlike my fellow patients who found the whole thing very distressing, I was very interested in all that went on about me. A timely warning about the demon drink, I thought.

The second incident was an event that I was to remember for the rest of my life. It was a demonstration of friendship that, when I remember it, I always find very moving. I was in the British Military Hospital near Khanaqin, one very hot afternoon just after lunch, when we were all dozing the time away waiting for the relative cool of the evening. The noise of some heavy transport could be heard approaching the hospital, and suddenly the peace of the afternoon was shattered as the transport drove into the hospital compound with the accompanying noise of shouted orders, and of heavy metal objects being moved about. I got off my bed to go and see what the row was all about, and was amazed to see that several lorries from a Royal Artillery Field regiment had entered the hospital compound and had drawn up quite close to the ward I was in. "Bloody idiots," I said to another patient who had also got up to have a look. "Don't they know it's against the Geneva Convention for fighting units to occupy Red Cross designated areas?" I went back to my bed as all was now quiet again, and I lay back, wondering why the battery had chosen to come into the hospital compound. Then, in the distance, I heard a voice I thought I vaguely recognised and looking towards the entrance to the ward I saw a gunner officer, covered from head to foot in desert dust, talking to one of the medical orderlies who was pointing towards me. The officer turned in my direction, saw me lying there almost naked, and with a broad smile showing through the dust he walked across to greet me. It was Ian Beddows, whom I had thought was still in the UK.

"Hello, old cock," he grinned, "good to see you."

"What on earth are you doing up here?" I asked him, "I thought you were still back at home living it up with all the fillies! And however did you find out that I was in this God forsaken dump?"

"Well, I knew that you had gone down with the plague, as your old man had told mine the bad news. I was then just about to embark with my regiment for the long voyage round the Cape, and before we got to Egypt we were diverted to Basra, and finished up in Mosul, where we are now deployed. I'm Mess Secretary, and I've been down to Baghdad with the regimental quartermaster buying 'goodies' to supplement the rations, both solid and liquid! Somehow I got lost on the way back and here I am."

We both had a good laugh and I said, "Well Ian, nothing changes does it? But tell me how you found out where I was?"

"I found out from the Military Secretary where your regiment was, and he very kindly also found out for me where you were, and I just couldn't resist the temptation to drop in and cheer you up a bit."

"You've certainly done that, old boy," I replied, " It's absolutely great seeing you. How long can you stay?"

"Not very long, I'm afraid. I've made a diversion of about ninety miles anyway and I must get back to Mosul and get everything we've bought safely stashed away". Ian and I had only a few minutes more to exchange news, as a Warrant Officer in the Military Police soon appeared at the door and the ward orderly came over to ask Ian to leave. We shook hands warmly, wished each other well, and this sudden but brief episode was over. Outside, the Warrant Officer saluted Ian, and asked him politely to get his vehicles out of the hospital compound without delay. I felt choked with emotion as I heard the lorries drive away. Would we ever see each other again? It was a question of living each day as it came.

A few days after Ian's visit, I was moved to a Combined General hospital in Baghdad to go before a medical board. After four months of the most intensive treatment they could give me, my condition was steadily deteriorating. I had long since lost interest in pretty well everything, and when the medical specialist suggested that it seemed unlikely that I would get rid of the amoebic cysts (which had apparently become completely resistant) until I returned to a temperate climate, I began to see some light at the end of the tunnel. I started to look forward to an early return to Britain, although that would mean returning to the British Army, and loss of my temporary majority and the higher rates of pay I was getting at present. But the future for me out here looked bleak; my life had turned sour on me and I hoped to be invalided back home where I could get properly cured of this disgusting disease.

On the way down to Baghdad in the ambulance train, something happened to my inside. Without warning I suffered a violent attack of what seemed like stomach cramp that spread throughout my abdomen. I was folded over, and lay there in the most awful pain I had ever had to endure. After several minutes it eased off, and I found myself sweating profusely with the sheer agony of the attack. But by the time I got to the Combined General Hospital in Baghdad, it had all subsided and I felt relaxed and comfortable and it was not until the next morning that a doctor came to see me. That morning however, I hadn't had diarrhoea for the first time in four months. It was the turning point. My doctor and I kept our fingers crossed and over the next few days my condition improved, and the plans for me to be medically boarded were put on hold.

I started to take an interest in what was going on around me, and I even did some studying. I acquired a physiology textbook and was seen reading it by one of the surgeons. When I told him that I had interrupted my medical studies to join the Army, the surgeon asked me if I would like to assist him in the operating theatre. He warned me that they would have to keep me in the hospital for another three weeks to be certain that I had got rid of my amoebae, and he thought I might as well make myself useful. I was delighted and I took part in some very interesting work that re-kindled my interest in *materia medica* and intention to return to Oxford as soon as the war ended.

The next few weeks passed very quickly, there was no recurrence of the *amoebiasis*, and I was sent back to the battalion that was still in the Kermanshah area. I had been warned that even a slight excess of alcohol would in all probability irritate the still inflamed lining of my intestines, and I would get the same symptoms I had suffered for the past six months. If this happened I was not to worry unless the problem did not quickly go away. The advice I was given was not to drink more than one tot of Scotch a day, and I made up my mind that I would toe the line and stick to just one. I also had to watch my diet, as anything too fibrous would have the same irritating effect.

I received a warm welcome in the mess, but Colonel Ted decided that I should take two weeks leave, and as Mike Baily was about to leave us to take command of another battalion, it was suggested that one of the other company commanders, George McMunn, whose father had commanded the Mesopotamian Force in the Great War, should accompany me on a fortnight's leave to the Caspian Sea. It was all agreed, and we soon went down to Baghdad together and caught a plane to Tehran. We would stay there for a few days and then go to the State-run hotel at Ramsar on the coast for a week. This seemed a splendid idea to me, especially as the battalion was under orders to move down to Baghdad for a short tour of duty before going across the desert to the Mountain Warfare Training Centre high up in the Lebanese mountains. This meant that when we flew back to Baghdad at the end of our leave the battalion would already be installed in Quetta Camp.

There were no problems, and George and I quickly made all the necessary travel arrangements through Army HQ. Two days after I had been discharged from hospital, I was back in Baghdad again on my way to the airport with George. But my excitement was somewhat quenched when I saw the plane we were to fly in. It was a very ancient Avro Anson, a good reliable 'kite' in its day, but this one looked as though it had seen many better days, and I wondered how long it was since it had been inside a maintenance hangar. However, the engine started up without faltering, and to my inexpert ear it sounded sweet and smooth. As we taxied to the end of the runway, I noticed oil seeping underneath one of the engine cowls. Too late now, I thought to myself, and I looked away, not once glancing at the oil until we were safely on the ground at Tehran. It had been a pleasant flight, and only once did I feel nervous, when we crossed the 12 000 feet mountains just before passing over Hamadan. We flew through a gap between two peaks, and to my surprise I saw large snowfields up there that remained from the previous winter. A bit of turbulence was all we experienced and once clear of the high mountains the Anson went easily on its way to a smooth touch down at Tehran.

# Chapter 10

## REST, RECUPERATION AND RUSSIANS

---

Tehran shimmered in the heat of late summer, but it was a great deal cooler than it had been down in the Iraqi desert. Up there we were already over 3000 feet above sea level. Not far to the north the Elburz mountains stretched more than 300 miles from Rasht, a short distance from the south west corner of the Caspian Sea, to beyond Gorgan to the east, to just under 19 000 feet. Like the mountains close to Hamadan, there was some glacier ice to be seen on the highest most inaccessible reaches. After my long sojourn in hospital in the desert at no more than 600 feet above sea level, to see and feel the proximity of such grand mountains was a tonic in itself.

Having taken it all in, George and I hired a cab and set off for the hotel where we booked in for three nights. It was nothing very spectacular, but fine for a short stay as we did not propose to spend much time inside. The idea of that leave was partly to get myself mountain fit again, walking for longer and longer periods each day. During that part of our leave we tried out various eating-places in the city, and learnt to eat spaghetti correctly.

After three very enjoyable days, it was time to move on to Ramsar. We had booked seats on the only method of transport available – the local mail bus which left Tehran at 6:00 am. At first sight I described it as a 'ramshackle old banger tied together with string' and the two of us very much doubted whether it would get us to our destination. The bus was packed and it reminded us of trains in India with people hanging on to the outside with baskets of goods and squawking chickens. Looking back, it was a most exciting and interesting journey that I wouldn't have missed for anything.

Although it was only 75 miles to Qasvin, from where we left the main Tehran–Rasht road to go over the Elburz mountains to the Caspian coastal plain, we did not arrive until midday. The bus ground its way along, seldom reaching its maximum speed because it was very overloaded. The road was far from smooth, and frequently the mudguards scraped the tyres sending out plumes of blue smoke. Then, of course, as anyone who has travelled in hot countries knows well, halts are made at every possible opportunity either to relieve the call of nature, or to replenish lost body moisture with endless cups of black tea. At every stopping place there was an exchange of passengers, mostly from those hanging on to the outside of the bus. Those going as far as Qasvin or beyond had all taken the precaution of booking seats, and we sat tight in case someone pinched our places whilst we were stretching our legs.

In Qasvin the driver announced that there was a serious fault in the engine. We could have told him that! But he insisted that we must delay our departure from Ramsar until 6:00 pm, which was the time George and I had expected to arrive at our hotel. Faced with the prospect of a tiring and uncomfortable night ahead of us, we decided to take some exercise. We made it clear to the driver that if we returned and found our seats taken by someone else, we would call the police and have him arrested. He understood, and the promise of 100 rials bought his acquiescence. We went off for a welcome walk, and wandered round the old city before arriving back at the bus station to reclaim our seats and part with our 100 rials.

It was well after 6:00 pm when the driver declared himself satisfied that his vehicle was ready for the daunting ascent over the Elburz. Once again the bus was festooned with 'hangers-on', and those passengers inside settled down to the long and tedious journey through the night. Darkness soon fell and we put our heads back for what little sleep we could. Fortunately there was a bright moon shining and, as the old bus struggled seemingly ever upwards, every now and then we caught a glimpse of the steep mountains either side of the road. It was past 2:00 am when we came to a coffee house almost at the top of the pass. Once again the bus stopped and because it was so cold up there, everyone left the vehicle to get a hot drink. We did not stop long as the driver was already seriously behind his schedule. He told us that we would shortly begin our descent to the coastal plain. By now all thoughts of sleep had gone, and as we crossed the ridge in the bright moonlight, we could see a dramatic change in the landscape around us. We soon descended to tree-level, and instead of the barren, dry, rocky slopes on the southern side of the range there were trees and scrub everywhere. It was an incredible change of scenery, and as we continued our descent, the trees became denser and taller as the influence of moist air from the sea became more pronounced.

At about 3:00 am the moon disappeared to the south of the mountains and for an hour or so we were in almost complete darkness until the first lightening of the sky appeared in the northeast, to herald the start of another day. The light spread in a broad band, steadily growing stronger and reddening as the unseen sun crept up beyond the horizon until suddenly the tip of a vast deep-orange ball showed above the horizon of the sea below. And as we watched the sun begin its ascent into the cloudless blue sky, we realised that we had at last reached the plain. The road presently arrived at a T-junction, and the driver turned left, westwards, towards Ramsar where we arrived soon after 7:00 am. It seemed as though all Hell had broken loose as the passengers struggled to collect their belongings and get off the bus as though every second was of vital importance. George and I waited until the turmoil had subsided a little, and then we too alighted. The driver pointed out where the hotel was, and rather than lug our bags up a long slope, we hired a horsed-cab and arrived in time for breakfast.

There were very few guests in the hotel, and one of them, whose name was Betty Moran, was the wife of a senior diplomat at the American Embassy in Tehran. She very soon took us under her wing and did all she could to make us feel at home. The only other guests who showed any interest in us were a naturalised Polish family on holiday from Tehran where Ludwig worked in the import-export business, obviously very successfully as his large limousine and general appearance proclaimed. We were famished after our twenty-four hour journey, but there was to be no cooked breakfast, just Persian-style, with junket and stewed or fresh fruit, and corn flakes. We tucked into it with gusto, and managed to persuade the waiter to get us plenty of toast as well.

Although we had very little sleep during the night neither of us felt like going to bed, and after breakfast we settled into our room then set out to explore the neighbourhood. The hotel was only a few hundred yards from the shoreline, and we walked down to the beach. Sand was no strange thing to us after two years in the desert, but this was quite different and the smell of the sea air and seaweed brought back happy memories of summer holidays at home. Ramsar itself was only a small town on the coast road, and had little to commend it. George and I walked first of all about two miles to the east, then turned about and came back to the town where we decided to have coffee. It was all a matter of exploration, and so we spent the rest of the day wandering here and there until we had a good idea of our whereabouts. One of the things that struck both of us was the lush green grass, something we had not seen for ages.

Back in the hotel, Betty Moran invited us to have a drink with her before dinner so that she could get to know us better. We all got on extremely well together, and it was not surprising that she asked us to share her table for dinner as well. Being on her own, she was rather lonely and yearned for someone to talk to. It had been a good evening when we bade each other goodnight, and George and I took another short stroll down to the beach. The weather seemed to be on the change, and there was a hint of dampness in the air, but it did not concern us too much as we planned how to spend our week in that lovely place. We had come armed with a reasonable map of the area, and when we returned to our hotel room, we sat down and worked out a route for a long walk the next day. We intended to do a high level walk in the mountains to the south of Ramsar eventually, but that could wait until I was a bit more mountain-fit. We both slept well and the noise of torrential rain did not disturb us in the least. After breakfast we looked out at the bleak sight, the sea barely visible through the downpour. Luckily we had both come with plenty of reading matter, and there was no alternative but to spend the day in the hotel, eating, resting and reading.

Betty Moran and Ludwig and his family did the same, and this routine continued for three days with no let-up in the weather.

It was at breakfast on the fourth day, when tempers were beginning to become a bit frayed due to sheer frustration, that the bad news came through. The road back to Qasvin was absolutely impassable as the main bridge along the coast road had been washed away, and several culverts on the mountain section had also been broken. We discussed our various options, and then asked advice from Betty Moran and Ludwig. All were of the same opinion; either we stayed where we were in the hotel for an indefinite period, probably for the whole winter, or we attempted to 'escape' to the west and try to reach the main supply route from Tehran to Russia at the little Caspian Sea port of Rasht. There was no news about the coast road westwards out of Ramsar and the first thing to do was to find out whether it was still passable. Betty Moran had by now made up her mind to stay put and get in touch with her husband in Tehran. Ludwig, George and I decided that the only feasible option open to us was to make every effort to get back to Tehran, and having satisfied ourselves that as far as could be ascertained the road was still open, we started to pack up our belongings and decided to get away as soon as possible. Ludwig offered to take us as far as Rasht in his car, and although it was going to be a tight squeeze to get the whole family, two fairly big men plus all our baggage into the saloon, we accepted with gratitude. We estimated that the road journey would be about eighty miles so we booked an early lunch in the hotel, giving ourselves what we thought would be enough time to get to Rasht before dark. I went to the local post office in Ramsar, and sent a cable to Army HQ in Tehran as our plan to escape from our predicament via Rasht involved entering Russian occupied territory and the sudden arrival of two British officers without authority might create some sort of incident.

After a quick lunch at midday and with flasks filled with hot drinks, we crammed ourselves into the car and set off for Rasht with hope but not much confidence. We soon found ourselves driving along a slightly raised road with extensively flooded fields on either side, and after fifteen miles we arrived at what we had feared most of all – a broken culvert. It was in the middle of a wooded area, and the stream that had caused the break was cascading in a mass of muddy white water towards the sea. George and I then realised why Ludwig had been so keen to take us with him; without us, he and his family would have been utterly helpless.

We made a quick plan and explained to Ludwig what we would have to do. The family must stay inside the saloon and keep warm and out of the way whilst the three of us set to work. There was plenty of good wood nearby, and with the help of the shovel which Ludwig always carried in his car, it was not difficult to get some useful timbers with which to repair the framework of the culvert, which was completed in little more than half an hour.

The final stage was to make a mat of smaller branches and leaves, and we were about to start collecting material for this when a truckload of surly looking Russian soldiers drew up on the other side of the culvert. They got out of their vehicle, and for a few moments our spirits rose, thinking that we had a gang of helpers. But no, the Russian officer smiled and expressed thanks to the three of us for repairing the culvert for the great Russian army! George had foreseen just such an eventuality, and had told Ludwig to get back into the driving seat and start the engine. While the Russians were getting back into their truck, George signalled to Ludwig, and the car dashed forwards. The heavily laden car just reached the other side of the culvert when part of the repair work collapsed into the swollen stream, and as George and I jumped aboard, the Russian officer raised his fist and shouted pretty vile imprecations. As we sped away we laughed at the obvious discomfiture of the Russians who, no doubt, must have looked even surlier than before!

The rest of the journey was uneventful and it was after dark when we drove into Rasht. Ludwig had been there before the war started, and he knew the way to the only hotel worthy of the name. We all booked in for the night, and joined each other for a good meal with plenty of local brew to warm us up after our adventurous drive. It was arranged to visit the British bank manager in the town immediately after breakfast, and Ludwig promised to take us to see him before he drove his family back to Tehran.

George and I slept soundly. When I awoke, I looked out of the window to see the town square just beginning to get busy. There was not a car to be seen anywhere, instead, plenty of horse-drawn cabs and bicycles, but the main thing I noticed was that it had stopped raining. I went to the bedroom door to go to the bathroom and, to my horror, found a Russian soldier with bayonet fixed standing outside. We had heard stories of Russian discipline and how they were reputed to shoot lorry drivers in the convoys passing through Persia with vital supplies, who might doze off at the wheel and drive their vehicles off the road. If they did that to their own men, I wondered how they would react to two British Officers of Field rank entering their zone unannounced and without any authority. I was allowed to continue to the bathroom, and the sentry moved down the passage to make sure I did not make a break for it. But where on earth the Russians thought the two of us would go was anybody's guess. The Russian sentry shadowed every move we made, and even stood guard at the door of the breakfast room.

When Ludwig and his family came down, he saw at once what was happening and acted as interpreter for us. He asked for the Russian commander to come and see us, which he did without delay. The commander was a young major and he explained that the two British Officers were in Russian occupied territory without permission and he was now waiting for instructions from Moscow as to what was to be done with us. In the meantime we were to be kept under arrest! Ludwig told him that we had an appointment with Mr Burrows the British bank manager, and would the major please allow this contact to take place as he had communication with Tehran. It was all agreed, and while Ludwig drove the short distance to Mr Burrow's house, George and

I were made to suffer the indignity of having to walk there under guard, with the major on one side of us and the sentry, still with fixed bayonet, on the other.

The meeting was pleasant and relaxed and lasted until the afternoon, with the sentry still watching every move we made. Mr Burrows had been in touch with the British Embassy in Tehran, who promised to start things moving from their end so that we could get out of Russian-occupied territory as quickly as possible. Feeling considerably reassured, we were then marched under guard to the Russian HQ in Rasht and were confined in a small, cold room with only a table and two or three hard chairs, and here we whiled away the 24 hours that followed until the major told us in his rather inadequate English that Moscow had authorised our release. We could go back to the hotel to collect our things, have a meal, and then a vehicle would pick us up and take us to the main road outside the town where we could stop a lorry returning to Tehran. It was all most unhelpful, but I was glad to know that on this occasion we would not be held under arrest and become pawns in a battle of prestige between the Russians and British.

In due course we were dumped at the side of the road and attempted to flag down a lorry; one or two drove on without stopping, but we soon managed to get aboard a 3-tonner belonging to the Indian Army Service Corps based in Tehran, and we then spent several hours being bumped and jogged in the back. It was a most unpleasant and painful journey and we were relieved and grateful when we reached the city. Dawn was beginning to break when our lorry drove into the transport depot, and our driver showed us the way to the officers' mess where we soon tucked into a typical English breakfast. Having cleaned ourselves up a bit, the commanding officer of the depot drove us to the Embassy where the First Secretary welcomed us. He knew the whole story and the reason why we had decided to make our way back to Tehran via Rasht. He thought we had acted correctly, but he had no knowledge of any message having been received from Ramsar where I had paid for a lengthy telegram to be sent, and the only conclusions we could draw were that either the post office clerk had just pocketed the money, or that the Russians had intercepted and stopped the telegram out of sheer bloody-mindedness. Before we left the Embassy the Ambassador came in for a brief chat before we were driven to a hotel. Here we found that there was no plane due to fly to Baghdad immediately, and we had to spend two more days of our leave in Tehran before flying back to Iraq. It had been an exciting adventure, and probably, if the truth be known, neither of us would have missed it for anything! We were certainly the centre of attention in the Mess as we told our extraordinary story.

# Chapter 11

## MOUNTAIN MOTORBIKE ASSIGNMENT

———

The battalion did not stay long in Quetta camp, and before the end of September 1943 we were once more on the move across the desert via Habbaniyah, Rutbah, and Damascus to Beirut. I was enchanted with the Lebanon; untouched by war it was a beautiful country with a fertile coastal strip bordering the eastern Mediterranean Sea. To the north and east lay Syria, to the south Palestine, and behind the coastal plain the Lebanese mountains rose to just over 10 000 feet. The climate was warm in summer, but during the six months we were there, until early April 1944, we endured an unusually hard winter. There was deep snow on the mountain roads that curtailed much of the planned mountain warfare training programme, and during those weeks most of the time was spent in the plains.

Towards the end of the training period, excitement grew with the expectation that the regiment would be joining the Eighth Army in Italy and I resumed command of my Pathan company before the battalion left Quetta camp.

I unexpectedly found myself in a situation in which I had to make a decision between the best interests of the battalion or of a brother officer Pat Phelps who had commanded my company when I had been in hospital. Pat, who was the same age as me, and was a big strapping man standing at least two inches taller than my six feet, asked me one evening in the mess if he could have a word in private. I was always ready to listen and give my advice if asked and the two of us left the mess and walked out of the camp so that we would not be overheard. Pat started by saying that he knew I didn't like him very much, but nevertheless I was the only one of his fellow officers in whom he felt he could confide. The problem was that his relationship with his *jawans* had reached a low and he was genuinely afraid that as soon as we went into battle, he would be quietly shot in the back with no evidence that his death was anything but a genuine battle casualty. I had known for some time that Pat's method of commanding Indian soldiers was bound to cause resentment in the long run and I had hinted as much to him previously. From what I heard from Indian officers in my own company, nothing had changed during my absence in hospital and the Pathans were relieved when Pat had been given command of the Sikh company.

I thought about telling Pat to change his ways as a matter of urgency, but it was probably too late for that now. I considered the dilemma I was in for some minutes, and then decided that rather than become involved myself, I had to advise Pat to tell Colonel Ted at once. If he failed to do so, I would then have had no alternative but tell the colonel about our conversation myself. The latter would be the best solution both for Pat and for the Regiment, and Pat agreed that I should do just that. I went to see the Adjutant the following morning and asked for an immediate and confidential meeting with Colonel Ted, who saw me straight away. There was no doubt in the colonel's mind about what had to be done. Even if after some discreet investigation by the *Subedar* Major (the equivalent of the Regimental Sergeant Major in the British Army), there was found to be no basis for Pat's fears, his self-confidence would have taken a severe knock and the colonel did not feel that he could rely on him to command a company successfully in battle. Before the end of the day, Pat had been removed from command of his company and had been posted away to a British unit that did not involve him in any sort of direct command of troops in action. A new company commander was appointed and the Sikh *jawans*, after a period of cautious assessment, accepted him and gave him all the support and loyalty they could.

During the latter part of our intensive training, when the snows had almost thawed, two incidents occurred, both of which endeared me to my *jawans*. During an exercise which lasted three days, the battalion had achieved its set objectives by the end of the second day, but the 'B' echelon, carrying the rations, cooking equipment and cooks, had become bogged down ten miles back. The only vehicle that had managed to arrive was the officers' mess truck, and the mess orderlies wasted no time in getting the evening meal prepared. Word was sent round to all the British officers that their meal was ready, but I was concerned first and foremost for my men, and as a matter of principle I refused to have my dinner until the *jawans* had been fed, and I stayed with them. All the men in the battalion were becoming restless and they were all hungry after the day's exercise, but my presence as their company commander was a calming influence. I realised quite soon that all the other company commanders had left their men to put up with their misfortune and hunger whilst they went to the officers' mess and had their dinner. I was absolutely amazed, as two of the company commanders were pre-war regular officers of the Guides and I thought that they should have known better. I had been taught that in the cavalry or horsed unit that, the first priority at the end of the day was to 'feed and look after your horse before all else'. There was one other officer who had not eaten, namely the MTO, Wyon Stansfield, who was with the bogged-down 'B' echelon and thanks to his efforts the rest of the battalion were eventually fed after a delay of about two hours. During our long wait, the other companies had become quite noisy and tetchy and the situation had called for intervention by the *Subedar* Major. Colonel Ted had of course been kept informed and the next day he had a great deal to say to company commanders who had looked after themselves while their *jawans* went hungry; they were given a well-deserved rocket, in fact.

Some days later I had arranged an all-day driving exercise high up in the hills. It involved every driver in the company, and with the agreement of the MTO the Bren gun carrier platoon was to take part. The object was to give every driver practice in driving on narrow mountain roads. Packed lunches were to be taken, and when one of my *naiks* (corporals) drew his rations from the cookhouse, he asked the *bawarchi* (cook) for a bit extra as he was "going on a very long journey today and he would need extra food". He didn't get it, but those who heard him ask for it were apprehensive for him and felt that his request was in some way intuitive.

At about midday the column was moving down a steep, winding, narrow road, and I had gone ahead a little way down the hill to watch the drivers negotiating some sharp bends. I had noticed that the road surface here was very soft from melting snow, but I failed to foresee what effect that was going to have on the heavier tracked vehicles. It is always easy to be wise with hindsight, and I felt afterwards that I should have instructed the drivers to keep close to the inside of the road. The *naik* was in the first carrier to come down the hill, and he was standing up in the passenger's compartment directing the driver. The carrier swung a bit too wide, the left-hand track coming right over the top of the retaining stone wall. I watched, shocked, as the wall began to crumble and the carrier slowly rolled over just once, coming to rest upside down below the base of the wall. The driver was shouting for help, but it was some time before the recovery vehicle at the rear of the column was brought up and the carrier was lifted sufficiently for the driver, who was unhurt although suffering from shock, to be pulled out. The *naik* had tried to duck down inside the carrier as it rolled over, but he was not quite quick enough and his head had been crushed under the armour plating. His face was at peace, the long journey he had foretold had begun. Showing every respect to the dead man, I arranged for his body to be taken back to camp. He had been a very popular NCO and in the circumstances I decided that the feelings of the *jawans* must take precedence. The exercise was aborted and we returned to camp.

The battalion was in for a huge disappointment at the end of the six-month training period. We were told that plans had been changed and we were to return to Persia for guard duties on the now vitally important railway line from Bandar-y-Shahpur on the Persian Gulf, through Qom to Tehran. Morale had dropped to a low pitch as it seemed that the Guides were destined to remain side-lined and to play no active part in the war which by then was turning in the Allies' favour. The high spirits that were so evident only two or three weeks previously had completely disappeared. When we had settled in at Do Rud on the River Arak, the battalion spent the rest of the summer setting up and manning a number of strategically placed strong-points to cover possible approach routes on the railway line. There were no roads in this wild and inhospitable countryside, only a few goat tracks leading to places where it was possible to cross the deep gorges with raging white water cascading down, hundreds of feet below the railway cutting. The area to the south west of Qom was extremely mountainous, and the railway line had been carved across the steep slopes above deep ravines. There had apparently been some terrorist activity recently, and it was an obvious target for enemy demolition squads who could be infiltrated, possibly by parachute, to destroy the rail link to Russia.

Shortly before the battalion was due to leave the Lebanon, I was given a temporary instructor's appointment at the Mountain Warfare Training Centre. It was something I really enjoyed and I was sad that after two months I had to rejoin the battalion in Persia. The journey across the desert back to Do Rud was hot, tedious and uneventful. However soon after entering the foothills between Iraq and Persia, we were passing through a narrow, winding defile when we were suddenly confronted by a large 10-ton civilian lorry which had slewed right across the road and ended up with its nose hard against the inside of the cutting. I saw flames licking the inside of the cab, and the driver and his mate had abandoned the vehicle and were sitting some way up the hill, watching helplessly. They shouted in *Farsi* (Persian), which the two *jawans* understood, saying that the lorry might blow up as it was loaded with high explosives. I didn't know what sort of explosive was in the lorry, so I had to assume that their warning had to be taken at face value. It was immediately obvious that if it did explode, the main supply route to Russia would be impassable and it would take a big engineering job over several days to repair and re-open it. We backed away from the crashed lorry and parked the jeep round the bend and out of harms way, and with shirts off we started to unload the boxes. I also found detonators packed neatly near the front of the lorry. Whilst we kept a watchful eye on the fire in the cab that did not appear to be spreading, we carefully unloaded the cargo, starting at the point nearest the seat of the fire.

Just as we finished, black with sweat and filth, the leading vehicle of a British battalion from the Home Counties, with the second-in-command Major Stewart in his jeep close behind, came round the bend on the other side of the burning lorry. They were leaving Persia to join a newly formed division in India, and the major was not in a mood to be held up! I explained exactly what had happened, and he ordered some of his men to come forward and the lorry was pushed unceremoniously over the edge. It took no more than a few seconds to reach the bottom of the defile where it came to rest in the riverbed. Major Stewart thanked my two *jawans* and me for what we had done, and said he would report the incident as soon as he reached Khanaqin.

When we arrived back at Do Rud, word soon got round about what had happened, and the story eventually came to the ears of the *Subedar* Major who in turn told Colonel Ted. I was summoned to his office and the colonel asked me why I had not reported the incident to him as soon as I returned to the battalion. I had certainly considered whether I should say anything, but I decided that it was a most unlikely story and it might well appear that I was making a minor incident into something much bigger. However, Colonel Ted saw it in a different light and said that in fairness to the two soldiers I should have recommended them for an award for what was clearly an act of considerable bravery. He saw my point, however, that in so doing I would be recommending myself as well! The matter was solved a few days later when Colonel Ted received a short letter from Major Stewart who had witnessed what we had done. In the light of what the major wrote, Colonel Ted told me that he was going to recommend us for a decoration since I had been instrumental in saving the main supply route to Russia for an indefinite period. The colonel felt that what we had done was not simply an act of transient bravery as we had worked in the heat of the day for almost two hours when at any moment, we might have been blown into eternity, continuing until the danger to the road had been removed. I was of course delighted that I was being recommended for an award, but I never thought that what I had done was worth a 'gong'. Neither, it seems, did the Divisional commander, for six weeks later Colonel Ted had to tell me that his recommendation had been turned down.

We soon settled down to the rather humdrum routine, but for me it was offset by the fact that there were many lofty peaks all around that I looked forward to tackling in due course. Almost immediately, however, I was to experience an expedition of a different type that was not at all to my liking. At a point fourteen miles to the south of Do Rud, there was a large water tank and a station with a passing place on an otherwise single-track railway line. This was clearly a vulnerable point with approaches from both the east and west. Colonel Ted was anxious to be able to reinforce our troops positioned there should they be attacked, and knowing that I was fairly competent on a motor bike he told me to take a reconnaissance patrol from the intelligence section and see if I could find a possible route from Do Rud down the gorge to the station.

I first of all carried out a foot patrol down the west side of the gorge, and although the slopes on the other side looked impossibly steep, I decided to set out with the intelligence *havildar* and two of his section, all of us on Norton 350cc motorcycles. It proved to be a hazardous and frightening journey, but I was not prepared to give up unless further progress was quite impossible. I pressed on although at times we had to push our bikes across rock-strewn slopes, and sometimes lift them over large boulders. After struggling in this way for some ten miles, and with at least three miles still to cover to the station, we had to cross a bare slope where I thought that perhaps not even a goat would dare to tread! There was no other way apart from turning back and retracing our steps, and we inched our way across the loose gritty hillside, until I panicked when the *havildar's* machine fell over and began to slide towards the bottom of the gorge. The *havildar* jumped clear and threw himself flat on the ground with his legs spread-eagled to stop his fall, a ploy that certainly saved his life. The Norton gathered speed as it careered down the slope, finally disappearing into the turbulent river more than two hundred feet below.

Quite shaken by this episode, we very cautiously journeyed the remaining few miles to the station. Each of the three intelligence men took it in turns to walk, which by then they all preferred to do rather than try to remain upright on a motorbike on such a steep slope. At last we reached the station and I told our story to the *Jemadar* in charge. While we relaxed and nursed our sore muscles, a meal with mugs of refreshing *char* was prepared for us. It had been a tremendous strain on the human body, and at the end of it all my curt report simply said that the route was impractical.

When the next supply train came in later in the day, the *Jemadar*, who had picked up a few words of Russian, spoke to the escort commander and somehow made him understand that my patrol and I had to get back to the station at Do Rud, and we needed to get our bikes on to the train. For some time the answer was 'Niet'. The Russians had no authority to take any passengers, even if we were allied soldiers actually guarding the vital supply route. Eventually it was agreed that we could go in the escort's van at the end of the train with the three remaining motorbikes, and we started to load the machines. The Russian sentries in the van just stood and watched, making no effort to help lift the heavy bikes up – a difficult job since there was no platform and we had to lift the machines from ground level. Furious with the lack of co-operation shown towards us, I jumped into the van, pushed the Russian soldiers out of the way and started to haul the bikes on board. The only reaction from the Russians was to stand back and look surly. It was a repetition of the attitude I had first experienced at the broken culvert on the road from Ramsar to Rasht just a year ago.

Soon after this exhausting exercise, I went down with an attack of sand-fly fever. To begin with the symptoms are very similar to those of malaria, but there was little danger of anyone in the battalion contracting that particular disease as discipline was extremely strict, with daily doses of 'mepacrine' taken under supervision by all ranks. Mosquito nets were always rigged up, especially when out on manoeuvres, under orders of the Commanding Officer. The MO recognised my fever straightaway, and assured me that it would last only a week at the most and that the only treatment was to stay in bed. He told me that the fever would probably reach its peak after three or four days, and he gave me some quinine that would help to reduce my temperature, but I still had to sweat it out.

For four days I suffered the most devastating headache, my eyes were dreadfully sore, I was constantly thirsty due to dehydration and I had little appetite. Abdul Khan, my Pathan orderly, looked after me as though he was a trained hospital nurse and was always within earshot in case I needed him. As the fourth night approached I felt hotter than ever and shortly after dusk I went into a rigor and was shaking so violently that I thought that I must be suffering from malaria. I had seen my cousin, on leave from Nigeria before the war, lying on his bed shaking incessantly and I knew how terrible he must have felt. As the evening wore on, I slept fitfully and sweated so freely that I was in a complete lather. Towards midnight I seemed to reach a crisis after which the rigor stopped and the sweating rapidly diminished. As I became aware that I was feeling more relaxed and better in myself than I had since the onset of the illness, I half rose in my bed and saw Abdul Khan sitting on the floor in the corner of the room watching me closely. "How long have you been sitting there, Abdul?" I asked.

"Since you started shaking, Sahib," came the reply. "I had to watch over you while you fought your fever, but now you are better and soon you will be well again." I was extremely moved by such loyalty. In the morning my temperature was almost normal and within two days I was back with my company although the fever had left me weak and it was several days before I had completely recovered.

Before I got sandfly fever, I had been giving my future a great deal of thought. It looked as though the war would go on for at least another two years, and since I would have been away from my medical studies for at least six years, it would need a great effort to start all over again, which I was not sure I wanted to do. I knew that my father would be terribly disappointed if I didn't go back to medicine, but I also felt that it would hardly be fair to expect him to pay for my medical training again. What I didn't know was that the government had already announced that adequate grants would be made available to all ex-servicemen to go back to university or college to carry on with studies that had been disrupted by war service.

Eventually I decided that I really enjoyed Army life and when the opportunity came I would apply for a regular commission. The chance to do so was not long in coming, and a few weeks later an ACI was published announcing that regular commissions would once again be granted to successful applicants. They would not, however, be given to British officers in the Indian Army as it seemed that the inevitable partition of India would mean that the Indian Army would be divided into two armies, those of India and Pakistan. The rise of nationalism and the departure of the Raj also meant that the two new armies would be officered by their own nationals. So any British officers of the Indian Army who wished to take regular commissions would have to transfer to the British Army. I had a short discussion with my friend George, and then put in my application for a regular commission.

Within a month the first Regular Officers Selection Board was set up and I spent three days being put through my paces down in the desert near Habbaniyah. The old chestnut of having to cross a strip of water with only a plank, a couple of empty barrels and a rope or something similar, was one of the tests and having done it all before at Sandhurst, I got through with no difficulty. I returned to the battalion in Do Rud and in my own mind I was already a regular officer in the British Army, but remaining seconded to the Indian Army. I applied to join the South Wales Borderers as my first choice, mainly because of my Welsh descent, and the King's Shropshire Light Infantry as my second. The Borderers were in great demand, probably because they were one of the most elite and popular line regiments with a remarkable and glorious regimental history, especially during the Boer War, and also because the officers wore most attractive buttons and rank insignia on their uniforms! They were already over-subscribed, but I was fortunate that I was accepted for the KSLI, a regiment with an equally fine record, and from my point of view it would be more convenient for me as the depot was in Shrewsbury, only 30 miles from home. I need hardly say that I couldn't have served with a finer regiment.

*The sleeve badge of the King's Shropshire Light Infantry*

# Chapter 12

## CASUALTIES OF WAR

———

In October, word came through that as the Italian campaign was to all intents and purposes over, 6 Indian Division was to be disbanded and all the infantry units were to be withdrawn to India and retrained in jungle warfare. 27 Brigade was put on stand-by and a number of officers and NCOs were detailed to go back to India to undergo a jungle battle course at Gudalur in the Nilgiri hills, not far from Bangalore. Colonel Ted told me that I would be in command of the training team which would be responsible for an intensive programme in jungle warfare when the battalion arrived back in India, and it would start as soon as the officers and men had returned from long overdue leave.

My training team and I were taken down to Habbaniyah just as the first snows of winter fell on the Persian mountains. I was sorry to say goodbye to the mountains, but on the other hand glad to be doing something more positive than security duties, or training for a more active role in Italy, a theatre of war which seemed to be getting progressively more remote. After waiting a few days at the RAF base in Habbaniyah we embarked on a brand new Dakota *en route* for the Burma front. At this stage of the war, these aircraft were shipped across the Atlantic from America and assembled in various bases in West Africa. From there they were flown across Africa to Iraq and then down the Persian Gulf to Karachi. Spirits had risen as we took off and headed south for Bahrain where we had a short stop for breakfast and refuelling.

Karachi was reached late in the afternoon and everybody on board went through Customs and Health clearance where we were asked for our yellow fever certificates. Not one of my party had one; no one had thought about inoculations, and normally anyone entering India from Iraq would not have needed to be inoculated against yellow fever. The problem was that the aircraft in which we had travelled from Habbaniyah had been assembled in a country where yellow fever was endemic. If an infected mosquito had hidden itself away in the plane before it left West Africa, it could have bitten unprotected passengers who would then have become carriers and risked spreading the disease in India. It was a disastrous situation, and the whole party was immediately transported in a mosquito-proof vehicle through the streets of Karachi to an isolation hospital out in the country. And here we found ourselves imprisoned without option for four whole weeks, living cheek by jowl with soldiers of all ranks from many different countries. It was a most frustrating period for us all, although we were well fed and looked after. In the meantime I had got word through to the local Army HQ who had sent a GSO 2 out to see me, and in due course arrangements were made for the party to be flown down to Bangalore as soon as we were released from isolation. The plan was that we would be included on the next course, which meant that we would still be ready to start training the battalion when it eventually returned to India.

By the end of the four weeks in isolation we were all utterly fed up with life in general and with most of our fellow detainees. To walk out of the building into fresh air was a most incredible experience – freedom at last! – but one had the feeling that until we arrived at Bangalore airport we had to keep our fingers crossed. We were taken up to the Battle School at Gudalur, and after being given a warm welcome by the commandant we began the course straight away after drawing essential equipment from the stores. I made a huge effort to learn everything I could about jungle fighting, and I thoroughly enjoyed being taught to be self-reliant and how to live off the land. At the end of the course I was awarded a 'D' (distinguished) classification that I was absolutely delighted with. I was really looking forward to running the battalion training course, but my pleasure was short-lived, for at the end of the course the Military Secretary visited the battle school to tell the students where they were to report. To my horror, I heard him announce that the party from the Guides and other units in 6 Indian Division were to return to PAI Force as the plans to disband the Division and bring the troops back to India had been shelved.

I arranged for my party to be flown to Delhi and for us all to have a month's leave, but I myself had no intention of going back to the desert. I had planned to spend my four-week's leave first of all visiting Uncle Eric and then the North West Frontier where a friend of my father, a senior officer in the Frontier Constabulary named Chokra Wood, was stationed in a small town called Hangu.

But first I went to see the Military Secretary in Delhi and requested a transfer to the 4th Battalion Frontier Force Regiment which was fighting in Burma with 17th Indian 'Black Cat' Division. I explained that if I did not do this, when the war ended I would not have qualified for a campaign medal at all, and as a regular officer I felt that it would be a source of considerable embarrassment to me throughout my service. The Military Secretary was very understanding and promised that he would post me to the 4th FFR and I was most grateful to him.

I then went to see Uncle Eric, and stayed with him and Aunty Kitty for a few days before making for Mardan, the home of the Guides. I was very moved to see their own chapel where I found so many memorials to deeds of bravery. Then I visited Hangu where I was given another warm welcome and spent almost a week being shown as much of the North West Frontier as possible. I saw some of the isolated forts where the various Scouts were based, and I realised how wise I had been to end my love affair with Penny and not end up sentenced to a celibate existence for the duration of the war as my commanding officer had threatened in Secunderabad.

At the end of my stay in Hangu with Chokra Wood and his wife, I moved on to Sialkot, not far from Lahore in the Punjab, to stay at the 12th Frontier Force regimental training centre where I was able to relax. I spent most of the day swimming in the club pool and drinking iced *nimbu pani* (lime juice), and dancing in the evening. It was here that I met Molly Sawday, the wife of one of my fellow officers in the Guides, who had recently arrived at the centre to be an instructor. George had been a solicitor in Calcutta before enlisting and getting his commission at the OCTU in Bangalore. He and I had become very good friends and it was a joy to meet such a fun person as Molly. George had been home on leave eight months previously and Molly was by then not far off producing their first-born son, Alastair, who was to be my first godson.

Before the end of my leave my posting order arrived and I reported to a holding battalion near Saharanpur. By now I was getting itchy feet, and was anxious to get into Burma where the action was gathering momentum. Christmas came and went, and it was not until early February that I was ordered to take a draft of reinforcements from the holding battalion and proceed to the base at Comilla, 200 miles east-northeast of Calcutta. Once again we were kept waiting and I kept my draft fit for battle by daily route marches interspersed with routine weapon training; it was all very frustrating.

In the meantime, Mandalay in Burma fell to the 14th Army on 20th March, but it was early April before General Slim was ready to start his big offensive. Taking a leaf out of Monty's notebook, he was not prepared to commit his forces until he was sure he had an overwhelming superiority of troops and weaponry. In this case, plans to reinforce and resupply had been put into effect before the battle for Mandalay had even begun, so that the delay after the battle was reduced to a minimum. Slim planned to make a two-pronged thrust towards Rangoon some 350 miles to the south with 33 Corps moving down the Irrawaddy valley with Prome as the first major objective. General Messervy's 4 Corps would make the main drive down the Sittang valley, following the road through Pyawbwe, Toungoo (about half way to Rangoon), and Pegu. Both Corps would push on as fast as they could and rely on air supply as each airfield *en route* was captured. Time was to be the main factor, the aim being to take Rangoon before the monsoon broke. At all events it was going to be a close-run thing.

It was mid April when 17 Division moved forward and joined the 4 Corps' advance. General Messervy carried out a brilliant manoeuvre in which he completely outwitted the Japs and took them by surprise by cutting the road from Pyawbwe to Rangoon behind their main defences. The road southwards was now open, but both prongs of the advance met very stubborn resistance at first and progress was slower than had been anticipated. The fall of Pyawbwe had a noticeable effect on Japanese morale and the advance gathered momentum as British and Indian troops realised that for the first time they had got the enemy on the run. They swept on towards Meiktila, an important road and rail junction thought to be stubbornly defended. As soon as 48 Brigade, of 17 Division, launched their assault, a prolonged and fierce battle ensued. As the Japs were at last seen to be pulling out, the squadron of Dakota aircraft waiting for the word 'go' at Comilla was called forward.

We were taken to the airfield where we spent most of the night sleeping under the wings of the Dakotas. Our take-off was scheduled for well before dawn to arrive at Meiktila at first light. Meiktila was 350 miles southeast of Comilla, and to reach it we had to fly over the 7000 feet high Chin Hills and Arakan Yomas which often gave rise to a lot of turbulence. But in the event the flight was quite smooth, and within an hour of take-off we were warned to prepare for a rapid disembarkation as soon as the planes touched down. Apparently there was some slight problem on Meiktila airfield!

By midnight, while we were sleeping (albeit fitfully) under the wings of our aircraft, Meiktila airfield had fallen into Allied hands, and the order had then been given for the Dakotas to take off as planned an hour before first light. But a strong counter-attack by the Japs while the aircraft were well on their way was partially successful, and when the Dakotas touched down, the far end of the runway was once again in enemy hands. As small arms fire swept across the open ground the planes were forced to do a quick U-turn and taxi away from the battle area as fast as they could while a battalion of the Border regiment set about dislodging the enemy. It was all over fairly quickly but the incident showed how determined General Slim was to press on to Rangoon to beat the onset of the monsoon, and the risks involved in doing so.

After Meiktila had fallen, 17 Division was leap-frogged by 5 Division that pressed on towards Pyawbwe, and my draft and I were taken to join our new battalion. After meeting the commanding officer, Lt. Colonel Alan McLeod, and the Adjutant, Captain John Beazley and I spent most of the day taking over command of A Company, the Pathans, whose previous company commander had been wounded in the battle for Meiktila and was already on his way back to a hospital somewhere in India. I was most impressed with my new battalion, a superb bunch of battle-hardened Pathan frontiersmen, exultant and proud of their recent successes. Not unsurprisingly, they viewed me with some suspicion. "What did this young *sahib* know about leading veterans like us into battle?" they thought, and while comparisons are often odious, I understood that they would naturally compare me with my predecessor, Major Baxter. I was confident, however, that I would prove to be every bit as good as Baxter had been, and I had the advantage of being able to speak Pushtu, the Pathan language, fluently. And so it turned out; as soon as it was known that I could converse with them, and furthermore that I had learned to take part in the Khattack dance – a lively exercise to say the least – the men muttered amongst themselves with approving looks in my direction.

Two days later 17 Division was called forward to rejoin the advance in the wake of 5 Division which had stormed into Pyinmana on 19 April and gone thundering on to take Toungoo 3 days later. As we stormed down the road to Pegu, signs of the ruthless advance were to be seen everywhere. The grotesque sight of dead Japanese, some already bloated by the hot sun, lay stinking where they had fallen or been dragged to the side of the road. The advance was so rapid that no cleaning up or identification of casualties had yet been possible, but in any case priority had to be given to our own troops amongst whom, happily, there were surprisingly few casualties. The overwhelming superiority in the equipment of the 14th Army saw to that.

After the fall of Toungoo, 17 Division overtook 5 Division and led the advance at tremendous speed to Pyu, a small township on the road south that fell to us after a brief battle in which the Japs showed little stomach for the fight. In fact the defenders were once again taken by surprise at the speed of the Allies' advance, and even civilians found themselves caught up in the fighting having had no time to flee.

During the assault on Pyu, we were confronted by a force of Japs occupying a small outlying village. They had to be mopped up, and I called in my gunner officer and the battalion's mortar commander, and very quickly the village was subjected to a short but heavy artillery and mortar attack followed by my Pathans going in with the bayonet. I had moved a platoon round to the rear of the village which effectively cut off the escape route, and as the Japs were flushed out of the houses they blew themselves up with their own grenades rather than lose their honour by surrendering to their enemy. As I moved through the village, making sure that there were no enemy left inside the houses, I was suddenly confronted with a heart-rending sight that has stayed with me for the rest of my life. On the floor of their humble abode lay an old Burmese peasant with a gaping shrapnel wound; he was already dead. Kneeling beside him was an old woman with huge tears flowing down her gnarled cheeks. She was his wife and in their old age he had been taken from her through no fault of their own. As I watched, stifling my emotion, she turned towards me with a look of bewilderment on her poor face, a look that said 'why have you done this to us?' Then she held out her hands as though in supplication, but she was showing me that the shelling had cut off both her hands, and all she had been left with were two bloody, raw stumps. I was distraught and wanted to be sick but I had to get on with the job in hand. The stretcher-bearers were called up and did what they could to help her. It was the first time I had seen the bitter reality of what war meant to unfortunate civilians who got caught up in it. It revolted me.

The advance continued, but it seemed increasingly likely that the monsoon was going to break much earlier than usual as heavy clouds began to build up. Alarmed by the forecasts of imminent heavy rains, Admiral Lord Louis Mountbatten, the Allied Commander-in-Chief, decided to attack Rangoon from the sea and the operation was launched on 27th April. At the same time 4 Corps had reached the outskirts of Pegu, only 50 miles from Rangoon, and the town fell to us on 1st May.

It was on the morning of 3rd May, my birthday, that Rangoon also fell to the Allies when a battalion of 50 Gurkha Parachute Brigade leading the assault on the city, defeated a small rearguard of Japs. Forward elements of 26 Indian Division in landing craft were then able to proceed up-river to the city itself which they entered unopposed. Early that morning an Air OP pilot of C flight 656 squadron RAF, which had been supporting the sea borne attack from the aircraft carrier HMS Khedive, flew over Rangoon gaol and saw the immortal words painted on the roof "Japs gone; extract digit". Only someone with knowledge of British service slang would know what those last two words meant, and the pilot at once passed the information to 26 Division. The many allied prisoners-of-war who had been held in the gaol were quickly released, and the capture of Rangoon was complete.

In the meantime the rest of 17 Division had pressed on through Pegu, but a night of torrential rain had put the river in spate and the main bridge in the town was not thought to be safe enough to carry tanks and other heavy vehicles. My A Company had gone on through the night with orders to secure the bridge over the next river which was 20 miles further on towards Rangoon. The incessant torrential downpour made me apprehensive, and I kept my whole company on the Pegu side of the river taking up a position on relatively high ground incase the river burst its banks. None of the men slept very much during that night; the river was rising minute by minute, and the noise of the swirling, rushing water grew steadily louder. Shortly before dawn the bridge itself collapsed under the weight of the water bearing down on it, and my foreboding was not unfounded. It meant that in spite of its incredible advance, 4 Corps had lost the race against the monsoon, and with it 17 Division lost the coveted prize of retaking Rangoon. This was particularly disappointing as the Division had been the last troops to leave Rangoon in February 1942. Apart from a period for refitting and reinforcement in India, shortly after the survivors of the harrowing rearguard action reached the relative sanctuary of the Kohima area, they had been fighting the Japanese continuously ever since. At the forefront of the final push, I had to suffer the frustration of seeing British troops from 26 Division, who had already walked into Rangoon without hearing a shot fired in anger, come up to the far bank of the river and shout across to us in a derisory manner, "What's keeping you then?"

The opening rains of the monsoon did not relent for several days and everywhere there were unusually severe floods; conditions were appalling with movement being restricted almost entirely to the metalled roads. Although to all intents and purposes Burma had been recaptured, the Japs had spilt up into small groups and disappeared northwards into the Pegu Yomas, a 75-mile wide strip of jungle-covered hills running 200 miles between the Irrawaddy and Sittang valleys. During the few weeks that followed, radio instructions from Japanese HQ in Siam were monitored by the Allies. It became obvious that the disorganised groups in the Yomas were being directed to various rendezvous points where they would come under command of the

28th Japanese Army HQ. The plan was to attempt a massive breakout when the monsoon rains had stopped and the ground had dried out a bit.

It was to be the task of 4 Corps to prevent the Japs escaping across the Sittang into the Malay peninsula and Siam (now Thailand) where they would be able to reform and help in prolonging the war in the Far East. The Japanese troops in the Yomas were far from fit, living almost entirely off the land as far as they could, with field rations being supplied by air during the night. How much of that food was retrieved by the Japs it was hard to estimate, and they became increasingly active in raiding villages on the edge of the jungle that put great fear into the Burmese peasants.

Following the capture of Rangoon, movement was necessarily restricted to the absolute minimum as the paddy fields on both sides of the road were impassable to vehicles. The roads were waterlogged and in danger of rapid deterioration. All units were for the time being grounded, and it was not until the end of May that 17 Division was moved north to take up defence positions along the Meiktila-Pegu road. Their task was to deny all possible crossing-places to the Japs. 4 FFR was located 100 miles north of Pegu in Pyu, the scene of that vicious battle in which my company had been involved in the advance south, where I had seen the tragic effects of friendly shellfire on the old Burmese couple.

The first priority was to make the battalion as comfortable and secure as possible, and life inside the company perimeter at once became more static including guard duties, maintenance of arms and equipment, and general reorganisation after weeks of hard fighting. At first I planned a series of familiarity patrols within a few miles of the company position so that every man would know his way about. Important points such as track junctions, villages and so on were given code names that were recorded by the supporting Artillery battery and the mortar platoon. The patrols not only moved westwards towards the jungle-covered Yomas, which rose from the valley bottom 5 miles from the main road, but also included the ground to the east as far as the broad Sittang river. There was a real danger that Japanese patrols involving troops which had not been defeated in the battle for Burma, would cross the Sittang to make contact with the regrouping forces that had sought refuge in the Yomas. This meant that 48 Brigade, which had the responsibility for refusing the enemy the middle piece of the Divisional front around Nyaunglebin, had to face both ways.

During this static phase in the final battle for Burma, the mail situation improved and I received several letters that had been held up until the postal unit could deliver them. The time taken for mail to travel to and from Britain had been considerably reduced, and planes could now fly a much shorter route across North Africa, previously denied to us by the Axis air forces. To my surprise I received a letter from my brother Ted from the northwest of Burma, where he'd been with his Air OP squadron since the end of February the previous year. It was full of news, and finished with a typically modest statement that "they seem to have been pleased with my

efforts as they've given me a couple of gongs – the MC and DFC. I can't think why!"
I felt very proud of Ted and as I told my brother officers about it, I basked in a
measure of reflected glory. There was no doubt that my image amongst the *jawans* in
the battalion was also given a pretty good boost. Soon after I received this letter, I met
a gunner officer who had been with the divisional artillery in the Arakan whom Ted
had been supporting. "You're not related to Ted Maslen-Jones, an Air OP, are you?"
he asked. When I said he was my elder brother, the whole story came out about how
Ted had flown extremely long hours spotting Jap positions and making sketches
which, when the infantry attacked, saved a great many Allied casualties. Time after
time his Auster plane had returned to the airstrip riddled with bullet holes, and how
Ted had escaped unwounded nobody could understand. All this had apparently gone
on day after day, week after week for 9 months before his work was recognised and
he was given the two immediate awards. He had also collected two mentions in
despatches and a Certificate of Gallantry signed by Admiral Lord Mountbatten.

# Chapter 13

## ENEMY ALL AROUND

———

The Japs were becoming increasingly active, pushing out probing patrols along the whole length of the Toungoo–Pegu road, with most of the activity building up around Pyu and Nyaunglebin. Intelligence reports suggested that there was a considerable concentration of Jap troops 25 miles inside the jungle immediately west of Pyu. This greatly concerned Brigadier Headley, commanding 48 Brigade, who asked 4 FFR to detail a company to carry out a fighting patrol that he would personally brief. His intention was to send the patrol deep into the Pegu Yomas with the specific task of capturing a prisoner. It was vital to get information about the re-organisation of the Japanese 28th Army, and Colonel Mac asked me to carry out the patrol. He stressed that it was a task of extreme importance, and that the Brigade Commander would brief me personally. I reported to him for my briefing on 20th June.

What lay in store was to teach me far more about the tribal feuding and vendettas on the North West Frontier of India than I would otherwise have learned. The three Pathan tribes recruited into the FFR were the Yusufzai, Orakzai and Khattaks, and they all had a reputation as brave, skilful and cunning fighters. In their own country these Pathan tribes were usually involved in internecine feuds that frequently developed into open warfare, but more often were limited to raiding each others' villages. In the Indian Army all inter-tribal rivalry was strictly forbidden, and it was this understanding that, in spite of all the different religions and sects that existed in the Army, enabled it to become the largest and most efficient volunteer force the world had ever known.

When I went to Brigade HQ, 9 miles north of Pyu, the Brigadier first of all gave me an up-date on the situation as he knew it. Together we discussed how best to organise and carry out the patrol, but I insisted that before I could make a detailed plan I must get more information about the lay-out of the Japanese position, approximate strength, type of weaponry and transport, if any, and routes in and out. It was agreed that a small reconnaissance patrol should go first, travelling light and moving fast, and I chose a *Havildar* (sergeant) called Abdul Qayum to take three *jawans* with him to do

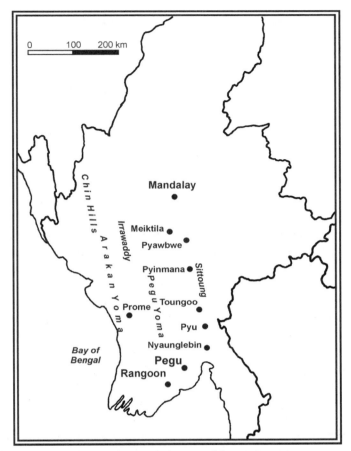

*Burma, showing the location of the Pegu Yomas*
*where we were sent to capture a prisoner*

the job. Qayum's tribe was Yusufzai and he had only recently joined the company after a two-year period of training recruits at the regimental centre in Sialkot, and like me he had felt that the chance of proving himself in battle was rapidly passing him by. He had a burning ambition to be involved in some real fighting, and achieve an award for bravery before the war ended. All Indian soldiers regarded the award of a medal as a matter of great pride, not only within their own families and villages but throughout their tribes. I was certain that Qayum was the best man for this job, and together we selected the three *jawans* to make up the patrol. As soon as they were ready, I briefed them and they set out with an expected time of return at the end of day five.

It was very surprising then that during the afternoon of the fourth day Qayum led his 'tired', dishevelled patrol out of the jungle and across the 5 miles of flat open ground to Pyu. I was astonished to see them back a day earlier than expected, but assumed that the route must have been much easier-going than we had thought, and Qayum confirmed this when he was de-briefed. He made sketches of the track through the jungle, and went into minute detail about the enemy, noting sentry posts, machine-gun and mortar positions, and even mule and elephant lines! It was a fantastic report and exactly what I needed to prepare my plan for the prisoner-snatching operation.

I went to see the Brigadier, showed him Qayum's report, and outlined my plan for the fighting patrol. The Brigadier approved and told me that he would send a spotter plane out each day at noon to make radio contact, as ordinary communications with either battalion or Brigade HQ would almost certainly be impossible once I was screened by the jungle-covered hills. I checked radio call signs and frequencies with the Brigade signals officer, returned to my company position in Nyaunglebin and walked over to have a word with Qayum. "Havildar Qayum", I said, "I shall want you to come with me on the fighting patrol as you know the route, so I suggest that you go and get cleaned up and have a good sleep. We will move out first thing tomorrow morning."

Qayum showed momentary surprise and his eyes narrowed in a way that I found disarming. Then he quickly regained his composure, saluted, and said, "Thank you Sahib, it will be an honour." I remember thinking that no doubt he thought he'd already done enough. With his report he must already be in line for that coveted decoration and surely it wouldn't be reasonable to expect him to go out again so soon?

My orderly, Jabin Khan, was a strapping young Orakzai and he'd been with me long enough for me to realise that he was a typical Pathan, and crafty to the point of slyness. But to me, for whom Jabin felt he was personally responsible, he was unswervingly loyal. He saw himself as my personal bodyguard and my enemy became his.

I told Jabin about Qayum's reconnaissance patrol and the detailed report he had prepared. But Jabin looked impassive and unimpressed. "Do you believe him, Sahib?" he asked.

"Yes I do, Jabin. I have no reason to doubt him. Do you?" Jabin's reply was to the point.

"I do not believe that he could have done all he said he did and covered 50 miles of rough-going in less than 5 days. And I heard the other men in the patrol saying that the jungle is very dense, and the path overgrown." Then, as he turned away, he muttered, "and anyway, he's a Yusufzai".

This remark was enough to bring to my mind the instruction all new officers were given about the make-up of the Regiment. The North West Frontier province is a country of wild valleys where the Pathans' prosperity comes from their cattle and the crops they grow. There are many tribes, all of similar character and living in like conditions. Their main occupation is farming, but except from seedtime and harvest, a continual state of feud and strife prevails. Tribe wars with tribe, one valley invades and attempts to steal crops and cattle from another. It is a state of war between communities and between individuals. Every tribesman has a blood feud with his neighbour, and they are ferocious, crafty, cruel, treacherous and violent; they are also excellent marksmen.

"Enough, Jabin," I replied after a pause. "This is the Pathan company and in this regiment we do not recognise different tribes. There are no Yusufzais or Orakzais here, remember. Qayum will be coming on the patrol with us and we'll soon see if your doubts are justified." Jabin smiled knowingly, leaving me with a niggling doubt that would not go away.

At about mid-afternoon next day we set out on what I expected would be at least a 9-day patrol. I had a full strength platoon of 32 men, a section each of 3-inch mortars and Vickers machine guns on pack mules, a signaller with a long range radio which was also carried on a mule, and two medical orderlies making 56 men altogether. I planned to cover the five miles to the edge of the Yomas before dark, find the track we would be following, and bivouac for the night just inside the jungle. We arrived on schedule, and having put out my sentries, I told my signaller to call up Brigade and had a brief talk with the Brigade Major as the Brigadier was otherwise occupied.

The following morning we set out soon after first light, and made slow but steady progress along the so-called track. For a while I was able to follow Qayum's sketch map. Then the map suddenly lost all resemblance to the route we were following which was heavily overgrown and showed no sign of having been used recently. We had to hack our way through the undergrowth and progress became much slower. Qayum appeared puzzled and ventured, "I think we must have missed a fork in the track, Sahib," but there had been no fork. At noon the signaller tried to make radio contact with Brigade, but the screening effect of the jungle already blanked out all horizontal communication. Then we heard the spotter plane circling around above the carpet of trees, and I spoke to the pilot. There was little to report other than to say that so far all was well. I made no mention of the doubts that were building up in my mind, and we signed off until noon the following day. The patrol pressed on and when we stopped for the night I reckoned we had covered no more than 9 miles.

I was determined not to let my doubts affect my judgement; I had been personally briefed by the Brigadier to do this job and I was going to see it through, come what may. So far I had given Qayum no reason to think that my suspicions had been aroused, and outwardly I gave the impression of being completely in command of the situation. And so the second night drew nigh, another bivouac, another dawn, and we were into the second full day. Fires for cooking or hot water were not allowed, and already we were beginning to look dirty and unkempt. Cold breakfast was not the best morale-booster after a chilly, damp night in the open, and after carefully concealing all signs of our camp site we set off again, glad to be moving and warming up our cold, stiff muscles and joints. Just before midday we tried to make radio contact with Brigade, but again there was no reply, and minutes later the spotter plane was on station. It was only a routine check and neither the pilot nor I had anything to report other than all's well.

As the day wore on, surprisingly it was Qayum who started showing signs of anxiety. "Supposing we don't find any Japs?" he asked. "What will you report to the Brigade commander, sahib?" My suspicions were slowly but surely being confirmed. I now had little doubt that Qayum hadn't come this far, and his sketches and whole report must be a complete fabrication. It all began to fit together, and this realisation aroused new fears in me. I had to play it cool, and I decided that I must take Jabin into my confidence.

"I know all that, sahib," Jabin replied when I had explained my suspicions to him. "He is a bad man and he has lied to you. His patrol never came this far; they just camped in the jungle for three days while *havildar* Qayum made up his report – and anyway he is a Yusufzai."

The tribal hatred between these two men would not go away and perhaps that was the one thing which kept me alive, for I knew that Jabin would fight to the death to defend me against Qayum, the hated Yusufzai. More than once Qayum went back to the same question urging me to say what I would report to the Brigadier when we got back to Pyu. My answer was clear and unwavering, "If the Japs have gone, I will say so. We can't take a prisoner if there aren't any Japs there, can we?"

We pressed on, and once again at noon the spotter plane flew over us and I spoke to the pilot. I checked my map reference and asked the pilot to make a sweep over the whole area to see if he could spot any sign of enemy troops. He flew at treetop height for almost half an hour, but eventually reported that he could see nothing below the thick blanket of trees, and even in the few clearances in the jungle there was no obvious sign that there had been any troops in the vicinity recently. As the pilot bade us farewell, I knew I had heard that voice somewhere before, but I could not place it and eventually thought no more about it. A couple of hours later I reckoned we had reached our target area, but there were no Japs, and neither had there been any. We were able to confirm what the pilot had told us; there were no signs of recent occupation and the whole area was undisturbed. There was no longer any point in pretending that I still believed Qayum's story, but before aborting the operation I must be quite certain that we had, in fact, reached the correct location. I set up a defensive perimeter and decided to go forward with Jabin and two *jawans* to make a thorough reconnaissance in case we had stopped short of our objective. If we travelled light, we could cover quite a wide area before dark, and I could satisfy myself that there were in fact no Japs in the vicinity.

Qayum's demeanour told me that he knew I had 'rumbled' him, and the situation was becoming very tense. Qayum's burning ambition to get a medal had become an obsession with him and there was no knowing what he might do to prevent his deception being revealed, with the inevitable court-martial that would follow.

After placing outposts round the perimeter, I chose a spot where Jabin and I would bivouac near each other, took off my equipment, and left it with my pack on the ground. I had marked a route on the map that roughly followed the line of streambeds and contours, and for navigating I could use the sun that was beating down from a cloudless sky. I wouldn't need my compass, and I left it in my equipment on the ground. The reconnaissance was uneventful and four hours later we came back to the perimeter in good time to brief the men for the next day's withdrawal operation while it was still daylight. Qayum showed by his body language that he was becoming desperate and I realised that he would try everything he could to prevent the true story ever being told. I felt I was living out a nightmare from which I could not wake up. The longer I stayed in this dreadful place, the more the jungle and events crowded in on me and there seemed to be no escape. Escape: perhaps that was the answer, and I should quickly disappear during the night and try to make my own way back to Pyu. However, the complications of doing that were too serious to contemplate, and I would be court-martialled for deserting my soldiers in the face of the enemy. I made up my mind to face my predicament and carry on as though nothing untoward had happened. After all, as far as I knew, only Qayum, Jabin and myself knew the real story.

I warned Jabin to be extra alert and to listen carefully to anything the other *jawans* might be discussing. In the meantime my imagination started playing tricks; every crackling twig alerted me and I kept a loaded 'Tommy gun' constantly by my side. I figured it would be easy for Qayum to stage an enemy attack on our position after dark during which the major *sahib*, displaying superb bravery and leadership, would be killed, shot in the back by Qayum no doubt, who would then take over command and lead the patrol safely back to Pyu. He would win his coveted medal without having encountered any Japs whatsoever. Of course he would see to it that anyone like Jabin who might spill the beans, would not live to tell the tale either. It all seemed too easy, and I prepared for a long and sleepless night.

I decided to move at dawn, and set about writing my orders on a scrap of paper. Halfway through I reached for my compass to check the general bearing back to base, but it was missing. "Jabin", I called, "where's my compass?"

"It's in your equipment, sahib," he replied.

I checked again, but it was definitely not there. I had left my equipment on the ground when we did our reconnaissance patrol during the previous afternoon, and someone must have taken it out of the pouch. Who but Qayum would have any reason to do that? I needed no more confirmation and it was beyond doubt that Jabin and I were in serious danger – an Orakzai and his British officer playing at cat and mouse with a crafty and desperate Yusufzai. The tension was almost at breaking point.

As soon as I was ready, I called the NCOs together and gave out my orders. I would keep Qayum in front of me and ordered him to retrace our route, and make all possible speed. It would not be lost on him that I would be watching every move he made, and his chances of carrying out some nefarious act would be reduced to a minimum. With Jabin and a section of ten men acting as my bodyguard I would follow a short distance behind Qayum with the rest of the patrol, the mules, mortars and machine guns behind us, and a third section bringing up the rear. While I felt that there was very little chance of meeting any Japs on the return journey, we couldn't relax our security, and I stressed that we must make every effort to cover the 20-odd miles to the edge of the jungle by nightfall. This suited the men who were becoming disenchanted with what had turned out to be a pretty futile patrol, and we were looking forward to the comparative comfort of our *bashas* back in the company perimeter at Nyaunglebin.

For the next 24 hours Jabin and I would have to remain alert and watchful. We set ourselves down for the night a few yards apart, and attached a cord to each other's wrists so that every so often a tug from either of us would ensure that we stayed awake. The night passed slowly, the silence broken only by the continuous chirping of cicadas, and eventually they, too, fell silent. When dawn had broken and my imaginary 'death in action' had not happened, I was immensely relieved and my anxiety gave way to renewed determination to be out of the jungle by the end of the day.

After another cold breakfast we moved off. No need to cover our tracks; the sooner we got away the better. For an hour or so Qayum found no difficulty in retracing our steps. Then he blundered away from the track we had made the previous day and we found ourselves on unfamiliar ground. Rather than waste time trying to find our previous route, I decided to use the sun and my watch to navigate by, and having determined the direction of due south, and keeping the sun roughly to our right, we would head eastwards down towards the Sittang valley. Without a compass I had to improvise, but this simple but effective method did not last long. At noon we heard the spotter plane and reported that we were heading down towards the valley. Quite suddenly huge black clouds that we had not been able to see through the jungle foliage came up with surprising speed and completely obliterated the sun. With our navigation beacon gone, we stopped for a short rest while a refreshing, cleansing deluge fell on us. At any other time it would have been sheer bliss after the humid heat of the past few days, but not then. We were lost and the *jawans* knew it.

I then remembered that I had an escaper's compass sewn into my flies. It consisted of two brass buttons, one of which had a small sharp needle which fitted into a cup on the reverse side of the other so that it spun round until a small luminous dot came to rest pointing north. "Jabin," I said, "cut these two buttons off, please."

Jabin looked at me, aghast. "No, sahib, do not ask me to do that," he said, passing me his knife.

His modesty knew no bounds, so, temporarily amused by such shyness, I took the knife and cut the buttons off myself. Watched by a circle of curious and disbelieving *jawans*, I put the two buttons together, allowed the makeshift compass to settle, then proudly said, "that's north, we go in that direction." The scowl on Qayum's face proved that he had been foiled. "Havildar Qayum," I said, "follow the line of the contour we are on now, and in about a mile we should reach a small river and we'll follow it down to the valley."

By the time we reached the river the deluge was easing off and it was still only knee deep. The bottom was smooth and sandy, and rather than try to work our way through the lush jungle along the bank which would have slowed us down to a crawl, I decided to walk the patrol down the actual river bed. The danger of being ambushed was now very small, and the only real disadvantage would be the leeches. We were all well-versed in how to deal with those detestable creatures, having woken up many times when out on patrol with our legs and arms covered with them, firmly anchored to our skin, and already bloated with blood. On one occasion I woke to find no fewer than 29 leeches on my legs.

The rest of the day passed without any serious incident, although Qayum walked too close to a hornet's nest on the river bank, and we had to suffer some angry hornets 'dive-bombing' us as we passed as close to the opposite bank as possible. Eventually we reached the valley in time to set up camp just before dark and as soon as this was done I told the signaller to call up Brigade HQ. There had been no direct communication since entering the jungle five days earlier, and my message was simply that we were all well and expected to return to Pyu by noon the next day.

I was still afraid that Qayum might try something desperate, and Jabin and I spent another wretched night. As dawn broke and the sun's warming rays fell on us from the far side of the Sittang River, I began to look forward to our return to relative civilisation and safety. I knew I could never trust Qayum again, and that I would always feel a marked man as long as the *havildar* was around. I had made up my mind that I would tell the Brigadier and Colonel Mac exactly what had happened, and that I would demand that Qayum be immediately transferred out of the battalion, avoiding the hassle of a court-martial. Of course Qayum would deny it, and it would be virtually impossible to prove anything.

As the sun climbed away from the horizon and warmed the patrol, I was in no hurry to move on. We were all tired and enjoying the relaxation after our long forced march through the jungle, and luxuriated in drying out and warming up after the deluge of the previous day. There were more clouds piling up to the west and I knew that before long we could expect another drenching. I had given permission for fires to be lit and we ate a good hot breakfast, the first for several days.

While we were clearing up and getting ready for the last five-mile stretch to Pyu, some sort of commotion in a village less than a mile away attracted our attention. Even through binoculars it was too far to see exactly what was happening, but something sinister had clearly upset and frightened the villagers. Then we saw men, women, and children running panic-stricken along the track into the Yomas. It was only two or three hundred yards from our position, and I ordered the patrol to stand-to in our overnight defence positions until I could assess the situation. Some of the leading villagers saw our patrol and ran towards us shouting excitedly, "Japani come, Japani come", before escaping into the safety of the jungle.

I raised my binoculars again, and as I looked towards the village I saw two figures walking along the path from the Pyu track. One was carrying a rifle over his shoulder, and I recognised him at once as one of the locally enlisted militiamen who had been recruited to assist in keeping law and order in the towns and villages as they were liberated. He was probably on his way back home after a spell of duty in the Pyu area, and the two men seemed completely unaware of the disturbance in the village. I watched in horror as they walked straight into the ambush the Japs had laid for them. I saw them both spin round and fall to the ground as the bullets hit them, and a split-second later I heard the staccato burst of the automatic fire which had killed them.

There were now Japs all over the place, at least 120 of them, which meant that my patrol was out-numbered by at least two to one. At that stage, the Japs seemed to be unaware of our presence, and I watched the group of Japs go to where the two Burmese were lying to make quite sure they were dead by mutilating them. When they were found later, their noses had been slashed off. The village was only half a mile north of the track back to Brigade HQ and was far too close to even consider trying to take the patrol through. We might have been able to by-pass the Japs without mules, but those heavily loaded animals were too big a target and too slow. We would have been seen coming and the Japs would have had plenty of time to move across and cut us off.

We still needed a prisoner, and this was clearly the only chance we would get. I quickly made a plan to create a diversion to bring the Japs out into the open ground where we could use our machine guns and mortars to best effect. Meanwhile I would send a snatch squad left-handed to the far side of the village to try and grab a prisoner. Qayum was the one man whom I thought I could rely on to do this successfully; apart from his initiative and experience, he was still hungry for that medal, and this might be the last chance he would get before the war came to an end. If he succeeded, it would go a long way to make up for his perfidy, and I called him over.

"*Havildar* Abdul Qayum," I began, "you realise that I know all about your lies and deceit, and also what made you act in that perverse way". Qayum nodded his assent. "Then I am going to give you the chance to redeem yourself and save both your reputation and your career in the army. We cannot get past the Japs out there, and we have still not taken the prisoner we were sent out to get six days ago. So I've made a plan, and if you succeed in your part of the operation, I give you my word that nothing will be said about your miserable performance during the past two weeks. And you will have the opportunity of getting the medal you so badly want. Is that a fair deal?"

Qayum's face lit up and he smiled broadly. "Thank you, *sahib*." he said, "I will do whatever you ask of me. I am truly sorry and I will prove it to you."

I then called my 'O' group together and explained the plan. First, a section would move right handed to the far side of the Pyu track, and set up a position to deny the track to the Japs. At a signal from me, this section would open fire towards the village and create a diversion. In the meantime *havildar* Qayum and three *jawans* would have made their way to the rear of the village to try to snatch a prisoner and bring him back to our present position. At that stage I would have reassessed the situation and decided whether to fight our way back to Pyu or remain where we were for another night. In view of the numerical odds in favour of the Japs I didn't much fancy either option.

Qayum chose three of my best men, and set off to the north to work his way round the back of the houses. I allowed him exactly one hour to get into position for the snatch operation. In the meantime the other section under another *havildar* crossed the Pyu track and then made a wide sweep eastwards to a point about three quarters of a mile beyond the village before turning north and taking up a position astride the track. All was now ready, and exactly on the hour this diversionary group made its presence known by firing at the Japs who responded by taking up positions in the paddy fields between the track and the village. That was precisely what I wanted, as all attention was now on that side of the village, leaving Qayum free to approach the rear houses unobserved. After a short while small parties of Japs moved from their original positions to outflank my diversionary group. Without knowing, they were exposing themselves to the machine gunners that were itching to open fire on them: they were sitting ducks. The mortar commander worked out the range, and reported that his men were ready to open fire. The Japs had done exactly what I hoped they would do, and the machine guns and mortars would keep them pinned down until Qayum's squad was on its way back with their prize. I sent a message to Brigade HQ – short and to the point – "Am engaging enemy force approximate strength 120 plus, 5 miles west of Pyu". Then I gave the order, "FIRE!" The machine-gun and mortar fire was extremely accurate and achieved the desired effect of keeping the enemy pinned down. The diversionary group, their job well done, withdrew and legged it back to the patrol position without loss, but the Japs now knew exactly where we were and they turned their mortars and automatics on us. The first casualty in this encounter was my signaller who was hit in the arm with a couple of bullets. The radio was shattered, and we now had no communication at all with Brigade HQ.

I was looking through my binoculars to see if there was any sign of Qayum when there was a sharp and vicious crack behind me. I thought I had been punched in the small of the back; just then my webbing equipment fell off. A mortar bomb had landed just behind me and a piece of shrapnel had struck the point where the webbing straps cross over each other, cutting clean through them. My legs were paralysed, and I was aware of a hot, searing pain in the middle of my back. The metal shard had gone through the straps, which had absorbed most of its momentum, and had come to rest firmly lodged against my spine. For a few moments I was near to panic and my imagination rather ran away with me. Would I ever walk again? I was in shock and agony but my legs soon recovered their feeling and in a few minutes I was able to relax and once again take command of the situation even though I remained lying on the ground. The medical orderly tended my wound and made me as comfortable as possible on a stretcher. He told me that he was sure the shrapnel had not penetrated too deeply. Meanwhile I told Jemadar to supervise the battle and I waited for Qayum to return.

Soon after midday Qayum proudly brought his prisoner back and presented him to me. I was delighted as he turned out to be a senior Japanese NCO who had gone into one of the houses to attend to the call of nature, and was caught fairly and squarely with his trousers down! He was captured without a shot being fired which was a stroke of luck as Qayum had been able to get his man and withdraw without any other Japs being aware of his presence. I congratulated Qayum on a superb operation, shook him firmly by the hand, and confirmed what I had promised before he had set out: that not a word of his previous treachery would be said to anyone.

The fire-fight continued spasmodically until it was nearly dark, and then everything fell silent. It was not long before we clearly heard the sound of digging, and assumed that the Japs were preparing to defend their position. But sometime during the night they withdrew and at first light I sent Qayum out to *reconnoitre* the whole area and find out from the few villagers (who had returned to their homes during the night) whether the Japs had in fact gone and if it was safe for us to start the final stretch of our march back to Pyu. There was no sign of the enemy other than several freshly dug graves and two discarded officers' swords, one of which Qayum handed to me. He kept the other, the better of the two of course, as a prized battle trophy. In the meantime, three *jawans* who had been killed in the battle were buried and their graves carefully marked so that they could be identified and properly re-buried in a military cemetery later.

As soon as we had eaten some food, we set out for Pyu. I had sent a small party ahead to make sure that there were no ambushes, and to let the Brigadier know that we were on our way with our prisoner plus a number of walking wounded and a couple of stretcher cases. We met no trouble on the way, and pressed on towards Brigade HQ. However, acting on the last message the signaller had been able to send just as the battle was beginning the previous day, the Brigade Major had arranged for a jeep patrol to go out to contact us, and my advance party met them about halfway to Pyu.

It was well into the afternoon when we arrived at Brigade Headquarters and after a brief talk with the Brigade Major, the other wounded men and I were taken by ambulance to the Casualty Clearing Station where the Brigadier and Colonel Mac came to see me. It was vital that they heard my story, and I told them what had happened, embroidered a little to avoid making any reference to Qayum's early deceit. I told them briefly that we had found no signs of the Japanese force we had been sent out to contact, and gave a detailed account of the battle during which Qayum had acted with skill and bravery in capturing the prisoner, who was by then already being interrogated by the Brigade Intelligence officer. I said that I thought Qayum's performance was worthy of an award, and the Brigadier and Colonel Mac both agreed and told me to rest assured that they would recommend him for one. I was then taken to the operating theatre where the offending piece of shrapnel was easily removed.

When I came to, the Brigade Major came to visit me and handed me what looked like a folded map. I opened it up and saw a hand-written message on the back, and at once recognised my brother Ted's writing. The date was two days previously, and as I read the short note I remembered how I thought I had recognised the spotter plane pilot's voice on that day. The note read, "Dear Bob. Have just been overflying a patrol in the Yomas to make radio contact. Don't suppose it was you, was it? Am just going to UK for 28 days leave. Look after yourself. Ted."

For a moment I was a bit emotional. Ted and I had been so near to each other without knowing it, and now he was going halfway round the world on leave. What a missed chance! But there it was: "*C'est la guerre*", I thought, and it was no good regretting it. Maybe we would meet up sometime before the war ended, and it certainly looked as though it would go on for a while longer even though the war in Europe had ended.

# Chapter 14

## HERE'S TO COINCIDENCE

———

I was evacuated to the military hospital in Rangoon, but before I left, Jabin came to say farewell. It was an emotional meeting between us and to begin with we said very little, our thoughts going back to the anxious time we had shared in the Yomas. Jabin had tears in his eyes when he eventually asked, "Why did you forgive him, *sahib*? He deceived you, and when he knew you had found him out, he intended to kill you. But you let him off. I will avenge you, *sahib*".

"Jabin," I replied, "When it really mattered Abdul Qayum fought bravely and did what I asked of him. That is why I decided to overlook what he had done. You have been loyal to me and I will never forget your support during the past few days. But please, Jabin, do not think of revenge. If it hadn't been for Qayum's part in the battle, our Pathan company would have failed in its task and let the Brigadier *sahib* down. And that would have brought dishonour on all of us." Jabin did not reply, he just saluted and walked out of my life forever.

As the ambulance convoy trundled down towards Rangoon, I had a lot of time to think about what had happened during the past two weeks. Perhaps the one recurring thought was how near I had been to Ted, and how nice it would have been if we could have met, even while I lay wounded in the CCS. But it had not happened, and I wondered whether we would ever meet again. From all I had heard about his exploits, he had been lucky to have come through the fighting so far unscathed. But eventually the dice might fall the wrong way, and I felt very uneasy about the tough campaign that now lay ahead of the 14th Army.

I did not stay more than a few hours in Rangoon as the hospital ship was waiting to return to Calcutta, already almost fully loaded with wounded, and as soon as we arrived and the casualties had been taken on board, the ship edged away from the dockside and set sail across the Bay of Bengal. Within a couple of days I was declared to have suffered no serious damage to my back, and I was relieved to know that my spine had only been badly bruised. I was soon on my feet again and starting to exercise by walking round and round the decks. Fortunately the sea was calm and I had no problem keeping my balance.

When we were half way across the Bay of Bengal, it was announced on the radio that an atomic bomb had been exploded over Japan and had caused the almost complete destruction of Hiroshima. The bomb, which had been parachuted from a B29 of the American 21st Bomber Group, had an explosive force equivalent to 17 000 tons of TNT, which was almost beyond comprehension. The date was 6th August 1945, but in spite of the devastation it had caused, which followed months of increasingly heavy conventional bombing of Japan's industrial centres, the Emperor and his people would not capitulate. I knew enough about the devotion of the Japanese to the 'God Emperor' to realise that only when he, and he alone, gave the signal to surrender could they lay down their arms and accept defeat.

When on the 9th August, a second atomic bomb was dropped, this time over Nagasaki, the Japanese Emperor knew that the end was near and he held a meeting with his Service chiefs in his bunker at midnight on that day. It had been announced the day before the Nagasaki bomb, which was even bigger than the Hiroshima bomb by the equivalent of an additional 3000 tons of TNT, that the Russians had declared war on the Japanese and had launched a full scale offensive against the million Japanese troops in Manchuria. To any mortal it would have been time to quit unconditionally, but not the Emperor. He offered to surrender on the one condition that he personally would be allowed to retain his sovereignty. "Arrogant little bastard," I said when I heard the news on the radio, "over my dead body."

The allies refused to accept the conditional surrender and another meeting took place in Tokyo on 14th August. The following day the Emperor announced to his people that the war was over and that he had at last surrendered unconditionally. This wonderful news coincided with the hospital ship's arrival in Calcutta, and as soon as she was made fast to the dockside, all the casualties were disembarked and transferred in a fleet of ambulances to the Military hospital. My wound had healed well during the voyage from Rangoon, and apart from some nasty and very itchy 'prickly heat' which had become infected, I was to all intents and purposes fit enough to be discharged. I was told to check in at the Grand Hotel in Chowringee, the main thoroughfare in the city, which had been requisitioned by the Military and was now being used as the officers' transit camp. I was also told to report back in a week's time for a final check up, and was then taken to the hotel along with two other officers who had been discharged that afternoon. Although it was under military administration, it was, to my great surprise, still being run as a first class civilian hotel, and I was happy to think that it was to be my home for the next week or so.

It was well into the afternoon when I checked in at the reception desk of what had once been a showpiece hotel in this bustling city. It was showing signs of having been occupied by the military for a few years, but the Indian staff were courteous and efficient, and being a field officer I was given a single room. A young porter was summoned to take my baggage, such as it was, up to my room on the third floor. The room was pleasantly furnished, but not over luxurious, and I was pleased with my first taste of civilised living since my dramatic leave at Ramsar on the Caspian Sea. I lay on my bed and it was firm and comfortable. I had a bath, put on the only reasonably clean uniform I had with me and went down to dinner.

The main lounge was seething with officers, and there was an air of unsuppressed excitement. It was after all, the first night of peacetime, and although many of those present realised that some Japanese might decide to fight on regardless of their Emperor's surrender, this was an evening to be savoured. It would be an evening most of those present would look back on as one of the most momentous they would ever experience, and which they would remember for the rest of their days, and as little groups formed for pre-dinner drinks, it was clear that a great deal of celebratory drinking was going to take place. I sat alone since I had been dropped into this scenario without any idea of what the evening would be like, and I began to wonder how I could make the most of it. I knew no one, and the best I could hope for was that somebody would ask me to join their party. I sipped a gin and tonic looking round about me, and suddenly I spotted a familiar face across the lounge; it was the medical officer who had looked after me on the hospital ship and with whom I had got on very well indeed. He, too, was sitting alone, and I got up and went over to say hullo.

"Well, George, I certainly didn't expect to see you in here tonight. How come?" I said.

"I thought I would take a day's leave as the ship doesn't return to Rangoon for two days, and I decided it would be more fun here than in the ship's ward room," George replied. "So here I am, and looking for a good evening. Shall we join together, as I see you are on your own?"

I was absolutely delighted to have someone I knew to share this special evening, and I sat down at George's table and ordered a couple of G'n'Ts. There hadn't been much chance to talk to George on the voyage from *Rangoon*, as whenever we met he was on his rounds and always seemed to be anxious to get on to the next patient, so we had a chance to catch up. There was time for another drink before dinner, and George ordered the same again from the waiter. We picked up our glasses, said "Cheers", but before taking a sip, George suddenly paled, put down his glass, and said, "My God, you see that chap standing by the bar over there? He's my brother and we haven't met since the early days of the war. He's in the RAF, fighter pilot, who did bloody well in the Battle of Britain." He was by now somewhat overcome, and I told him to go over to him.

"This is going to be some night," I said as George went over to tap his brother on the shoulder. A turn of the head, immense smiles and a huge bear hug, and in a few minutes George was introducing his brother Jack and I ordered another G'n'T for him. The evening no longer looked quite so promising for me, however. As George and Jack chatted about family and friends, I wondered how to slip away. As they went on talking I ordered another drink and thought how near Ted and I had been to each other six weeks earlier in the Pegu Yomas.

As George and Jack went on talking I thought that the best thing I could do was to go to bed as I certainly didn't want to end up legless on my own just because the war had suddenly ended. However, I was quite hungry, so I decided to stay with the brothers and make the best of it until the meal was over. A few moments later, I felt my hair almost stand on end as I heard a voice I clearly recognised, not from the distant past, but from the patrol on which I had been wounded a little over five weeks ago. Before I turned round I knew it was Ted, and uttering the words, "He's here!" I turned round in my chair to see Ted walking behind me, chatting animatedly to another officer. On my feet in a second, I slowly walked the few paces to tap Ted on the shoulder and said " I think I know you, don't I?"

He turned round, saw me and said, "Oh, Christ!"

"No, not quite", I said "Still just your brother Bob". Then we embraced as George and Jack had done a short time earlier. "I thought you were still on leave in the UK," I said.

"So you got my message on the map," he replied, "What brings you to Calcutta? I thought you were still winkling the Japs out of the Yomas."

I told Ted briefly about the clash with the Jap patrol the day after we had unknowingly spoken to each other. I then introduced him to the other two and all four of us went into dinner. We drank toasts all round, to coincidence, luck and family. It was an emotional evening, and for Ted and me it was to begin a fortnight of celebration.

It was well into the small hours of 16th August when a group of officers, fortified with copious quantities of alcohol, went 'right over the top'. It was started by some gunners who went out on to Chowringee, grabbed a *gari* (horse-drawn carriage) and in spite of the impassioned pleas of the *gari-wala*, they drove it through the vestibule of the hotel into the main lounge where they unharnessed the terrified horse which promptly emptied itself on to the dance floor, then proceeded to dismantle the vehicle itself. A 'well-oiled' colonel did his best to control the situation that was getting quite out of hand, and in the end he called in the Military Police. We could hardly keep straight faces, and the final episode was when the ringleader of the group, who was an expert horseman, rode the horse bareback and coaxed it up the main staircase on to the landing. It was a superb piece of dressage, but then the alcohol took its toll and he was unable to persuade the animal to come down again. In the end it was the *gari-wala* who managed to coax his horse backwards down the stairs to the cheers of everyone in the lounge. To his delight some less inebriated officers then set to and reconstructed the *gari*. In all fairness someone suggested a whip round for the poor little man, and he went home a good deal richer than when he was pounced on out in the street. It was quite late when Ted and I surfaced the following morning, and the first thing we did was to send a cablegram to our parents telling them of our incredible meeting.

I went for my check up at the end of the first week, but Ted, who was on his way to rejoin his Air OP squadron for the invasion of the Malay peninsular, which would not now take place for real, took time off to enjoy the extra break with me. The fortnight soon went by, and each night brought forth some extraordinary caper to celebrate the defeat of the Japs. Nothing, however, could match that final event on the night of 15th August.

During our time together Ted and I did a lot of catching up on news of family and friends, and one of the things I particularly wanted to know about was his marriage to a girl called Muriel. My father had mentioned it very briefly in one of his letters, but he gave no details although what he wrote left me in no doubt whatsoever that he did not approve. A few *chota pegs* (tots of whisky) soon loosened Ted's tongue on the subject, and it was not a happy story. During his training as a pilot he had met Muriel, and had, so he thought, fallen in love with her. She already had a daughter although had not been married before, and Ted wondered why he had ignored all the warnings and pleas from his father not to marry her. All our strict upbringing had counted for nothing, and even when Dad had pleaded with him to go away and have a dirty weekend and get it out of his system, he still couldn't see that Muriel would never fit into our family circle. In short he got married in haste, a typical wartime shotgun marriage, and within a few weeks he was posted to India. When he arrived there, Ted admitted that he knew he had made a huge mistake, and he told me that when he was sent on spotting missions, he threw caution to the wind for he had nothing to lose. But all he had achieved was to get two 'gongs', the MC and DFC, a Certificate of Gallantry and two Mentions in Despatches, and he still had to face the future saddled with a woman he did not love and her daughter, without a career or job to go back to. His plan had been to continue his studies at Oxford University and get his degree in Agriculture; to do so now with a wife and daughter to support would be very difficult. "Of course I didn't sit down and count the cost, did I?" Ted said. "She was so attractive I just went head over heels and the sex part of it was out of this world. Of course Dad didn't come to the wedding and that hurt, but I'm beginning to think he was right, as usual."

"How did you get on during your leave?" I asked.

"That's what I mean," Ted replied. "It wasn't the same, she seemed to have lost some of the sparkle that attracted me to her in the first place. And that brat of hers, no discipline and as truculent as they come."

The conversation went on, leaving me rather concerned about Ted's plans for University now that the war had come to an end. "Why don't you stay in the Army, Ted?" I queried. "With a record like yours you've got a ready-made career with success assured."

"No, I won't do that," answered Ted. "In fact, just before I left my squadron to go on leave, I was interviewed by my Brigadier about taking a regular commission, and I had given it quite a lot of thought. But in the end I couldn't see myself as a career officer with a wife tagging round the world after me, and anyway as you know I've always set my heart on going into agriculture. You won't believe this, but when the Brig eventually realised that I meant what I said, he looked me straight in the eye and said, 'What a bloody waste of medals'. And that attitude was another reason why I couldn't make the army my career."

Another incident occurred during the two weeks Ted and I were in Calcutta together. The Americans had played a relatively small, but important part in the Burma campaign, and true to form the Hollywood film industry was quick to produce a classic of its kind featuring Errol Flynn, the swashbuckling star of many similar productions. A large number of officers and NCOs who happened to be in Calcutta at the time were invited to see a preview of the film and to vote on whether it would be wise to show it to British troops. The film was a brash pro-American production that suggested that the British and Indian armies might just as well have not been in Burma at all. Errol Flynn was at his flamboyant but inaccurate best and those who watched it came away with the impression that the Americans really believed that he, playing the part of the American commander General Joe Stilwell, had recaptured Burma single-handed. The vote was unanimously against letting British troops see the film as there would be such dented pride and intense anger that a violent reaction could be possible. That was the opinion of both of us who, like all the others present, were incensed at the appalling arrogance of the film director.

Ted and I made the best of the two weeks we had together, and before parting we bought each other a silver plated tankard engraved with each others names and 'Calcutta 15 August 1945'. These gifts would always remind us of two incredible coincidences from the day before I was wounded in the Yomas until two sets of brothers, first George and Jack, then Ted and me, met each other in the lounge for the first time in five years. The chance of that happening must be a million to one, especially on such an important day in world history.

Ted left Calcutta to rejoin his squadron somewhere in Madras, and I made an appointment to see the Military Secretary about my future. I realised that I was now perfectly fit to rejoin my battalion in Burma, but the war was over and I wondered what the point of that would be. Now that I was a regular officer in the British Army, I felt that the sooner I made myself known to my new regiment the better. The Military Secretary told me to stay in the Grand Hotel for the time being, and he even invited me to knock a golf ball about with him at the Tollygunge Club at the weekend. I accepted, mediocre golfer though I was, and during the coming weeks we enjoyed some rather unspectacular golf there. Some three weeks after my first meeting with him, I received an official letter from his department informing me that I was no longer attached to the Indian Army, and that my possessions, which I had left behind with the battalion in Burma, would be sent to me in Calcutta as soon as possible. Arrangements would also be made for me to be flown home from Dum Dum air base and that I should hold myself in readiness to go at a moment's notice. I was delighted at this turn of events, and I wrote home to warn my parents that I might arrive without further warning.

A few days after receiving this letter from the Military Secretary, one of my brother officers from the 4 FFR in Burma, John Peyton, booked into the Grand Hotel. Handshaking over, he said that he was on his way to the UK on leave, and he had brought my kit with him. He was staying in Calcutta for only one night, and we spent the evening together, chatting about the later stages in the battle for Burma. After dinner, I asked John whether *Havildar* Abdul Qayum had been awarded a decoration for his part in the battle near Pyu when I was wounded. "As a matter of fact he was," said John. "Haven't you heard the bizarre story which followed his award?" I said I hadn't, and John took a long sip of his *chota peg* and launched into the tale.

It was early in August when Abdul Qayum was given an immediate Indian Distinguished Service Medal for 'extreme bravery and resourcefulness in the face of the enemy', and the Brigadier had pinned the ribbon on his chest in front of the whole battalion drawn up on parade. Qayum was a very proud man indeed, but the wheels of fate, having given him the medal he had coveted for such a long time and at such cost, were beginning to turn against him. He wallowed in the *Izzat* (pride) his award had brought him, but soon afterwards he found himself in command of the battalion quarter-guard. As he paraded his men for inspection he came eye to eye with *sepoy* Jabin Khan. The two men looked at each other impassively, the silence of hatred broken only when Qayum told Jabin to wait behind when he had dismissed the remainder of the guard. According to Jabin, Qayum taunted him, saying, "You haven't got your white *sahib* to protect you now, have you? I'm in charge and you'll do as I tell you, understand?" It was too much for Jabin, for he had seen this Yusufzai cheat and lie in order to get the IDSM that he felt Qayum in no way deserved.

"No," said Jabin, "He is not here, no thanks to you. But you won't enjoy the medal for long, I promise you." Qayum had leered at him, but before he could defend himself, Jabin struck him in the face. He was immediately put under close arrest and confined in the quarter-guard.

There were still a lot of Japs about in the area, some trying to escape across the River Sittang and others probing the Allied positions prior to the expected mass breakout attempt. Because of this, when any prisoners in the quarter-guard were sent outside the perimeter for exercise under escort, they were allowed to carry arms for self-protection. Due to an extraordinary muddle, one day the prisoners were escorted on their daily exercise by a detail from A Company under the command of *Havildar* Abdul Qayum. The party had stopped on the railway line for a rest when Jabin suddenly got up and shot Qayum before he could be overpowered and restrained. A runner was sent back to battalion HQ with the news and the Adjutant sent out a stretcher party to fetch the *havildar* in. As soon as he arrived, the regimental MO sent him straight down the line to the Field Ambulance about eight miles away. The Adjutant had meanwhile sent a jeep ahead to clear the road, but Qayum died in the ambulance before he got there.

At the court martial that followed, the prisoner, Jabin, told the whole story of Qayum's dishonourable conduct. It was confirmed by others on the patrol, some of whom were not of Jabin's tribe and therefore had no axe to grind, but whatever was said in mitigation it made no difference, for Jabin had murdered Qayum in cold blood. He was found guilty and sentenced to death by firing squad, and as soon as the sentence had been confirmed by the Army commander, the whole battalion was formed up on parade and Jabin, handcuffed to an escort, was marched on. The adjutant, John Beazley, promulgated the finding and sentence, first in Urdu then in Pushtu, and announced that the execution by shooting would be carried out at dawn the next morning. Jabin was then marched back to the guardroom to await his punishment.

For the second time fate looked kindly on Jabin Khan, for by another extra-ordinary oversight the guard that night was once again from the Pathan company. It seemed amazing to me that this should have been allowed to happen, but many years later back in England I met John Beazley and asked him about the incident. John, who was well steeped in the sensitivities of the various tribes, felt that it would have been most insulting to the Pathan company if he had changed the guard. It would have implied that they were not to be trusted, but in the event, that's how it turned out and he would have been perfectly justified in doing so. The senior Pathan VCOs were so intent on seeing justice done, and expunging this appalling blot on the fine record of inter-tribal accord in the FFR, that they overlooked the fact that the new guard to be mounted that evening would be Orakzais, Jabin's own tribe.

Shortly before dawn the commander of the Yusufzai firing party went to collect Jabin from the guardroom. He would have the satisfaction of avenging the murder of one of their own, but when the Orakzai guard commander went inside with him and unlocked the door of Jabin's cell, it was empty. On the far side of the small room there was a hole in the outside wall through which Jabin had been spirited away during the night. What the guard knew about it will never be known, but Jabin was never heard of again.

After Ted had left for his squadron, rather than let time hang heavily on my hands, I went to the Tollygunge Golf Club almost daily. I soon met some of the British community in Calcutta, and was made welcome by their families and at the Saturday Club, the exclusive establishment where I was made a temporary member. The affection of the community in Calcutta was immense; I was extremely grateful for the kind way so many people took me into their homes and entertained me so generously. However the days dragged into weeks, since the Military Secretary was unable to get me on a flight to the UK as every seat was reserved for officers going back home for a month's leave, who had to be given priority.

There was still a great deal for the Allied armies to do in the Far East, not least being the collection and incarceration of hundreds of thousands of Japs in prisoner-of war-camps. In fact, I soon received a letter from Ted who had already arrived at Kuala Lumpur in Malaya, telling me that one of his first flights had been to take the

Japanese Commander-in-Chief on a reconnaissance mission over a group of islands off the Singapore coast. The General was then able to plan where his defeated soldiers would be sent to, and had given Ted a signed photograph of himself with the words: "Thank you very much for flying me safely over the Kep Riau islands". A nice gesture, but it hadn't gone down too well with Ted who had kept his revolver within immediate reach and I rather agreed with him that whatever your rank you couldn't trust the Japs further than you could throw them. Ted happily did not have to defend himself, and quite soon afterwards the General got his comeuppance when he was tried by a War Crimes tribunal, found guilty and executed.

September came and went, and it was not until the last week in October that I was ordered to get out to Dum Dum airport immediately. My excitement was immense; I threw my kit together and grabbed a lift to the airfield on a 15 cwt truck. I didn't even have time to contact my friends to thank them for taking me under their wing or to say good-bye. I reported to the Air Traffic Control Officer and was told to go to the canteen and have a good meal as the plane was not due to take off for a couple of hours and it would be some time before I would get the chance of another meal as the first stop was Karachi, 1400 miles away.

I reported back to the ATCO at the appointed time, and joined a group of officers and a few other ranks in a sparsely furnished building where in due course we were joined by the ATCO himself. He checked everyone on his list and directed us to the embarkation point where a Liberator bomber was waiting to receive us. The aircrew were loading our gear on board, and while the pilot started up the engines, his co-pilot introduced himself and told us that this crew would take us as far as Lydda in Palestine where we would have a day's rest before continuing our journey to Waterbeach airfield in Cambridgeshire with a fresh crew. We would fly via Libya, where we would make a short stop at Castel Benito airfield, have something to eat, and another pilot would take over for the last leg of the flight to England.

He explained that we would be travelling in the converted bomb bay of the aircraft that we would probably find pretty uncomfortable, as bench seats had been fixed along each side of the plane and the passengers would be sitting facing each other with knees touching. As soon as we boarded the plane and entered the bomb bay, we saw exactly what he had meant. There was no reasonable way of getting out of our seats once we had settled in, even to be airsick or relieve ourselves at the bucket at the end of the plane. It was going to be a most unpleasant journey and to add to the discomfort, the poor lighting meant that reading a book was out of the question. The only solution was to shut one's eyes and try to sleep, but wearing jungle battle dress, flying at 25 000 feet and with no heating system, was intensely cold. For over five hours we endured it all simply because we were going home; had we been heading the other way our tolerance would have been zero.

The journey was uneventful and without turbulence, and we arrived at Karachi on schedule. We were allowed time to have a good meal in the canteen, and to stretch our cramped legs. The next part of the journey was almost 2000 miles, but I managed to get some spare clothing out of my holdall that I put on before take-off. It was now night-time, and the excitement of the day and discomfort of the journey to Karachi helped to make sleep come more easily. Almost before we knew it, we were circling Lydda airport as dawn broke and after a smooth touch down, we said farewell to the crew and were taken to the transit camp where we were able to clean ourselves up and shave, and have an extremely satisfying breakfast. The ATCO at Lydda arrived to brief us about the final part of our journey home, and told us that take-off would be the following evening, so we had a break of 36 hours. It was an irritating delay, but I had been in Tel Aviv three years ago and persuaded a few of my colleagues to let me show them some of the town. We asked about transport to and from the city, and this was laid on courtesy of the RAF. The ATCO did, however, warn us that various terrorist organisations were becoming increasingly active in their campaign for a Jewish state, which would be free of British domination once our League of Nations mandate ended in 1947.

The Gat Rimon bar and restaurant had been one of my favourite places, and I made a beeline for it. It was exactly as I remembered it, and we enjoyed some ice-cold beer and a most enjoyable lunch that took us well into the afternoon. Most of us were rather short of cash, and we returned to the transit camp mess for dinner. The sun was already beginning to dip as we were taken to the embarkation point, where our baggage had been reloaded into another Liberator. When we started to taxi for take-off, the plane was clearly tail-heavy as it banged repeatedly on the tarmac, filling some of the passengers with apprehension. The pilot decided not to attempt to take off until he had sorted the problem out, and he taxied back to have a go at restacking the baggage. Although there was a slight improvement, the aircraft still felt unbalanced and I held my breath as we gathered speed. At last we were airborne, and I could see the Mediterranean stretching away in front of us as we climbed steadily into the darkening sky. I fell asleep almost immediately, and woke up four and a half hours later as the Liberator started descending over Tripoli and came in to land at Castel Benito.

The runway lights came up to meet us, but something didn't feel right and I remembered how even after reloading, the plane had still seemed to be tail-heavy. I was apprehensive to say the least. The plane touched down but after a few seconds, during which it did not seem to be slowing sufficiently, the pilot boosted all four engines and took off again to make another attempt. I looked at my watch; it was just before 2:00 am and I thought, "What a silly time to die".

The pilot knew that we were anxious, as he told us over the intercom not to worry and everything was under control. Nerves remained tense as he touched down a second time and although his timing was better, as he applied the brakes the tail hit the ground several times and once again put the fear of God into us. At last we were down and were told to disembark, go into the canteen where there would be a hot drink and something to eat, and wait for further orders.

While we were enjoying our hot drinks and cake, another pilot came into the canteen and introduced himself as the relief who would fly us the rest of the way to Waterbeach. "But first," he said, "I'm not flying that machine until it has been properly reloaded – the damn thing is far too tail-heavy." What he said to the pilot who had brought us this far was a matter for speculation, but there was no doubt that he didn't think much of the risk he had taken. Having watched the plane come into land there was every reason for him to be somewhat disparaging about the pilot's flying performance. Our confidence had been restored as we re-embarked and were glad to be airborne again soon after 3:00 am. The excitement amongst us all was now growing minute by minute, and any further sleep was impossible.

The pilot knew that nearly all of us had been away from Britain for a number of years, and he fuelled our excitement by giving us a running commentary every now and then, telling us where we were and our expected time of arrival at Waterbeach. Soon it was light enough for us to see the ground below, though it was difficult to get a good view as the windows were small and we had to peer past the person sitting opposite, or twist right round in our seats to look out of the window behind us. This procedure was quite uncomfortable after a while, and not to be recommended. At last we passed over the French coast, and those who could get a view peered down to see if there were any signs of the invasion beaches. Then the English Channel and the white cliffs of Dover were behind us and we made a beeline for Cambridge. "Pity it couldn't have been Oxford", I thought to myself. "I could have recognised exactly where we are then." The pilot announced that we would be landing in ten minutes, and that it was a cold, raw and drizzly morning, but not to worry, there would be a good English breakfast waiting for us as soon as we had gone through the usual formalities.

The Liberator nosed down steadily and the pilot made a smooth landing. He taxied back to the airfield buildings, and as we disembarked he wished us farewell and a safe journey home. He had played his part, and now that at last we were back in England we were profuse in our thanks to the aircrew. I walked down the steps on to the tarmac, and there I knelt down on the wet ground and kissed it. Others did the same, and we then walked over to the customs shed. As each of us was carrying only a holdall no one had anything to declare, and impatience got the better of several of the passengers who thought it was really rather a pointless operation and a waste of time. Each of us was checked through by a Flight Sergeant, and we then went over to the canteen for that promised English breakfast. Seldom had bacon and eggs tasted so good.

The next port of call was the RTO's office where we were given rail warrants to London and onwards to our ultimate destinations. I quickly worked out that it would probably take us about two hours to get to Liverpool Street station in London, then I had to go by Underground to Paddington and unless my memory had let me down, there would be two trains to Wolverhampton, one at 6:10 pm and the second exactly an hour later. As far back as I could remember those were the two early evening trains on that line, and the journey took about two hours. I would get to Liverpool Street in the early afternoon, have something to eat, and then make my way to Paddington in good time to catch the 6:10 pm train. Although I had been away for five years, crossing London by tube was just as I remembered it, and it was as though I had done it only yesterday. I arrived at Paddington station soon after 4:30 pm, and the first thing I did was to telephone home. The phone rang three times and then I heard my mother answer.

"Who's speaking?" she asked.

"It's me, Bob", I said, and for a moment no more words would come.

"Bob? My Bob?" she said excitedly.

"Yes, mum, I'm at Paddington now and I'm coming home on the 6:10 train. Can you meet me? I think it arrives at quarter past eight."

"Of course, Bob darling", my mother said, by now so excited that she too was finding it hard to speak. "We'll be there to meet you."

I said that I had to ring off as I hadn't enough cash left, but I did manage to tell her that I would be starving by the time I got home. In my excitement I had forgotten about rationing which was still very much a problem every one had to live with. But after I had put the phone down I knew she would rustle up something good for me; surely there must be a fatted calf somewhere in the larder that she had kept for this special moment! But even if there was nothing else, I knew that there would be a celebratory drink waiting for me.

I suddenly realised that the jungle battledress I was wearing had not been designed for a bleak and raw November day in Britain, and I began to feel distinctly chilly. I went to the gents and took out all the extra clothing I could find in my holdall and put it on under my battle dress, but even wearing my last reserves to keep warm, I still felt cold. I went over to the station buffet and had a mug of hot tea and a stodgy bun, and I felt a bit warmer. I walked about the station, from one platform to another, enjoying the fact that I was back in England in one piece, in spite of one very lucky break in July. The time went by ever so slowly as I looked forward impatiently to getting back home. As soon as the 6:10 train pulled into the platform, I was one of the first to get in the queue, and I was lucky to find some empty places facing the engine. I was soon comfortably settled in a corner seat of what had once been a very smart compartment. The years of war and lack of adequate maintenance had taken its toll and the seats were now very tatty, to say the least. "Not to worry", I thought, "as long as it gets me home safely I'll be happy."

At precisely ten minutes past six the guard blew his whistle, the engine let out its surplus steam and the train, by now completely full, slowly pulled out of the station on its journey to Wolverhampton. As I sat back savouring this very special moment, I thought back to the same sort of feeling I had experienced four years and nine months ago when I said good-bye to my sad parents on the very station to which I was now returning. Then, however, I was starting out on a great adventure as a mere stripling. Now the adventure had run its course and I was returning home, almost five years older and much wiser.

There was no way I could doze as my mind took me back over so many incidents during those years, and once the train had gathered speed, the time kept pace with it and almost before I realised it, the train was slowing to stop at Birmingham Snow Hill station. Nothing seemed to have changed there, but I knew that outside the station tremendous damage had been incurred during the blitz. The train pulled out again and less than half an hour later we entered the tunnel immediately after which was my home station. Once clear of the tunnel I made a move for the door, let down the window, and oblivious of the cold night air, I leant out to scan the platform where I hoped my parents would be waiting to greet me. There was a seething mass of people standing there, all craning their necks to try to spot the people they had come to meet, and by the time the train had stopped I had not been able to pick out Dad and Mum. I got out and started walking towards the ticket collector at the exit when I suddenly saw Dad peering over the heads of the crowd. But my mother, only a little more than five feet tall, was not to be seen; she was hidden behind the crowd of people squashed around her. Dad and I saw each other at almost the same moment, and huge grins spread over our faces. We drew closer through the crowd and then we were together, clasping each other in great bear hugs. "Hey, what about me?" said Mum, and I grasped her to me and she wept into my chest. It was a scene which went unnoticed by those about us, a scene which was being repeated many times a day as husbands and sons – the lucky ones – came back home, our duty to family and country well and truly done.

# Chapter 15

## LIVING LOST TIME

———

The following morning I went along to the regimental depot at Copthorne Barracks in Shrewsbury, which was only 30 miles away. I was warmly welcomed into my new regiment by the commanding officer and a retired major, Victor Crane, who was administering regimental affairs. Over a cup of coffee, they told me that they had just been notified by the War Office that I had been mentioned in Despatches for my patrol in the Pegu Yomas. I was as delighted as I was surprised at this news, but I felt that if I was to get an award for what I had done under the most unusual circumstances, it was surely worthy of something better than just a mention. But it was the luck of the draw and an immediate mention was better than a 'gong' that came up with the rations.

I was given a month's leave which meant that I would have to report back just before Christmas. Mum was furious that after being abroad for the past four Christmases, it didn't look as though I would be able to join the family again this time. I told her I would get on to the admin officer about it and she should assume that I would get an extension and be with them, and make plans accordingly. After being away for nearly five years, it was hardly likely, I explained, that they wouldn't give me an extension of a week or two. "Bank on it, anyway, Mum," I said.

I immediately set about picking up the pieces of my disrupted life but I found it strange that regardless of so much water having flowed under the bridge I didn't feel a day older than when I sailed out of Liverpool early in February 1941, and I planned to spend my leave as though nothing had changed. But as I met old friends and caught up with the news it soon dawned on me that very much had in fact changed. People I had known as youngsters had grown up and matured, and as I learned that so many of my old colleagues would not be coming back, and others were maimed for life, I realised that the Maslen-Jones family had been extremely lucky. Three sons had gone away to fight, and all three had come back unscathed. My heart went out to the less fortunate, especially to the parents of one family, close friends of my parents, whose three sons had been playmates of ours. All three of them had been killed and I tried to understand how their parents must feel about the rotten hand they had been dealt.

By the KING'S Order the name of
Captain R. G. Maslen-Jones,
The King's Shropshire Light Infantry,
was published in the London Gazette on
19 September, 1946,
as mentioned in a Despatch for distinguished service.
I am charged to record
His Majesty's high appreciation.

*J. J. Lawson*

Secretary of State for War

*A copy of my certificate of Mention in Despatches*

Joy was stationed at a nearby RAF hospital in Cosford where she was a nursing sister, and one of the first things I did was telephone her and find out when she was next coming home. I was a bit diffident about meeting her again, and after five long years away without the chance of meeting many girls, my strict upbringing was still a dominant feature in my life. I looked on the opposite sex as special people to be respected and cherished, not used or abused as so many of my acquaintances in the army considered to be their right. I wondered if I would still feel the same about her, for when I last saw her she was still a schoolgirl, and the five long years we had been apart must have matured and changed her like so many of my other friends. I was pleasantly surprised at her obvious excitement when she heard my voice, for I had half-expected that she would be going out with some dashing young RAF doctor. "Not so", she assured me, and she would get home to see me as soon as she could. It wasn't long before she telephoned suggesting that the two of us should join a party of our friends at a dinner dance in aid of the Red Cross in the Civic Hall in Wolverhampton. I agreed, and looked forward to the party the following week. It was to be uniform or a black tie affair, and I dug out my dinner jacket suit only to find that I had completely outgrown it. The only presentable uniform I had brought home with me was my Service Dress that I'd had the foresight to have sent to me in Calcutta during my long stay there. I had no option but to wear it, but I arranged to be measured for what were still called 'Patrols' (but soon to be renamed 'Number One Dress'), and I was determined to get those made as a matter of urgency.

Although petrol rationing was still in force, I bought a 1937 MG (TA) with a re-conditioned engine from a second hand car dealer called Wolf whose premises were just round the corner from Dad's private nursing home in Wolverhampton. I figured that because of his position in the town the dealer wouldn't dare to try to cheat me, and I parted with the princely sum of £350. Then I proudly drove over to see Joy and show her my new purchase. The car was a pleasure to drive and I really fancied myself, driving along with the hood down and the loose ends of my old school rugger scarf trailing in the breeze behind me. I arranged to pick Joy up in the MG (with the hood up) to go to the dinner dance, and when she greeted me in the Mess looking more beautiful than I had ever imagined, all looked set for a wonderful and romantic evening.

We were a little late arriving at the Civic Hall, and our friends were already well into their second drinks. I knew every one there except for one couple who had only recently moved to the area. He was an executive director in a big boiler-making company and as we were approaching our table, I overheard him say in a very loud voice "Oh my God, NOT uniform, surely? We've all been through *so* much. Surely we can forget the war now?" My hackles rose but I managed to control myself until I was being introduced to that obnoxious person who was called Cedric Baker. He rather reluctantly held out his hand when I was introduced to him, but my body language made it clear that I was going to shake hands and not react to the remark that had clearly been made for me to hear. I let his weak, flabby hand slip out of my grasp and I suddenly lost some of my self-control. As he took his hand away, I snapped, "I heard your unfair and unnecessary remark, and for your information I only arrived home from Burma a few days ago and my dinner jacket no longer fits me. So either I wear the uniform I, at least, am proud of, or I don't come". Cedric knew that he had landed himself in an awkward predicament and was not going to get off lightly. He rather lost his head, and blustered that what he had really meant to say was that the war had been over for at least seven months and surely that was enough time for people to get back to normal.

"Haven't you heard that since the end of the war in Europe, hundreds of thousands of men who had been involved there have already been moved to the Far East to join the 'Forgotten Army'?" I replied. "I was in that army, and we were already beating the Japanese in Burma and preparing to invade Malaya and Siam and carry the war through to Japan itself before Hiroshima and Nagasaki had been atomised. And if it hadn't been for those atomic bombs I and thousands like me would probably be buried in some Godforsaken bit of jungle out there. And for what? So that people like you who never had the guts to go and fight could become executive directors of Daddy's firm and grow fat and flabby on the backs of those who did."

I was suddenly aware that the whole party had been shocked into silence. I was so upset that I couldn't face remaining with them a moment longer. I apologised to my old friends, and to Joy for spoiling her evening, and said that if she wanted to stay

I would understand and I would return to take her back to the hospital later. But I could not stay in the company of that dreadful man a moment longer. To my surprise Joy replied that she entirely agreed with what I had said and we could go and have a quiet dinner on our own somewhere else. I heard later that Cedric had excused himself and his wife soon after we had left, as the rest of the party completely cold-shouldered him.

When Joy and I were in the car, I relaxed and told her about my meeting with Brian Parsons in the Victoria Hotel bar just before I sailed for India. It was still a sore point with me, and to be greeted with Cedric's snide remark brought it all to the boil.

"Don't worry about it," she said, "I'm sure that everyone else understood how you felt and from the looks on their faces I would guess that they agreed with every word you said – as I certainly did. You have been very unlucky to have those two experiences", she continued. "The first just before you went away, and the second just after you got back. If you count all our friends who did join the services, it leaves only an insignificant number who didn't have the guts to do their bit. And they are not worth worrying about".

I was temporarily overcome and leaning over I stole a kiss, and she took my hand in hers. For a few moments neither of us spoke, then Joy said that perhaps we should find somewhere to eat, and she knew a super little restaurant only three or four miles out of town.

"The food is really good, and we think they have a number of suppliers where they get scarce items, but it is quite expensive".

"You mean they get it on the black market, don't you," I grinned. "Let's go there, then. After my embarrassing outburst tonight I owe you something special, don't I?" From then on it became an enchanted evening for both of us. Our feelings for each other had matured over the years of being apart, and when I took Joy back to her hospital quarters, all my diffidence had disappeared and we savoured a long and passionate embrace. I drove home almost in a trance, the unpleasantness of the evening temporarily forgotten. For the first time in my life, including my brief flirtation with Penny Somerset when my amorous activities in Secunderabad in 1941 almost got me banished to a life of celibacy for the duration of the war, I imagined myself head over heels in love. "Wow" I shouted into the night air as my beloved MG purred its way homewards.

Next morning I told Dad what had happened at the party and rather expected him to give me a rocket for my lack of self-control. But his only reaction was to tell me to ignore people like Cedric and to remember that his sort were few and far between. "They're just not worth worrying about. You and your friends who went out to fight are all who really matter, so forget the others even exist." That was the end of that particular conversation, and I went on to tell him about my new car. "I wish you had asked me before you bought it from that place", he said. "He's a known twister and even though my nursing home is so close to his show room, I doubt if that would stop him trying to make an easy bob out of you. Keep an eye on the car, and if anything goes wrong, talk to me about it". I felt that even though I had been an Army officer for close on five years, Dad suspected that I was still not very street-wise and somewhat naive about the unprotected world outside the Army.

I had to ration my mileage as petrol was still in short supply and on coupons, but Dad managed to let me have a few of his quite generous ration now and then which made my purchase more worth-while. But before I had done 500 miles in the MG, I detected a knock in the engine. Although only slight at first, it very quickly developed into a serious and very worrying noise. I went straight back to the dealer, who of course didn't want to know. I then went to Barnett's garage just across the road from Wolf's, and sought out one of the mechanics, Jack Law, who had taught me to drive before the war. He was in the showroom and after telling him what the problem was, we went out for a test run and as I feared the verdict was that the big end had gone.

"But Wolf sold me this car with a reconditioned engine," I said.

"And he sold you a pup into the bargain," came the reply.

At lunch I told Dad the sad story and asked what I should do now. "Get Law to strip the engine down and see exactly what is wrong with it. Then, if it's as bad as Law says, go back to Wolf and demand your money back, as he has sold you the car fraudulently. Tell him that the evidence is open to inspection in Barnett's garage, and that unless he pays you back every penny you paid him, we will take him to court. And furthermore, tell him he can collect the parts of the engine from Barnett's place".

"Thanks Dad, I'll do just that," I replied, and immediately after the meal I went to confront Wolf. The boot was now on the other foot, and reassured by my father, I was determined not to be kicked around by this crook. With a degree of self-assurance I had seldom experienced before, I went for Wolf's jugular and like all bullyboys he folded under my onslaught. The meeting was short and sweet, Wolf paid the money back in cash, and I walked out of the shabby little office to tell Law what had happened. Law refused to take anything for his trouble, saying that those like him who were too old to join up, owed a tremendous debt to those who did go. But I couldn't leave it at that, and I gave him £5, which in those days was quite a lot of money. I went home feeling that I had learned a salutary lesson, but at the same time I was disappointed to have lost my new toy. Soon afterwards I went back to Barnett's garage and saw the MG still parked in a corner with the engine lying in pieces beside it. I didn't mention it to the salesman whom I had gone to see, and to cut a long story short, I drove away in a smart little Morris 8 Tourer which was to serve me well until a few months later when I was once again posted overseas.

Two weeks before Christmas, I drove over to the Regimental depot again and as I expected, they didn't want me there. I collected another fourteen days leave that would take me up to 6th January, and went home to tell Mum who was absolutely delighted. Christmas and New Year were one long round of parties, and with brothers

Ted and Freddy at home for the whole holiday period, and of course the 'aunts' who had never missed a Christmas with the family until 1939, the clock slipped back five years. At our dinner party on Christmas night we played charades and other silly games that would probably never have happened without the excellent wine Dad had provided, and it was as though that long break in our Christmas tradition had never occurred. Just for a moment, however, Dad brought us all back to reality when he raised his glass and asked us all to "Be upstanding and drink to absent friends". For a few moments I remembered many of my old friends who would never again enjoy Christmas but this was not the time to let the past spoil the present, and after a brief pause the party was once again in full swing.

I saw Joy two or three times before my leave came to an end, and my feelings for her grew ever more romantic. Demobilisation was in full swing, and she expected to be released within the next six months. We couldn't make any firm plans to see each other again until I knew where I would be posted, and I was given this information when I reported back to the depot. I was to join 20th Holding battalion in Court-y-Gollen Camp near Crickhowell in South Wales, and that effectively destroyed our hopes of being able to see each other fairly frequently. Time started to drag a little, but I was able to play rugger for the battalion although the standard was rather rough and ready and I found playing local teams up in the 'valleys' a bit daunting, with huge miners throwing their weight around with little abandon. After six weeks at Crickhowell, I was posted to South Wales District HQ in Abergavenny as a Staff Captain, a job I found extremely boring as I spent most of the day sitting at a desk shuffling paper which by no stretch of the imagination could be called productive. I had found some excellent digs in the town, and the one redeeming feature of the posting was that I was within a few minutes walk of the golf club where I saw to it that my handicap improved and was soon almost in single figures.

Not very far from my digs, I found a riding stables. I had never been an experienced rider, but I saw the chance to improve my performance and build on the short but intensive training course I had done with the Guides. The owner of the stables was a retired mounted policeman called Allen, assisted by his son Graham who had just been demobilised from the Royal Marine Commandos. Graham and I were much the same age and soon became very good friends, always ending an evening ride with a few 'jars' at the local pub where we reminisced about our wartime experiences. At first I felt that Graham's exploits in the Commandos put my own war record rather into second place. But on reflection, some of Graham's stories were a bit far-fetched. Beer gives licence to the imagination!

At the beginning of May, South Wales District was disbanded. In the meantime 20th Holding battalion moved to Pembroke Dock and I held my breath wondering whether Joy and I were to be separated by another 150 miles. My uncertainty did not last long and much to my relief I was posted back to the depot in Shrewsbury. As soon as I arrived there, I was put in charge of a detachment of 100 men and given the job of occupying no fewer than three large airfields that had been decommissioned to prevent the buildings being taken over by squatters. I set up my HQ in what had been the Officers Mess on the airfield nearest to the RAF Hospital in Cosford where Joy was stationed, and I settled down to a summer of comparative content. I had taken my car with me, but by good route planning frequent inspections of my detachments enabled me to use my official transport to make equally frequent visits to see Joy.

The job of guarding the empty buildings was for the most part without incident and became progressively less interesting. Occasionally I had to deal with a confrontation between my soldiers and some irate families who thought the buildings were there for the taking. It was a problem brought about by the sudden release of servicemen whose one intention was to get their families together and make a home for them. It seemed to us that these people deserved better than a blank refusal to use buildings which the forces no longer needed, but it was my unpleasant duty to keep squatters out, using minimum force to do so. On the very few occasions when things looked as though they were getting nasty, I immediately sought police assistance as briefed as the Army did not get closely involved. As most of my men were waiting for their own release anyway, and some of them might soon find themselves 'on the other side' of that particular situation, it could have put us in a difficult position to have to use force to keep the would-be squatters out. The often dreary routine of daily inspections of the airfields was relieved only by my visits to see Joy, and occasional visits home.

We had received instructions from District Headquarters that in view of the sensitive nature of our anti-squatter role, everything possible must be done to keep up the morale of the troops involved, most of who were de-mob happy conscripts. To achieve this I had asked our Quartermaster to ensure that we were given the best possible rations and plenty of well cooked food. He had achieved the almost impossible and had received plenty of praise from the men. The few officers on airfield duty with me enjoyed exactly the same fare as the soldiers.

One lunchtime, the mess orderly on duty was called Alan Smith. He was a real Black Country lad with an accent so thick you could cut it with a knife, and he was one of those disarmingly pleasant individuals who was universally liked. When I arrived in the Mess all my colleagues had finished their meal, and only Smith, who liked to be known as Smithee, was in the building. He was still dressed in his white Mess waiter's jacket, standing by the serving table, and said that he had already dished up my dinner and had kept it hot for me. He brought in a plate piled high with steaming stew and vegetables, and I was soon tucking into my meal. As usual it was extremely tasty and I was thoroughly enjoying it when I noticed Smithee looking at me with an expression of disbelief on his face.

"What's the matter, Smithee?" I asked.

"Yow've aiten that lot, I s'pose yow'd like another 'elping, Sir?" he replied.

"It was great Smithee, and if you can manage to scrape up a bit more, yes please."

Knowing my appetite, Smithee had kept a second helping hot for me, and as he placed it in front of me, he said in his broad Brummy accent, "Cor, yow car 'arf scoff, yow car, Sir". He never failed to use that final little word; that reminded me of my days with the Indian Army and the doubts I had had about how I would get on with British soldiers. I realised now that there was little difference between them if you treated them firmly but kindly, and I felt encouraged that Smithee, whom I had known for only a few weeks, had gone to such trouble to look after me.

In July I took a fortnight's leave and drove to Bisley to shoot in the National Rifle Association meeting. Since I had first come to this Mecca of Rifle Shooting in 1936, I had grown to love Bisley camp with the all-pervading smell of lime trees in flower, and the smell of burnt cordite on the firing points. I had to buy a rifle and equipment, but it needed 'zeroing' and until this had been done to my satisfaction, my performance was far from brilliant. Nevertheless, before the end of the meeting I was selected to represent Burma in the Kolapur Cup competition, and I also shot for the Welsh Twenty Club.

On my return to the depot, I was told that I was to be posted to the 2nd battalion in Cyprus and would be sailing with a draft of reinforcements in the latter half of September. In the meantime I was put in charge of a holding company and it was my job to look after the administration and organise training for those who were detailed to join the reinforcement draft. It was not the sort of job I could put much effort into, and it certainly didn't occupy all my time.

The weather in August had turned warm and sunny; Joy had been demobilised and whenever possible I drove over to Wolverhampton to see her and we played tennis on their hard court. On 23rd September we embarked for the relatively short sea journey across the Mediterranean to Alexandria. I had been given two weeks embarkation leave, and Joy and I spent the few days together before I left for the Middle East. I also made a short visit to Abergavenny to see Graham. The two of us had become good friends, and we played a round of golf together and enjoyed some excellent beer in a real country pub. We said goodbye to each other, and Graham promised to write to me and keep me informed of local news.

My leave passed far too quickly but Joy and I enjoyed a hectic round of tennis parties, swimming in her parents' pool in the garden, and dinner dances in the evenings. The last evening came all too soon and the two of us dined together with my parents before I returned to the depot, and to them it looked as though we were nearing the point of no return. It was a match that both sets of parents dearly wished to end in a happy marriage. But I was still not sure about it.

# Chapter 16

## CYPRIOT ROUND BALL GAME

———

There were two days in which I and my draft of 72 all ranks, including three newly commissioned subalterns, had to be kitted out, documented, inoculated and made ready. We entrained without incident and on arrival in Southampton we immediately embarked on the troopship *Empire Orwell*. The ship was already almost full, mostly with an infantry battalion starting a tour of duty in Egypt, but there were also a number of drafts for battalions and other units already stationed in the Middle East. After seeing that my men were properly accommodated on our troop deck, my subalterns and I found our own cabin and after settling in, we reported to the ship's adjutant. He told us that the commanding officer of the infantry battalion would have overall command of all service personnel on board, but that Major Jack Thatcher, Brigade of Guards, would be responsible to him for the drafts. On arrival in Alexandria, Major Thatcher would take over sole command of the drafts as far as Cairo, where Movement Control would give fresh orders to each draft commander.

Before we docked in Alexandria, Major Thatcher ordered the drafts to parade on the after deck where he wished to give the men a few words of advice. He had spent several years in the Middle East during and before the war, and there were one or two things he felt he should tell the drafts who were mostly young National Servicemen away from home for the first time. His final piece of advice was to take every precaution to prevent local thieves from stealing their personal possessions, such as watches, wallets and the like, but above all to safeguard their weapons. He warned that any soldier who had his personal weapon stolen could expect short shrift from his commanding officer. To have your weapon stolen was considered a cardinal crime.

When the *Empire Orwell* came alongside, the infantry battalion disembarked first, followed by the drafts. The battalion marched smartly away from the docks to be loaded into Service Corps transport, and the drafts were marched to the railway platform that was parallel to the dockside. Here Major Thatcher ordered each draft to get into the waiting train, while he satisfied himself that every seat was occupied and every serviceman was on board. My draft was in the last carriage, and the Major himself was in the last compartment. A few miles out of Alexandria the train stopped for a minute or two at a station that was crowded with local inhabitants, and as it began to gather speed again, Major Thatcher leant out of the carriage window. Most of the Arabs on the platform were well clear of the moving train, but some Arab porters remained only a few feet from it, and in a flash all Jack Thatcher's advice about sneak thieves was lost on one person – himself. The train was almost clear of the platform when a keen-eyed Arab who had spotted Major Thatcher's gold wristwatch dashed forward and snatched it off his wrist. I heard a shout, and turning, saw Major Thatcher holding his wrist. "That little bastard snatched my watch," he shouted to me. While I felt sorry for Jack I couldn't help but be amused that so soon after warning the men about just such a trick, he was the one with scrambled egg all over his face.

The rest of the journey to Cairo was uneventful, and Major Thatcher saw the drafts safely to the transit camp just outside the city where he relinquished his command and went on his way to join his own regiment in Palestine. The RTO duly appeared and issued instructions to each individual draft commander, and I was told that my draft would be leaving by train for Haifa that same evening. There we would embark on the ferry for the short sea journey to Famagusta in Cyprus. It was dawn the next morning when the train drew into Haifa station, which was heavily guarded by British troops. The local RTO was there to meet us and after asking if we'd had a reasonable journey, directed us to the dockside where the ferry to Cyprus was waiting.

"You'll get breakfast on board", he said, and then as an afterthought added "I don't suppose you've heard the news have you?"

"What particular news is that?" I asked.

"Oh, they blew up the King David Hotel in Jerusalem last night. Huge loss of life, and a serious blow. We had our HQ housed in part of the building, you know". I hadn't known, and I was quite shaken that once again I seemed to be in the middle of a war. "So that's what the heavy military presence is about, is it?"

"That's right," replied the RTO, "from now on it looks as though the gloves are well and truly off. It's all blown up very quickly and the Stern Gang and Irgun Svai Leumi have threatened to carry out more attacks like last night's until their demands for an independent Jewish state are fully met".

"Well, I hope we'll be out of the firing line in Cyprus," I said. "You keep your head down here, and let's hope it can be sorted out quickly. Cheerio, then", I said as I instructed the junior subaltern to move the men on board the ferry.

When we arrived in Famagusta, it was like a different world after the tense atmosphere of Haifa. The battalion transport was lined up on the dockside, and disembarking and loading onto the lorries was simple and well organised. The adjutant, Captain Jim Darlington, was waiting to meet the draft, and when the men were all embussed and accounted for he told me to go with him in his jeep, gave the order to move off, and drove ahead of the convoy to the battalion camp at Dekhelia near

Larnaca. There were no signs of any unusual security precautions during the drive along the coast road westwards from Famagusta until suddenly we were passing a heavily wired and guarded camp.

"Looks like a POW camp," I commented.

"You might say that, for that's exactly what it is if you think of illegal Jewish immigrants as 'enemy'," replied Jim. "Hardly a day goes by without boatloads of refugees from Europe arriving off the Palestine seaboard, and the camps are already full of the unlucky ones who have been intercepted by the Navy just before reaching their promised land. You can't help feeling sorry for the blighters in a way, but they are determined people and will stop at nothing to get to Palestine. So security in the camps has to be extremely rigid, as though we are at war with these people."

I asked who was responsible for guarding the camps, and was told that duties were shared by the garrison battalions centred around Larnaca, of which the 2nd battalion of the KSLI was one. "We don't carry personal arms unless we are actually on guard duty," Jim told me, "unless you count your 12-bore as a personal weapon!"

"I'd heard that the blackcock and partridge shooting is pretty good in the olive groves. How often do you manage to have a day's shooting?" I asked.

"Well, we are lucky as our camp is between the sea and a big estate belonging to a very friendly Cypriot landowner. So far we have been asked to shoot once a week, and we've had some pretty good sport. I hope you've brought your gun?"

I had indeed brought my gun with me, and I began to look forward to using it before very much longer.

Before we reached the battalion camp at Dekhelia Jim told me about the officer set-up. The commanding officer was Lt. Colonel Peter Shaw-Ball DSO, and his second in command was Major Chris Hill, both excellent shots, and both of whom had been decorated during the Normandy fighting. The company commanders were a good lot, and it was altogether a very happy battalion. I didn't know what the commanding officer had decided to do with me, but I thought I would be taking over command of HQ company as Captain Ted Taylor, the company commander, was going to the UK to do a month's course at the School of Infantry.

On arrival at battalion HQ, I handed over the draft to the Regimental Sergeant Major, and the three subalterns and I reported to the orderly room. As expected, I was told I would be taking over command of HQ company for the time being, and I was also asked whether I knew anything about football. I was a rugby player, but during the summer holidays of 1938, Ted, Ken Spray and I had spent five mornings each week training with our local 1st Division football team, Wolverhampton Wanderers ('The Wolves'), to get fit for the school rugger season. Inevitably I had picked up a liking for the round ball game as well as many useful tips on training a soccer team, and I volunteered this information to the colonel who was affectionately known as Snowy.

"Splendid," he said. "How about taking over the job of Football Officer? We don't have one at the moment, and Sergeant Major Bill Strong runs the team.

Naturally it is always the same side, many of them from the Sergeants' Mess, and frankly it does nothing to help maintain morale when we know that we have a lot of damned good players in the battalion. What I would like to see, though I shan't be here by then, is a really good battalion football team able to take on any of the local Army and civilian sides and of course Service teams visiting the island. What d'you think about that, eh?"

"Off the cuff I think it's a jolly good idea, Colonel," I said. "When can I start?" Before I took over command of HQ company, I met Sergeant Major Strong and made up my mind not to clash with him. I told him exactly what I planned to do, and I would start with the appointment of a selection committee with representatives from each company, and a series of trial games. Rather surprisingly I got the fullest co-operation from Strong, who confided that he was in a very difficult position in the Mess as so many of the 'old hands' felt that they had a divine right to be in the team whether or not they were good enough footballers. I experienced a feeling of relief that this situation was now changed and that he and I would work together to build up the best possible team. It all went according to plan, and a fixture list was drawn up to start after Christmas that included playing every unit on the island as well as local teams such as Larnaca, Nicosia and Limassol. In the meantime, I enjoyed some excellent days out with the guns and there were memorable drives of French partridge and blackcock. I also found time to visit the Troodos mountains where I spent a few days climbing, and I also visited the small port of Kyrenia on the north coast where I spent a night in the Dome Hotel – a delightful spot, and completely peaceful.

Some of the other officers and I developed a habit of visiting the Goldfish Cabaret in Larnaca once or twice a week. There were hardly any decent places where off-duty soldiers could enjoy an evening's drinking, and that applied to the officers as well. The Goldfish was well policed and although there were usually officers and other ranks drinking in the same building, there was never any trouble. I rather liked the local brandy and salted peanuts, and this became my routine drink when I went out on the town.

My enthusiasm and complete involvement as battalion football officer virtually took over all my other interests. For example I would rather train my team than go out with the guns, and gradually I thought less and less about Joy. It must have been conveyed to her in my letters that were full of my new interest and had also become less frequent. My ardour for her was no longer as hot as it had been only a few months before, and in turn her letters to me became less passionate and fewer and further between.

Soon after Christmas the football team was ready to play its first match against one of the other battalions. The promise shown in training was maintained, and we won by a single goal. I felt that we could probably have done better if we'd had good vociferous support, and it was agreed that transport would be laid on to take supporters to all the away matches. Snowy decided also that a few buglers should accompany the team to every match and blow fanfares to add to the vocal support. It was an excellent idea, and before long there was a new spirit in the battalion, based entirely on the football team. Throughout the rest of the season, the team was unbeaten by any Army side, and suffered only two defeats, both to Limassol FC. In fact, probably our best performance was to draw with a visiting British Army team from Egypt that included some professional players from the Football League. It was all very exciting, but like all good things it had to come to an end, and this was early in March when orders were received for the battalion to send a strong detachment, amounting to approximately half our total strength, to Cyrenaica in Libya. I was chosen to command the detachment, and at the same time to take over command of X Company, whose commander was being posted to a staff job in Cairo. This coincided with the departure of Colonel Snowy who was leaving the battalion to command a Brigade, and until his replacement arrived, Chris Hill would be left in command. I discussed with Chris how best to deploy my troops, and it was decided to have one rifle company in Tobruk, and the remainder of the detachment with the supporting arms in Benghazi, where District HQ was established. The detachment from the 2nd Battalion KSLI was in fact the only infantry force between El Alamein and Tripoli, but there were no specific reasons for our presence there other than to act as garrison troops. There was also a regiment of armoured cars, the Derbyshire Yeomanry, stationed on the Jebel el Akhdar at Barce, where the local airport was located.

The move to Cyrenaica was immediate, but shortly before the detachment left, word came through that Neville Thursby, who had the misfortune to have spent most of the war suffering the privations of a Japanese Prisoner-of-War camp, was going to take over command of the battalion. He was due from the UK within a few days. No one knew very much about Neville, who was a pre-war regular officer in the regiment and had been a useful hockey player. His war had been a short and very unhappy one as he was a staff officer in Singapore when the Japs attacked, and had spent the rest of the war years 'in the bag'. It had been rumoured that his nerves had been badly affected by his ordeal, but how this was manifested was not known. We were soon to find out.

The detachment sailed from Famagusta in a Royal Navy corvette that had the reputation of being able to roll on a damp lawn. The weather she sailed into was very much rougher than that, and as we rounded the southeastern point of Cyprus and headed across the Mediterranean towards Tobruk, we were sailing diagonally across a full westerly gale and conditions aboard the little ship became chaotic. To start with the ship was filled to capacity, and many of the soldiers were soon lying in the scuppers on deck feeling so ill that they did not care whether they lived or died. I had always prided myself on being a good sailor, and even in February 1941 when the *Mulbera* ploughed into that tremendous gale in the north Atlantic, I had come through without succumbing to the violent twisting and rolling of the ship. But the motion of this much smaller and narrower ship was quite different and for the first time in my life I knew what seasickness felt like. On the first morning, after having managed to survive the night, I had filled the washbasin with hot water to shave when one of my colleagues, Captain Freeman-Green who was occupying the top bunk, leapt out of bed and was violently sick into my shaving water. That did it for me and I was then relegated to the ranks of the seasick.

By the time we reached Tobruk, the storm had passed and the sun was shining warmly again. Spirits soon recovered and I saw Z Company, commanded by Peter Excell MC, settled into their barracks in a delightful part of the small seaside town which had suffered so much during the North African campaign. Much had been done to repair shattered buildings, and the dock area was a hive of activity. Many sunken vessels still lay on the seabed with masts and funnels pointing skywards, memorials to those who had gone down with them. The next morning I led my convoy out of Tobruk and headed for Benghazi, following the coast road through Derna, a name made famous during the ebb and flow of the desert campaign. Then, skirting the northern side of the Jebel el Akhdar, we arrived in Benghazi during the afternoon, and I reported to the Brigade Major at District HQ. We were escorted to the outskirts of the town where we were introduced to Berka Barracks, a gaunt and not very clean building that had in turn been used by Italian and German forces. My first impression was one of horror. My men were two miles from the small NAAFI building that had been pointed out on our way through the town. To have to live in what seemed at first sight to be a sub-standard building was not what we had expected to find, especially after seeing the excellent accommodation Z Company had been put into in Tobruk. I delivered a short morale-boosting talk to my men and promised them that we would transform Berka Barracks into something to be proud of.

The following morning my officers and I took a long, hard look at what we had inherited, and I made it clear that we would have to pull out all the stops to get the place decent and to maintain the men's morale. Plans for the transformation of the barracks were quickly drawn up, and I made myself busy finding out whether the NAAFI could help in setting up our own canteen. There was no money available, and as Colonel Snowy had left the battalion for his new appointment in Palestine, and Neville Thursby had somehow missed his flight and was still in the UK, I could get no positive reply from Larnaca asking for a grant from Regimental funds. I therefore decided to provide the money myself, and I made £100 available to start up the detachment canteen. I made it clear that from then on it had to be self-financing, and very soon it proved to be a very popular and profitable little business.

From the point of view of brightening up the building itself, I handed the responsibility over to the Sergeant Major, and within two or three days, the whole appearance of Berka Barracks had changed. Everywhere there was newly applied whitewash, the detachment guard spruced itself up in sympathy with the new-look barracks, and everyone reflected my determination to create an impression fitting for the KSLI's fine reputation. Word soon reached the Brigadier, and he came to see for himself what a remarkable change had taken place. He was quite amazed and told me that he would personally tell my new commanding officer what we had achieved. Inevitably one of my priorities was to get a football team going, and to play any team that happened to be around. Unfortunately there were very few of us, but soon after arriving at Berka Barracks, a flotilla of Royal Navy minesweepers sailed into Benghazi, and the Brigade Major asked me to do all I could to organise some entertainment for the crews. It was only a short visit, but apart from some pretty heavy drinking in the canteen, a football match was played which resulted in a draw.

I suddenly realised that I had not written to Joy since leaving Larnaca, and I wrote a long account of our journey from Famagusta and everything that had happened since then. Somehow I couldn't raise much warmth, and I wondered if it wasn't time to stop pretending that we were still in love with each other. "I'll give it one more try," I thought to myself, but there was no letter from Joy in reply, and I knew then that it was all over between us.

Not all my soldiers appreciated what I had done to improve their accommodation and to provide them with a canteen, especially one private soldier named Turner who had an inherent dislike of whitewash, the application of which he considered to be entirely unproductive. This bolshie young man, whose mental capacity was distinctly substandard, also took exception to discipline both on and off duty, and on one occasion the duty corporal had to remove him from the canteen where he was stirring it up and slagging off the officers. The next morning an unpleasant graffiti was scrawled across the gleaming white wall at the entrance to the building, and I saw it before the Sergeant Major could have it removed. The message was short but succinct, and it was directed me. It read, "Major, you're a —-t". I was furious, and perhaps I overacted to this gratuitous insult when I ordered the Sergeant Major to have the whole detachment on parade in ten minutes. I believed in striking while the iron was hot, and I was going to say just what I felt about this display of ingratitude. In those days £100 was a considerable sum for me living on my pay with no private income, and I was going to tell the culprit so. At that point, I did not know who he was although we had a pretty shrewd ideas it was private Turner, so I had to address my feelings to the whole detachment.

The Sergeant Major brought the company to attention and duly reported "X Company ready for your address, SIR". I told him to stand the men easy and then in a quiet and deliberate tone I told the men exactly what I felt about the graffiti. I was almost at the end of my address when I saw one of the men screwing his eyes up, and thinking the man was grinning at what I had said, I lost my temper – and some respect with it, no doubt. I yelled at the soldier, not realising that he was screwing up his eyes because he was looking straight into the sun. The incident was quickly forgotten after the parade when the soldier explained that he wasn't laughing at me, and having cooled down I was once again my normal friendly self and the soldier, the Sergeant Major and I had a bit of a laugh about it. The rest of the detachment certainly appreciated what I had done for them, and it wasn't long before they found out who the culprit was. The following morning even I knew that Turner was the guilty man, but there was no need for me to take any further action as his black eye indicated.

Everyone in Benghazi District had been so helpful and co-operative that I decided to show my gratitude by having a cocktail party in the NAAFI officers' club, and I made the preliminary arrangements for it when I heard that the new commanding officer, Neville Thursby, had arrived in Cyprus and would soon be visiting the detachment. The plan for the visit was for the colonel to fly via Cairo to Barce airfield and for me to meet him there and bring him back to Benghazi. The next day would be devoted to inspecting the barracks and meeting the Brigadier and others, and of course speaking to as many of the men as possible. I had also arranged a football match against a scratch District team, knowing how keen he was on sport. That evening the party would take place as planned, and the following day I would drive him to Tobruk to meet Z Company. I would then drive him back to Barce where the colonel would stay until the next scheduled flight to Cairo was due, and I would then return to Benghazi.

When the Cairo flight touched down at Barce, I was excited to meet Neville Thursby and was determined to make his visit a success. As the passengers disembarked from the plane, I spotted the tall figure of the commanding officer of the Derbyshire Yeomanry who was coming to the party later that evening, and as he came towards me he drew me to one side and said, very apologetically, "I don't think your commanding officer will be coming to see you, Major Maslen-Jones". I was taken aback, my hopes to impress Colonel Neville collapsing.

"Why not, Colonel?" I asked.

He looked embarrassed, rather wishing he had not seen me to give me the bad news. "Because when I last saw him he was legless in Shepherd's", he replied. "And unless he has a magic carpet there is no way he can be here until tomorrow".

I thought quickly, and said with a smile, "Thank you Colonel, but my party will still go ahead and I hope you will not disappoint me twice in one day!" The colonel reassured me by promising to be there to support me, knowing how important this visit of my new commanding officer was to me.

The party was in one sense a huge success, but in another it was an embarrassment to me having to explain that my commanding officer had gone down with an attack of 'gippy tummy'; it may not have been quite accurate, but it sounded better than saying he was drunk in a Cairo bar! Furthermore, I had hoped and expected that as the party had been arranged as part of a regimental function, Colonel Thursby would pay for it out of regimental funds, if not all of it, then at least in part. But Neville Thursby never did come over to Cyrenaica, and it was not until the detachment moved back to Alexandria after a tour of duty lasting six months, that I met the man. By then I really did not want to know him. I had been humiliated and even when we met, the colonel made no effort to apologise for his appalling behaviour. I soon learnt that Neville Thursby, having spent so much of the war in a Japanese Prisoner-of-War camp, was in fact a very sick man and it was going to take a long time for him to fully recover. To some extent this gave him an excuse for his behaviour and I felt genuinely sorry for him. With hindsight one could only wonder why a man in his condition was appointed to command a battalion.

It was good to be back with the rest of the battalion again, but it had been announced that as soon as we reached the UK the battalion was to be disbanded. I was relieved that I would not have to serve under Colonel Thursby for very much longer. I decided to try to get a place at Oxford University under the Army scheme for seconding officers to universities to get degrees that would be useful to the Army. It was July now, and if I applied to go up to Oxford at the beginning of the next academic year in little less than three months, there should be just enough time for the necessary arrangements to be made and hopefully I would be able to take up my place in my old college which would make it so much more enjoyable.

The journey back to the UK was uneventful, but the excitement of going home was tinged with regret amongst the regular soldiers that the 2nd battalion, which had done so well in 3rd British Division during the Normandy campaign, was soon to go into suspended animation. The National Servicemen, who made up more than half the battalion strength, did not share the same feelings; it was all the same to the majority of them where they served and for the most part they counted the days to their release.

The battalion disembarked in Liverpool and was transported by train to the small town of Gobowen in Shropshire from where we marched some six miles to an old US Army hospital in the grounds of a large country house, Halston Hall, a mile from the village of Whittington which had been reoccupied by its owners. The hospital buildings were in excellent order, and the battalion quickly settled in to spend its final days there. As soon as I could get to a telephone, I rang Joy who was very surprised that I was back in Britain so soon. There was no enthusiasm in her voice, but we agreed to meet the next day, and she told me that there was now someone else in her life. He was a young qualified dentist from the Liverpool area whom she had met in the RAF. While I realised that a glittering prize had slipped from my grasp, I was relieved that I knew where I stood, and that my plans for the future could now go ahead with only myself to think about.

I put in my application to read Natural Science that had been my faculty before I joined the Brigade of Guards in 1940, and I asked to be sent back to my old college. From then on it was a matter of keeping the troops disciplined and occupied, and it was my responsibility to organise sports and football. I enjoyed it, and as an extra activity I arranged for parties of my X Company men to visit a local coalmine and other industries to widen their views on what they might decide to do when they left the Army. It was after one of those educational visits that the party was involved in an accident on our way back to camp, and one soldier suffered very severe head injuries. He was Bob Mills, the corporal cook, and had always been one of the most popular men in the company. When I heard about the accident I rushed to the hospital in Shrewsbury where I was allowed to see the unconscious man for a brief moment. I was used to seeing my soldiers wounded in battle, but to see Bob Mills lying there, dying, simply because of someone else's error of judgement, seemed to be grossly unfair. We were all very upset, and I immediately got in touch with Bob's family who were shattered by the news. Bob died during the early hours of the morning with his parents at his bedside. With a large number of men from X Company, I attended his funeral a few days later. It was a sombre affair, and the family were grateful for the support they had received from Bob's old mates and from the company officers. The Mills family had provided a generous spread for us in their small house after the burial.

As the battalion strength dwindled, there was less work to do for those officers who were left, and I took two weeks leave to shoot at Bisley in the National meeting in July. I met many old friends, and soon found my form, being selected for the Army Twenty. One of the Army team was Captain Robert Maxwell whom I had met out in Burma and whose family had a long and distinguished record at Bisley. I was to meet Robert Maxwell again in the not too distant future much to my surprise.

At last only a rear party of the battalion was left, and in mid-August I received the news I was waiting for. I was to go back to New College, Oxford, to read 'science'. By this I assumed they meant Natural Science, which I had been reading as part of my pre-medical studies. There followed detailed instructions about my secondment, pay arrangements and so on, and I was absolutely delighted that things had turned out so well, particularly as my brother Ted would be reading Agriculture in Brasenose College at the same time. The day I left the rump of the battalion, I thought back over the past two years since I had made the change from the Indian to the British Army and on the whole I was well pleased with the transition. I had found my feet again and made my mark with my own sort, and after completing my degree I knew I would be able to take up the reins again where I was now dropping them.

On 28th September 1947, shortly before the 2nd Battalion went into suspended animation, an historic ceremony took place at The Chelsea Royal Hospital when Colours and Battle Honours, many of which had been captured by British regiments in the Napoleonic Wars, were restored to them for safe keeping.

Major General John Grover, Colonel of the King's Shropshire Light Infantry received from General Sir Clive Liddell, Governor of The Royal Hospital, the Guidon of the American 1st Hartford Dragoons and the Colour of the American 68th Regiment, both of which had been captured by the British 85th Regiment, now the 2nd Battalion of the KSLI, at Bladensburg, Maryland in 1814. This was the last ceremony in which our 2nd Battalion was to take part, and I was particularly proud to have been selected to represent the Regiment as commander of the Colour party. Both the trophies were already in a very fragile condition, and were handed over to the Shropshire Museum for framing and preservation.

The Colour escort included the oldest serving soldier in the KSLI, private Nick Carter, who had already completed 42 years service in the regiment, marching in the front row between the two trophies, and it was a fitting and well deserved finale to a lifelong career in the regiment.

*Battle Honours captured in the Napoleonic Wars being restored to British Regiments during a ceremony at Chelsea Royal Hospital, September 1947*

A few weeks' leave followed, during which I prepared myself for university life, and at the end of September I went up to Oxford for the second time in my life. Being a more mature student, I was not required to live in college, and I managed to find digs fairly close to Ted's in a quiet cul-de-sac off the Banbury road. It all seemed too good to be true, and sadly it proved to be so. When I met my tutor I discovered that a terrible mistake had been made. I was to read Advanced Physics. For a start, Differential Calculus and the like was something I had only heard about at school, and in which I had no interest or understanding. For a week I struggled to master the basics, but it was all Greek to me and on the advice of my tutor I telephoned the Military Secretary's department in the War Office and explained the situation. The reply clarified everything.

"What's the difference between Natural Science and the subject you are expected to study?" I was asked.

I explained the difference in clear, precise terms, finding it difficult not to put too much edge in my words. I suggested that I should be allowed to stay at Oxford and read Geography instead which I knew I could master, but the MS would have none of it. "Well, what am I to do?" I asked.

"You'd better come to the War Office and discuss the best course of action," I was told. On the following Monday I found myself waiting to be interviewed by the GSO 2 in the Military Secretary's department in Whitehall.

After a few pleasantries, the G2 asked me how I would like to do a tour of duty as a junior Staff Officer in London. I had never given the possibility any thought, but after only a brief moment I said I would enjoy it very much. "That's excellent, then," replied the G2, "because that's exactly what we've got lined up for you. You are being appointed to the Military Operations department – MO for short – as a G3, and your specific responsibilities will be to work in the section dealing with Commonwealth liaison. That means you will be writing briefs which eventually arrive on the Chief's desk."

"I take it you are referring to Monty?" I queried.

"Quite correct," answered the G2, and after telling me about the set-up in the War Office, he took me down to the Military Operations department and introduced me to the staff officers there. The G1 was Lt Colonel John Jervis-Reed who was in the Royal Engineers, and my two G2s were Majors Sam Chambers, also a Royal Engineer, and David Long-Price from the Essex Regiment. Each of the G2s had three G3s working for them. I would be under David Long-Price, and at first sight I thought we would get on well together. I was given two weeks leave and told to report to the Administration Officer who would tell me where I would be living.

I was quite excited about the prospect of the two-year tour of duty to which I had just been appointed, but the arrangements for my accommodation didn't sound so good. I would be living in the War Office Mess in the old Royal Artillery barracks on Shooter's Hill at Woolwich, which would mean a dreary train journey in and out every day. It would also mean a noisy tram journey from Woolwich Arsenal station to the top of Shooter's Hill, and the prospect rather dampened my enthusiasm. But I would make the best of it and see how things turned out, though I couldn't see how I would be able to take any girlfriends out in the West End and get back to my room in Woolwich late at night. I decided to go down to Woolwich while I was in London to have a look at where I would be living, and I was filled with gloom. I couldn't imagine how I was going to exist for two years in what I thought was a hell of a dump, and even before I left London for my leave, I was working out plans to improve my lot. I had found out during my short meeting with my new colleagues that not one of them was living in the Mess at Woolwich, and I was not in the least surprised now I had seen the place. I caught the evening train to Wolverhampton and at the first opportunity I asked Dad whether we had any relations living in or near London. If so, I could apply to go on the lodging list and get the appropriate allowance. But Dad could not think of anyone and I just smiled and said, "Never mind, Dad, I'll find one". He was not sure what I meant by that, but he was soon to find out.

# Chapter 17

## IT'S NOT THE WINNING THAT MATTERS

———

My leave passed all too quickly, and at the beginning of November I took the train to London and booked in at the Mess. My room was small, sparsely furnished, and overlooking the trams on Shooters Hill. It was cold and felt unlived in. There was a small open grate, and I was allowed one tiny bucket of coal per day. I soon found out that it didn't provide even sufficient heat to warm the little garret enough for me to sit and read, and I was therefore forced to use the Mess itself that was usually nearly empty, almost as cold as my room, and in which I did not find even one kindred spirit to whom I could talk. As I journeyed to the War Office to report for duty the following morning, I felt that I might as well have been in a prisoner-of-war camp, and the outlook for the next two years looked unattractive and very bleak indeed.

After a cold and rather sleepless night, due to the dankness of my room, the hard and lumpy horsehair mattress, and the clanking of trams late into the night and early in the morning, I had a breakfast that I would not have fed to pigs. The bacon was greasy and the scrambled eggs, clearly contrived from powdered egg, were utterly tasteless. The toast had been made too early, probably the night before, and was like leather. There was, in fact, nothing to commend it, and I wondered who was lining his pockets rather than providing a decent standard of cuisine for those officers that were unlucky enough to be accommodated there. As I sat in the constantly stopping and starting commuter's train to Charing Cross, I made up my mind that I would get out of this intolerable insult to my being at the earliest possible moment. One thing was certain, that I wouldn't be able to enjoy any social life until I had sorted out my affairs and got somewhere decent to live. For the time being, however, I must keep my discomfort under wraps, apply myself to my new job and make the best possible impression on my new colleagues.

I walked briskly out of the station, skirted Trafalgar Square into Whitehall, and turned left into Whitehall Place, joining a number of officers and civilian staff who entered the War Office building through a side entrance. I knew my way to the room on the first floor where I would be working, and was warmly greeted by David Long-Price and Hugo Trim, one of the G3s who had been detailed to take me under his wing for a few days while I found my feet. I was very soon initiated into the procedure for writing briefs, but I was rather disappointed when I was told that I would be responsible for matters dealing solely with Commonwealth Liaison. I had hoped that I might be involved occasionally with real operational matters. I soon learned that all the hard graft in this department was done by a G3, and in fact I found it quite interesting researching the background for any particular brief I was detailed to write.

When a brief was ready, the G3 would write a short memo to his G2 stating that he had "prepared the attached brief", and what the brief was about. It was then, and continued to be, a matter of some amusement to me that as the brief into which the G3 had put so much hard work went on its way to the CIGS, each succeeding staff officer, after perhaps making some slight alterations or adding some small and probably irrelevant item perjured himself by attaching an onwards transmission memo which stated, for example, "Sir, I have prepared the attached brief for your information and approval, please." Of course each senior officer knew full well that the memo slip was a little white lie, and that when he had read it, he too would tell the same fib. Ultimately the brief would arrive on Monty's desk, and soon after I had written my first brief, I was summoned to the CIGS's office at the end of the passage to discuss the brief in detail with the Chief himself. I knew that Monty had a clear, quick brain, and could not abide any sort of uncertainty or dithering. He always gave clear unequivocal answers himself, was entirely predictable, and expected his junior staff officers to have sufficiently mastered the subject to be able to do the same for him. I was in no way overawed by the great man and when I came out of my first interview with him, I felt very confident and found myself enjoying the experience. As time went on, Monty seldom asked me to discuss my briefs in detail, and I realised that the detailed discussion I had had with him about my first brief was his way of getting to know his junior staff officers and to assess their ability and reliability.

The system of Army Officers and senior NCOs working alongside civilian employees seemed to work well, and I and my colleagues in MO2 got on well with the messengers on whom we relied for cups of good strong tea. One morning one of the light bulbs went, and I climbed onto the desk to replace it. I was caught in the act when the messenger came into the room with a tray full of files, and he reacted as though I'd committed a serious crime! The man was furious that an officer had decided to do his job, and he proceeded to explain to me and others present that there was a clear demarcation of roles in the building, and that if anyone allowed his job to be done by anyone else, it would be a case of 'everybody out'. I could hardly believe that the act of changing a light bulb could bring the civilian staff out on strike and the whole War Office to a stop. It was, I was told, Union Law, and there was nothing I could do about it. I asked exactly who was responsible for various tasks in the office, and was told that the cleaners, who came in early in the morning, were responsible for the floor and walls up to desk height. The desktops and above, including the lights, were the messenger's responsibility, and above that any cleaning had to be done by another group of civilian employees. It was typically bureaucratic and my colleagues and I felt that if some small job such as changing a light bulb needed doing, the sooner it was done the better, no matter by whom. But that was not the way of the New Britain under Labour, or rather the Unions.

I continued to live in the Woolwich Mess, which I hated more each day. One day I was glancing through the personal advertisements in the Times when I saw 'Comfortable accommodation for paying guest – Harrow-on-the-Hill'. I telephoned and spoke to the lady who told me that her house was in a quiet residential area overlooking the Harrow School playing fields. It was a short bus ride from the Underground station, and the terms included Bed, Breakfast and a good evening meal. I went out to Harrow to see the accommodation the next day and asked Mrs Speight to keep the room for me until I had arranged to get myself onto the lodging list. Nothing, I figured, could be worse than Woolwich, and my only fear was that it might still be too far out for me to enjoy a bit of nightclubbing in the West End.

There was no problem about getting on to the lodging list, as my new landlady, unknown to her, assumed the status of a maiden aunt on my mother's side, and it was with a feeling of immense relief that within a few days I packed up my things in my miserable garret down at Woolwich and moved out to Harrow-on-the-Hill. At last I was living in a warm, comfortable home with excellent food, and my morale soared. But I was soon to find that my hopes of having an occasional evening out in the West End was not going to be possible as the last train left for Harrow-on-the-Hill well before midnight, and even then it meant that I would have a mile long walk back to my digs from the Underground station.

I decided to see how things worked out, and I stayed with Mrs Speight for some twelve weeks. By then winter was over, and I was often asked to join a party to go to the theatre, usually followed by dinner or a visit to a nightclub, and once again it was decision time. Early in April 1948 I found a bedsit in Palace Court on the Bayswater Road almost opposite Kensington Gardens, and as there was an optional evening meal, and it was much less money than Mrs Speight's comfortable establishment, I decided to take it. It was all done surreptitiously, and the administration officer presumably never found out that I had left my 'auntie'. Not only was my Palace Court bedsit ideal as a base for enjoying London life to the full, but I was able to start taking regular exercise again rather than sitting out a dreary and quite costly train journey to and from work. I could walk across Kensington Gardens and Hyde Park, cross Hyde Park Corner, and carry on down Constitution Hill and through St James's Park to Horse Guards Parade and Whitehall. Unless it was raining (when I would travel by bus), I did this walk twice a day, a total of about six and a half miles.

Although Palestine was not the responsibility of MO2, everyone in the War Office became aware of the deteriorating situation at the end of 1947 when the British mandate to govern the country was nearing its end. Of course, I had been interested in what was developing in the Middle East since my time in Cyprus when the 2nd KSLI had been guarding illegal Jewish immigrants. By the middle of March the situation had deteriorated very seriously and was in danger of getting out of hand as Arabs and Jews fought each other to gain the best possible advantages for themselves before the British mandate ended in mid-May. The British Army, for so long the target for attack by the Jews, found itself in the position of trying to be the honest broker to ensure a fair deal for both sides. Monty was very much involved in this scenario, and made it quite clear that if any important strategic centre was taken over by either side, the British Army would immediately recapture it and hand it back, even though on the termination of the mandate it might be destined to go to the side which tried to jump the gun and pre-empt the terms of the agreement.

At about 6:30 on the evening of 22nd April 1948, while working in the position of MO duty officer, I had gone out to have some supper. After seeing some startling headlines on the placards, I bought both the Evening News and the Evening Standard, and after having a quick bite I returned to the duty officers' room to check up on any outstanding matters that I might have to deal with during the night. There was nothing of note waiting for me, no reports of unusual trouble in Palestine, and I thought I would have a relatively uneventful night. It was about 7:35 pm when I sat down, put my feet up on the desk, and started reading the papers. The headlines were indeed stark and alarming, and told of up to 23 000 Arabs having been massacred by the Jews in Haifa. If this were true, why had no reports of it been received by the War Office during the day?

Presently I heard the door open and thought, "Oh, good, my cup of tea," for it was usually about that time that the night messenger brought the duty officer a brew. I did not turn round until I was aware that someone was standing behind me and I was just about to say, "Put it down here, please," when the well known voice of the CIGS said, "Well, what do you think of it then, Maslen-Jones?" I jumped out of my chair to see not only Monty, but also the Vice-CIGS, General Sir Gerald Templer, standing behind me. "Well, Sir", I said as I scrambled to my feet and proceeded to explain my views.

"Good thinking, Maslen-Jones," said Monty, "I agree. Now I am already late for a dinner at the Mansion House, and I have just had an urgent meeting with the Prime Minister, Foreign Secretary and Minister of Defence about the true situation in Haifa. I will be back here at 10:15 pm and I want you to have General Crocker on the line from Fayid with the answers to these questions. I shall speak to him myself." Monty then wrote out some questions on a sheet of foolscap.

At precisely 10:15 pm Monty came into the duty officers' room and I told him that General Crocker was standing by in Fayid to speak with him. Monty told me to call him up, and within seconds General Crocker was telling Monty what the real situation was. There had been a bit of fighting around the Haifa enclave, but the press reports in the London evening papers were wildly exaggerated. In short, there was no

Telephone Message to Fayid

Require following information at once
about situation in HAIFA which is
reported in Press and by MARRIOTT as
being serious :

1. Is heavy fighting between Jews and
Arabs going on in the town ?

2. Are British troops taking any part in
this fighting ?

3. Any British casualties ?

4. HAIFA is our final evacuation
port and it is important to
keep a firm hold on the town
and immediate surroundings so
that we can get our troops and
stores away according to plan.
Are we quite safe in this respect
or is our evacuation port in
jeopardy

5. As we evacuate the country can
we maintain law and order
in the Haifa enclave ? If this
is in doubt it will be
necessary to have enough troops
there to ensure ourselves in this
respect

*Monty's handwritten note with the questions he wanted answered by General Crocker*

danger to our evacuation port, and the allegation that the Foreign Secretary (Ernest Bevin) had made to Monty earlier in the evening that the British Army had let him down turned out to have been founded on rumour. Things continued to be very tense for several days, and exchanges between Monty and the Foreign Secretary were often heated and relations became strained. But Monty had always liked Ernest Bevin, and as soon as the mandate had ended, the two men were once again on friendly terms.

One weekend in May I went down to Bisley to shoot in a weekend competition, where I met my old friend Ronnie Maxwell who was in the Black Watch. On the Saturday evening we were drinking together in the Army Rifle Association Club House when Ronnie suddenly told me that he had been selected to shoot for Great Britain in the Olympic Games, and wondered why I hadn't been chosen. I was as good a shot as Ronnie, and I was a little put out that I had been overlooked. Ronnie saw my annoyance, and suggested that I might like to come down to Bisley two or three times a week to keep him company while he was practising, which I thought was a bit patronising.

He explained that the 'Free Rifle' weighed 19 lbs, had a ring foresight and was quite different to anything we had ever fired before. All the practices were at 300 metres, and each involved firing 40 rounds in the standing, prone and kneeling positions, each practice within two hours. This allowed just 3 minutes per round, and towards the end of the two hours, arm muscles would be tired and aching. I thought for a few moments, and realised that just supposing one of the selected team of three should fall out for any reason, I would be in a strong position to take his place if I had been practising regularly. "Can you fix it with the War Office?" I asked, and Ronnie then told me that he had already discussed the possibility of having some company when he was practising and Brigadier John Barlow, Captain of the Army Eight who was running the Olympic Free Rifle team, had agreed that it was a good idea. Ronnie was sure that he could persuade the Brigadier to contact the Director of Military Operations, and a telephone call from him to the DMO on the following Monday was all that was needed. I was given leave to spend two days each week at Bisley, and went down every weekend as my scores were very nearly as good as Maxwell's. In spite of what he had told me when the subject first arose, the team had not yet been chosen, and I was determined to be selected.

I decided that it would be much more convenient for me to buy another car, and one lunch time as I walked down St James' Street I noticed a smart silver-grey 1.5 litre MG sports tourer in a show room. I looked at it longingly, pictured myself driving with the hood down with a gorgeous girl by my side, and though it cost far too much, I went in to inspect it. My heart warmed to the car, and at £750 I felt I could just afford to buy it. The salesman eventually suggested that we should go for a test drive, and I drove along Pall Mall towards Trafalgar Square. Before I had reached the Square, I knew that the car was mine, and on return to the showroom, I completed the deal and proudly drove my new love to park by the War Office in Whitehall Place.

For the next two months I drove down to Bisley three times each week and soon found that I was scoring as well or better than anyone else in the squad, including Ronnie Maxwell. Although the National meeting was held at Bisley during July, the 'probables' for the Free Rifle Team were warned not to take part in it, but to concentrate on the Olympics practices. It was a bit disappointing but I felt it would be worthwhile sacrificing the fun of the Bisley meeting if it meant I would be selected to represent Great Britain in the Olympic Games. Early in July all the recorded scores were examined, and one final selection shoot took place in which I came first in all three practices. Ronnie came a close second, and both of us, together with a civilian called Knott, a gunsmith armourer from Kingston-on-Thames, were chosen to represent Great Britain at the Games in August. The selected team was published in the National newspapers on 15$^{th}$ August, and I received letters of congratulation from many old friends including the Colonel of the KSLI, General John Grover.

Suddenly I was living in a world of excitement, and my parents were proud of my selection. Articles appeared in the local papers and Dad also got a fair share of publicity for his service to the community as a brilliant gynaecologist. With only two weeks to go before the opening ceremony, the three members of the team had to be measured for the official Olympic uniform which consisted of a blue blazer with a Union Flag and 'Olympics 1948' embroidered on the breast pocket, white flannel trousers, tie and hat. In the event, everything was ready in time, but only just. Two days before the opening ceremony, Ronnie Maxwell went down with mumps and John Barlow stepped into his place. The opening ceremony was an emotional event and as I marched round Wembley Stadium past the King and Queen, I felt a huge surge of pride in being British and being able to represent my country at the highest level. I took heart from the fact that the principle of the Games was not so much in winning, as in taking part and doing one's best.

After the ceremony, I went down to Bisley to prepare for the shooting events, and was accommodated in the Army Rifle Association Club House. Almost immediately I found out that someone, and I never discovered who it was, had decided that the three rifles should be stripped down and re-bedded. It was not until the night before the competition began that the rifles were ready. There was no time to 'zero' them properly; it was a crazy thing to have done. I was absolutely livid, but calmed myself down as I knew that unless I put the bloody fool who was responsible out of my thoughts, I wouldn't be able to shoot at anything like my proper standard.

The Free Rifle practices were spread over three days and in all three of them I came out top of the British team. My overall position was 24th, which, considering that the team had only had a few weeks practice, and that we were shooting with un-zeroed rifles, was not too bad.

I had taken a few days leave and with my free pass I watched several of the events at Wembley, but all too soon the closing ceremony took place, and I resumed my duties at the War Office.

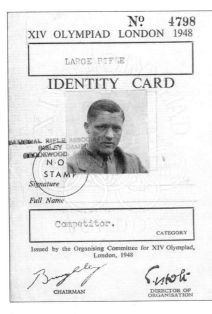

# Tettenhall Officer Is Youngest Member Of Britain's Rifle Team

CAPTAIN R. G. MASLEN-JONES, K.S.L.I., of Pavings, Wrottesley-road, Tettenhall, son of the Wolverhampton gynecologist, Mr. Maslen-Jones, has, it is understood, been selected as one of the three rifle shots who will represent Great Britain in the Olympic Games in August.

An official announcement of the team is expected within the next few days.

Captain Maslen-Jones, who is 27, will be the youngest member of the team, and his selection is the culmination of two months intensive practice.

He has been in the army for just over eight years. Starting as a private in the South Staffordshire Regiment, he was commissioned into the Indian Army and had a period of service in Burma before transferring to the King's Shropshire Light Infantry. He is at present a staff officer in the Military Operations Branch of the War Office.

The Olympic rifle shooting, for which competitors use a 19lb. rifle, consists of 20 shots in an hour in each of the standing, kneeling and lying positions. It is considered generally to take more stamina and powers of endurance than the normal competition shooting.

During the trials Captain Maslen-Jones made the highest single score in the standing and kneeling positions, and the highest average at each.

## Midlanders Win Bisley Prizes

In the *Times* service rifle competitions at Bisley for ten shots at 200 yards, with a possible 50. At D. Cullen (Worcesters) scored 46 and Captain R. G. Maslen-Jones (K.S.L.I.) 44.

Captain L. R. Godfrey (Denstone) was among 12 competitors scoring the highest possible (50) in the service rifle competition, who will shoot off for the first prize today.

Among lower-placed prizewinners in this competition were Flight Lieutenant A. E. Heather (Whitchurch) 48 and I. F. Kilson (Kidderminster) 48.

*My Olympics ID card, press cutting reporting the event and a photograph of the opening ceremony*

*The 1948 shooting team*

On 27th September 1948, Monty was appointed Chairman of the Commanders-in-Chief of the five Powers of the Western Union, and soon afterwards he bade farewell to everyone working in the War Office. Those who had worked closely with him, including me, were able to say our personal goodbyes, and I felt quite emotional as I shook hands with Monty for I had got to know and like the great man during the past months and I was extremely sorry to see him go. On his final day in the War Office, Monty summoned every officer, and all civilians of the equivalent rank of Captain and above, to attend a farewell talk to us at the Victoria Palace theatre during the lunch break. As we were filing in at the main entrance, I happened to glance upwards and saw a vast poster announcing 'The Crazy Gang'. For a moment I had a quiet laugh to myself, but little did I realise how true the words were to be. Monty, always the great showman, really excelled himself. He spoke for about fifteen minutes about his war service, and then announced what everyone present already knew, that he was leaving to become the commander of Western Union. "When I failed the Staff College Entrance examination for the third time," he said, "never, ever, did I think that I would eventually rise to command the British Army. But now look at me! I am going to command five armies". Great cheers rang out, and the applause continued for some minutes. Monty had sat down, and General Templer was on his feet to bid Monty a final farewell. But Monty was not yet finished. He rose again, thanked the vice-chief for his kind words and spoke for another five minutes. Even I, who held Monty in such high esteem, felt that he had got completely carried away. As we all made our way back to our offices, there were many sarcastic and disparaging remarks bandied around – what a great pity.

It was in October that the 1st battalion of the KSLI came to London to do public duties, as the Brigade of Guards was fully committed overseas and not one of their battalions was available for ceremonial duties. It was considered a great honour for the regiment to be selected to stand in for the Brigade, and when I heard that they were to be stationed in Chelsea Barracks, I decided to move once again, this time to a bedsit in Eaton Place. It was slightly more expensive than my room in Palace Court, but was only just round the corner from the barracks where I could have a lot of fun with my brother officers in the regiment. Throughout the winter I spent a lot of time and money nightclubbing and soon earned for myself the nickname of 'G3 social' – a tag that was to stay with me for many years. The favourite nightclubs were Churchills and The Bag of Nails, and at 96 Piccadilly there was a small unpretentious club where young lovers could smooch the night away to Bobby's gentle piano melodies. That was to be my choice whenever I wanted to get better acquainted with some new girlfriend.

Inevitably I met many eligible young 'fillies', one of whom was really too young for me. I happened to meet her in Hatchett's Restaurant in Piccadilly while I was waiting to meet some of my friends. Things moved fast, and after only a week or two, I was invited to spend a weekend with Jennifer Wimbush at Packwood Towers on the outskirts of Birmingham. The house was lavishly furnished and equipped, and there was a complete domestic staff including a butler. It was something I had seen in Joy's home, and I wondered if I was destined to marry into such opulence. It was a short stay, but although I noticed that Jenny was more interested in her horse than in me, I persevered, hoping that things would change. Before I returned to London, Jenny's father suggested that I should stay with them for the Gold Cup meeting at Cheltenham where he had a horse called Flaming Steel running in the big race. Without hesitation I accepted the invitation, and in due course I found myself back at The Towers.

The plan was to drive down to Cheltenham each day in the Bentley, and I was handed my members badge for the meeting that I tied to several others on my binocular case. To my disappointment Jenny had decided not to go with us on the first day as she wanted to do some dressage with her horse, but when she joined us on Gold Cup day, I found it very hard going, and though I did my best to find some common ground with her, I realised that, sweet as she was, she was not yet ready to have a meaningful relationship. When I returned to London, I could only think that it had all been great fun, as well as being quite an eye-opener, but there was no future in pursuing Jennifer any further. After that we didn't even write to each other.

During the winter I organised a party to attend a charity ball in the Park Lane Hotel. One of the men in the party was Captain Peter Baker in the Parachute

Regiment, whom I had met once or twice in 96 Piccadilly and we were already good friends. During the evening Peter asked me if I knew a friend of his in the Rifle Brigade called Alistair Mackie-Campbell whose mother had a large flat (to her, just a small *pied-a-terre*) on Park Lane, near the Dorchester Hotel. Alistair was due home on leave in a few days time and his mother, Isobel, was planning a dinner-dance for him in the Dorchester and had asked Peter to choose some nice young people to make up the party.

"What about it, Bob?" Peter asked me. "They are a super family who's home is in Ayrshire. Alistair's father, Geordie, is chairman of one of the big distillers and if you ever get asked to stay there, you'll always get a really splendid malt to go to bed with."

"Sounds good to me, Peter," I replied, "I'd love to come."

Peter promised to let me know the date and time, and a week later the party met in Isobel's flat for drinks before going to the Dorchester. I knew everyone there except Alistair, and we hit it off from the start. I was the only one in the party whom Isobel hadn't met before, and she had placed me on her right "so that we can have a good talk and get to know each other". She was absolutely charming, and the evening was tremendous fun, and during one of our dances together Isobel had asked me what I wanted out of life.

"I want to be a farmer eventually," I told her, and I was a little puzzled when she replied, "Oh well, I must see what we can do about that." Before the party ended, Isobel had invited me to spend a long weekend at their Scottish country home in Monkton, Ayrshire, not far from Troon and the Bogside racecourse and I gladly accepted. She had added that she would get some nice young girls along to meet me. It later turned out that Isobel had misheard what I said to her on the dance floor and thought I had said, "I want to be a father"!

Three weeks later I set off for Scotland in the MG feeling really excited about the prospects of meeting the whole Mackie-Campbell family and the girls Isobel had promised to find for me. It was a great weekend, and I was spoilt for choice. I enjoyed a splendid day's racing at the Scottish Grand National meeting at Bogside, and Peter's promise that I would get a malt last thing at night was quite correct. It was a dark, smooth liquid the like of which I had never tasted, and I mellowed to this type of lifestyle. Clearly I had, I thought, been accepted and before I returned to London, Isobel invited me to join her party at the Oban Ball in the summer. Alistair would be home on leave, and I thought it would be splendid fun. I accepted, and the whole party was booked into a large hotel in the town, only a few minutes walk from the hall where the Ball was to be held.

When I arrived at the hotel, I offered to pay for my accommodation, but Isobel would hear none of it. I was her guest and in return I would make sure I gave her more than a fair share of the dances. As soon as we arrived in the Hall, we were given our dance cards and I booked my dances with her. It was the first time I had been to such a gathering where dance cards were used, but I had been forewarned, and knew the form. During one of my dances with Isobel she told me that not one of her other young guests had booked a dance on her card and she was clearly quite hurt by this lack of manners. Manners Makyth Man! The party had dined well in the hotel, but at midnight there were more refreshments at the Ball. The night sped by, and between my dances with Isobel, I found a most eligible girl called Miriam who happened to live in the West Midlands, not far from Birmingham. "Could be quite convenient," I thought to myself. It was 4:00 am when a superb breakfast was served, and by then no one had any thoughts of sleep. Our appetites had been sharpened by the exertions of reels and other energetic capers, so that gorgeous Loch Fyne kippers and large helpings of bacon and eggs were more than welcome. The Ball ended at 5:30 am, and I escorted my new girlfriend Miriam back to her hotel. It was then that I found out that she was the daughter of an earl, and had the title of 'the Honourable'. The next day Miriam and I went for a long drive in the MG, and we arranged to meet again back in the Midlands.

On my way back to London after my visit to Oban, I told my parents everything I had done and how much I had enjoyed it all. Dad was quiet and thoughtful, eventually asking, "And how are you going to finance this new lifestyle, Bob? You cannot go on just accepting all this expensive hospitality – I suggest that with your flashy car you are giving the wrong impression to your new friends about your ability to pay your way." I knew that my father was right. I had already spent all the capital I had accumulated from my Indian Army pay during the war, and I now had nothing other than my army pay to live on. I had enjoyed getting into such a wealthy set, but I had to pull in my horns and however humiliating it might be, change down several gears to a lifestyle I could afford.

Back in London, I knew it was not going to be easy to change my lifestyle, but I determined to take my Army duties more seriously and be seen to be more interested in finishing a piece of work instead of clock-watching towards the end of the day and leaving the office 'on the dot'. Not only would this change of attitude help me overcome the problem I had created for myself, but I had no doubt that it would be noticed by my seniors and would be noted in my annual report. I also decided to start playing rugger again, and I joined Rosslyn Park whose ground was at that time at the Old Deer Park at Richmond. There was not much of the season left, but I was soon selected to play in the 1st XV, and I spent much of my spare time training.

I began to use the Officers' Mess in Chelsea Barracks more frequently, and soon built up a circle of friends whose financial situation was akin to my own. I still made occasional visits to nightclubs with a carload of my regimental friends, but my days of hobnobbing with the wealthy set were for the time being over, and I rarely met my erstwhile girlfriends.

The winter came to an end, and I turned my thoughts to the one sport in which I had achieved the ultimate success – rifle shooting – and I started spending my weekends at Bisley. By the time the National Rifle Association meeting came along in July, I had been selected to shoot for the Army, and I also competed in the King's Prize. I was satisfied to find myself in the 'King's Hundred' which meant that I would shoot in the final over 900 and 1000 yards, and when I came 50th I was well satisfied.

As the summer wore on, I began to get rather bored with the '9 to 5' office routine and I longed to get back to regimental soldiering, so it was with a glad heart that I heard in August I was to be appointed Adjutant of one of the KSLI's territorial battalions in Hereford. The Territorial Army had been reformed in 1947 and the Herefordshire Regiment was renamed The Herefordshire Light Infantry. Lt Colonel Henry Barneby who had served with great distinction during the war and was now back home looking after his estate was appointed to be the first post-war commanding officer.

# Chapter 18

## THAT'S JUST NOT CRICKET

———

I said goodbye to my colleagues and staff in the Military Operations Directorate on 15th September, and went home to spend a few days leave. I went to Hereford to see Henry Barneby whom I had met at a regimental dinner at the Army and Navy Club (The Rag) during my time at the War Office, and to find myself somewhere to live. I had telephoned to make sure the Colonel would be there, and on arrival I was pleased to see that the second in-command, Peter Crofts, had been asked to come along to meet me as well. After chatting for an hour, the three of us repaired to the Three Counties Country Club for a glass of sherry and a light lunch. The club, as it happened, was owned by Peter, which could have accounted for his somewhat florid complexion.

During lunch, I asked whether either of them knew where I could find somewhere nice to live, and I was directed to Hugh Hall and his wife who lived in Holmer Grange, just outside the city, with more rooms than they could use themselves. Hugh had commanded a company in the regiment during the war, and Peter telephoned him to see if he might be interested in taking in a paying guest. Lunch over, I drove out to meet Hugh and his wife Gwen, and after being shown over their large country house, it was agreed that I would be very welcome to live there. Gwen's old father, well into his eighties but still firing on all cylinders, was living in the house, as was young Sam Hall when he was home from Lucton School during the holidays. I was delighted with the arrangement and felt myself extremely lucky to have found such a nice place to live where I would have my own suite of bedroom, sitting room and almost exclusive use of a bathroom that I would share with Sam when he was at home. And above all, I would be paying no more than what my small bedsit in Eaton Place had cost me. Driving home I considered the day's achievements in more detail. I decided that Henry Barneby and I were very much kindred spirits and I looked forward to working with him. About Peter Crofts I was not so sure and I had a lurking suspicion that he drank more than was good for him as evidenced by his complexion and generally unfit condition. I hoped I was wrong, but only time would tell.

My arrival in Hereford coincided with the annual dinner of the local branch of the British Legion, and I was invited to attend as guest of honour which meant I would have to make a speech. A short article had appeared in the Hereford Times announcing my appointment as Adjutant of the TA battalion, and a larger number of members than in previous years attended the dinner. It was quite an experience for me to stand up and speak to men and women, many of whom were twice my age or more, without seeming to be patronising. Despite the fact that it was my first public speech other than addressing my soldiers on several diverse occasions, I managed to get through it, and received a very warm reception as I sat down. The speech was reported verbatim in the local paper.

A few days later, I was sitting alone in my office when the telephone rang. "My name is Margaret Bulmer," said a voice I did not recognise. "Your father once operated on my mother, and he also delivered my three sons. I am now living just outside Hereford, and when I read in the local paper that you had been posted here, I thought that as you probably don't yet know many of the local people, it would be nice if you could come and have dinner one evening. My husband, who was in the RAF, was killed in a surprise attack on his airfield by a lone German plane only twenty-four hours before the war in Europe ended, so I am living alone with my sons in a cottage on my father-in-law's estate. He lives in a large house and we have an arrangement that if I want to entertain and have a dinner party, we join forces and have it in his house." At last I could get a word in, and I thanked Margaret very much and said I would be delighted to meet her and her family.

A date was fixed and resplendent in my 'number one' dress to impress the lady, I turned up at the big house. I was shown into the sitting room by the butler, and after introducing myself to Margaret I met Howard Bulmer who it turned out had also lost his wife during the war and was now a staid widower who doted on his three grandsons. I was once again being entertained by very well-to-do people and I got on well with both Margaret and Howard. During the evening Howard asked me if I liked fishing; it was three years since I had spent that fishing holiday with my father and Ted up in Sedbergh, and I told Howard all about it. "Great then," he said, "I've got two good stretches of trout water, and as soon as the season starts next spring, you must make use of them whenever you're at a loose end." I was absolutely delighted at this generous offer and accepted graciously. Howard promised to contact me and show me both stretches of water on the Arrow and Monnow before the season opened.

Before winter had merged into spring, I had met many of the county gentry and had enjoyed two local hunt balls where I met the Lord Lieutenant, Sir Richard Cotterell Bt, and his wife, Lady Lettice and daughters Rosie and Anne. The girls were extremely attractive, lively and full of fun. Rosie, a brunette, was rather shorter than Anne who had fair hair and a most attractive figure. Rosie was in her mid-twenties, almost exactly the same age as me, and Anne was nearly three years younger.

It was not easy for me to choose, but the problem soon resolved itself when it became clear that Rosie was already very involved with Richard Brown-Rivers, a war-time Lieutenant Commander who was now farming the family estate quite close by, his father having decided to take a back seat and enjoy himself hunting, shooting and fishing. I liked Brown-Rivers, and it was not surprising that I was asked to shoot there once or twice during the rest of the shooting season. Over the next few weeks Anne and I met each other at a number of cocktail parties and dances, and we soon became close friends. I felt my feelings for her getting stronger day by day, and when I asked her to go with me to the next Point to Point meeting, her immediate and more than enthusiastic acceptance told me that her feelings for me had reached the same level. It was the signal Anne had been waiting for, and she took the opportunity to invite me to dinner with her parents at Garnons, their impressive country house some five miles west of Hereford.

As I drove through the immaculate wrought iron gates bearing their coat of arms, I remembered my father's advice not to live beyond my means. Yet this was exactly what I was in danger of doing once again, and I felt myself being drawn into a whirlpool from which it was going to get more and more difficult to drag myself out of. I had to play it cool and not let myself be completely swept off my feet, and the knowledge that I had only nine months left of my tour of duty gave me a measure of encouragement that my posting to the 1st battalion in Hong Kong would almost certainly save me from becoming irrevocably involved with Anne.

I was determined to make the most of my two-year tour of duty with the TA, and apart from the social side, I joined Hereford Rugby Club where I would be able to meet possible recruits for the TA battalion. After just one training session I was welcomed into the first XV as a wing forward, and although the standard of rugger was not very good, at least it helped me to keep fit. I also joined forces with a local farmer who had started up a pack of beagles, the Pembridge, and after seeing how inexpertly the man hunted his hounds, I virtually invited myself to carry a whip. In the end I found myself actually hunting the pack before the season finished, but sadly the farmer decided he had had enough and disbanded the pack during the following summer.

Before the cricket season began, one of the TA warrant officers, Walt Healey, asked if I would enter a battalion team in the local evening cricket league. Although I was not a great cricketer, I was keen on having a go at virtually any sport and I saw the chance of getting myself and the battalion better known with the possibility of doing a bit of recruiting on the side. The idea got the full support of the colonel who agreed to buy the necessary equipment – bats, pads and so on – out of battalion funds. When the league started, I soon found that I was every bit as good with the bat as any of the other team members, and I started getting a name as a bit of a 'slogger'. I also found that I could take the odd wicket with a crafty googly that I had learnt from the cricket coach at school. The team did well, and the commanding officer became sufficiently interested to spend an evening now and then watching us perform.

One morning in May I received a telephone call from a man who introduced himself as Peter Clay. He ran a Country House Hotel not far from Hereford, and he told me that he organised a cricket team that he called the 'Herefordshire Gentlemen'. They played three or four matches each summer against similar sides, and also one against the KSLI that was a regular event coinciding with the regimental reunion at the barracks in Shrewsbury. It was all pretty light-hearted stuff, he explained, and he would like me to play. I modestly said I really wasn't good enough to play at that standard, but Peter Clay would not hear of it. "Not what I've heard", he said. "You've already made a name for yourself in the evening league, and my scouts have told me all about it". I didn't need asking twice, and I agreed to turn out for the County subject to Henry Barneby giving his permission. I knew there would be no problem there, and so it turned out. I played in all five matches, scored in each innings, and took a few wickets.

TA camp in 1950 was held in North Wales, and for a time I had to forget the social side of my job and once again become the regular army officer. I found, somewhat to my surprise, that some of the TA officers resented my professional attitude, and rather looked on the fortnight's camp as their annual holiday even though they were being paid for it! They were certainly not going to have their fun spoiled by a regular officer, and there was considerable animosity at times, to which I did not take kindly. I had words with the company commanders, most of whom had seen service during the war, and I was not surprised that they took my side. But the fact that they had to speak firmly to the young officers concerned only resulted in them making occasional snide and unpleasant remarks to me. I was glad when camp came to an end, and I could revert to the more pleasant side of my appointment.

Summer gave way to autumn, and when a notice appeared in Command Orders about Army rugger trials, I decided to have a go. For the next month or so, I trained hard and in due course went up to Catterick for the trials. I was selected to play in the Command XV against a representative side and subsequently I was surprised and delighted to be asked to play for the Army against Cumberland and Westmorland. They breed big, tough men up there, and just before halftime, my achilles tendon was severely damaged under the full weight of an opponent's boot. I was in great pain and was taken to hospital by ambulance. The injury took weeks to heal, but by the time the hunt balls started again, I was able to walk and decided to test the tendon gently on the dance floor. It stood up to it, and from then on I didn't look back.

My friendship with Anne was developing nicely, but I had decided not to rush my fences. I had been home for Christmas, and on New Year's Eve I was invited to partner her at the Lord Lieutenant's Ball at Garnons. Anne had warned me that I would be closely vetted to see if I was a suitable partner for her. Laughingly, she said she had assured the family that I didn't eat my peas off my knife! When we went into dinner, Sir Richard asked me to sit on his left at the head of the table, with Anne opposite me on her father's right. On my left there was Lady Antonia Proudfoot, the

*Winning Army team at Bisley, 1950*

young sister of one of the premier Earls of England, whose family seat was in nearby Compton Court. She was for the most part in earnest conversation with a young man sitting next to her, and I guessed that she had lost her heart to him. At all events, barely a word passed between Antonia and I throughout dinner. It was a superb meal, and I had a most interesting and animated discussion with Sir Richard, mainly about farming and whether farmers were really feather bedded!

At last it was time to pass the port, and Sir Richard removed the stopper from the decanter and invited me to help myself "to a little Ruby, and pass it on". I poured myself a glass of port and passed the decanter to Lady Antonia. I had never tasted corked port, but the moment I smelt it I knew it would be undrinkable. I took a sip, and the taste was so foul I almost spat it out. I put the glass down and quietly pushed it an inch or two away from me. My reaction was not lost on Sir Richard who leaned towards me and, *sotto voce*, said, "What's the matter, Bob, is it corked?"

"I'm afraid it is, Sir Richard," I replied. He was clearly angry and embarrassed and told Cross, the butler, to clear it away and replace it from the cellar.

"I am so sorry, Bob," he said. "It should never have reached the table like that and I'll have something to say to Cross about this tomorrow morning. But where did you learn that little trick of pushing your glass away if the wine isn't right? Absolutely first class, young man, and you earned full marks. Hardly anyone else even noticed it and you saved me a lot of embarrassment."

"Thank you, Sir Richard," I replied. "Actually I remember my father telling me a similar story about a Mess night during the Great War when he was a half colonel in the RAMC in Cairo. The General was dining in Mess that night, and when he realised the port was corked 'Mr Vice' did exactly as I did a few minutes ago and saved my father a great deal of embarrassment. History repeats itself and I just did what came naturally!" Pleased with the good impression I had made I was not unaware of the beam of pleasure on Anne's face on the other side of the table. Things were definitely going my way.

At that time there was an expression in general use to emphasise one's satisfaction with some particular thing or event – nearly everything really good was 'a ball of fire'. In the early hours of New Year's Day, when the Ball was over and the guests were leaving, our hosts were standing in the main hall saying farewell to their guests. Sir Richard had asked Anne and me to stand by his side so that those who hadn't been able to have a few words with us during the evening might do so as we left. I saw Lady Antonia and her escort approaching and as they moved a bit closer to Anne's parents, Antonia gushed, "Thank you both so much for an absolutely fab party, Sir Richard and Lady Lettice. It was absolute balls in the fire!" There was a stunned silence and I caught sight of Sir Richard's smiling face turning red as he fought to control his amusement. I looked down at my feet, conscious that I was blushing as I, too, tried to stop myself laughing. "So glad you enjoyed it," said Lady Lettice who had not appreciated exactly what Antonia had said. Then suddenly they had gone, and giggles broke out all round to relieve the tension. Even those in the highest ranks of society can make gauche remarks, I thought later, as I lay in bed savouring once again what had been a very enjoyable and promising night for me to remember.

By early spring I was completely fit again, and was looking forward to the start of the cricket season. My commanding officer was replaced in April by a rather bad-tempered-looking officer called Bobby Armitstead. He was a member of the MCC, and had played for the Free Foresters. He was not well liked in the regiment, and had the reputation of being something of a bully. I wanted to work with him as I had done with Henry Barneby, but from the start it looked rather a remote hope that things would stay the same. Knowing my new commanding officer's reputation as a cricketer, I suggested that he might like to play for the battalion in the evening league, and I was shattered when I was told, "No, I don't think so. That sort of thing is for other ranks. I might come along and watch once or twice, you know, to lend moral support".

"Well, Colonel, have you any objections if I play in the side?" I answered. "After all, I started last season, and it will look very odd if I suddenly back out of it now."

"No, I've got no objection if you like that sort of thing, but don't expect me to play." I was amazed, but said no more about it.

One morning the colonel came into the office – he never arrived before 10:00 am – yawned loudly and said, "My God, how I hate my family". He did not enlarge, just sat down and looked through the mail that I had placed on his desk. Later it turned out that one of his children had been fractious during breakfast, and an unpleasant row had broken out between him and his wife Pat. It was no business of mine and I kept my mouth tightly closed. I was aware by now that my new Commanding Officer was not a very stable or nice man to know, and I knew that for the next six months my own life was going to be somewhat tense and that I would have to be very guarded in what I said. The carefree days of my first year in Hereford were a thing of the past.

Part of my job was to maintain regular contact with the companies in their outlying drill halls, and I spent as much time as possible out of the office combining my journeys with a few hours fishing on one of Howard Bulmer's waters. Every morning in the office, I had to put up with the moods and general unpleasantness of my commanding officer but between us we managed to survive what was a very marked difference in our personalities and I had to be careful not to allow them to develop into an open clash. That is, until Peter Clay telephoned me one morning to ask me to play for 'The Gentlemen' again, and I accepted the invitation without hesitation. But I told Peter that I must first clear it with the Colonel, adding that he rather fancied himself as a cricketer.

When Bobby Armitstead came into the office half an hour later, I immediately told him that Peter Clay had asked me to play for the Herefordshire Gentlemen the following Wednesday and that as I had played in all their matches last year, I had accepted "subject to your agreement, Sir". The reaction was wholly predictable.

"You? Play cricket? You get all the cricket you need in the evening league. No, you can't play, I'll play instead."

"All right, Colonel, I'll telephone Peter Clay and tell him exactly what you have just said, and I suggest that you tell him why you won't allow me to play. After all, it is a major part of our job to promote the image of our Regiment and this is one of the best ways of doing so. Peter Clay knows what sort of cricketer I am and in any case these matches are fun games, not pseudo-professional."

The Colonel scowled, and I picked up the telephone to speak to Peter Clay who listened carefully to what I said. "Not very surprised," Peter said, " I have of course heard about your Commanding Officer but I don't see why he should play and you be left out of it. I'd like to speak to him if he's there."

I gave the handset to the Colonel, and I winced as I heard him introduce himself in a suave, obsequious voice. I thought to myself, "What a creep", as the Colonel almost scraped and bowed, his words punctuated with 'Sir' and 'of course'. After a few minutes he handed the handset back to me, saying, "he wants another word with you". Peter then told me that he had felt bound to ask the Colonel to play but had made it clear that he expected me to play as well.

It was a fine day when the Colonel and I turned up for the first match of the season that was against a side from Gloucestershire. They batted first and the runs soon started mounting, and I was not surprised when the Colonel went over to Peter Clay and asked if he could have an over or two. It was perhaps as well that in his first over he took the wickets of the two batsmen who were seemingly well dug in, and I was pleased not so much for my Colonel as for the fact that if he hadn't had some success, life for me would have been made even more intolerable than it was already.

At lunch the Colonel was positively beaming at everyone and I saw a side of him I hadn't believed existed. But success was short-lived. During the afternoon he made a few paltry runs before being run out, and to add insult to injury, I made the highest score, just short of a half-century. The scowl had returned to Bobby Armitstead's face, and I did not look forward to seeing him the next morning.

For the rest of the season, both the Colonel and I turned out for Peter's team, although by now I would have willingly given my place to someone else. The Colonel had not forgiven me for scoring more runs than he had in the first match and I had an uneasy feeling that he would sooner or later make me pay for it. His chance came in mid-July, shortly before we went to annual camp at Castlemartin in South Wales. It was the day of the KSLI Garden Party-cum-cricket match at Copthorne barracks in Shrewsbury, a yearly fixture when the Regimental side played the Lord Lieutenant's eleven, and on this occasion both the Colonel and I were in the Regimental team. It was the sort of day that made the English summer something special. The sun shone in a sky flecked with just a few white cauliflower-like cumulus clouds, and everyone was thoroughly enjoying themselves. Bobby Armitstead was bowling his usual medium off breaks, and I was fielding fairly deep at third man. The batsman was deceived, played forward and got an outside edge, the ball lifting towards me. I was on my toes and running forward. But it landed several feet in front of me and I fielded it first bounce. There was not even the remotest chance of a catch, and as I was about to return the ball to the bowler, I saw him standing with his feet apart, hands on hips, and heard him shout, "You might at least try to catch it, you little shit". I saw a picture of the school prefect bullying and shouting at his fag, something I had never experienced at Oundle. I hurled the ball at Armitstead as hard as I could, but for me the fine day had become clouded.

I was furious, and apart from the hurt to my personal feelings, I was deeply embarrassed at being so abused in front of a large gathering of my brother officers and their families. But there was nothing I could do about it and when we went in for lunch I felt that my world had fallen in. I sat down next to one of the visiting team, and after a few attempts at making polite conversation with an obviously false smile, I gave up, sick at heart. I hadn't met the man sitting next to me before, and had no idea who he was. For that matter I didn't care very much either in my present frame of mind, but presently the other man spoke to me.

"Don't let it get to you," he said, "I heard the whole nasty incident, and frankly the man's not worth worrying about."

"But he's my Commanding Officer," I replied, "and I've got to live with this sort of thing. There wasn't a hope in hell of me catching that ball, and Colonel Armitstead knew it. He's just trying to put me down the whole time, and I've had enough of it. But I'll soldier on until the end of the summer when I'm off to rejoin the battalion in Hong Kong. I only hope he won't repeat this sort of thing in the meantime or I might be tempted to make an official complaint to the Brigadier."

"Well, for what it's worth, I wouldn't do that. In my experience you'd be very unwise to react in the way he clearly wants you to. You'd probably find that your senior officers would close ranks, and in the end it wouldn't get you anywhere, except possibly backwards." The conversation continued and I soon discovered that I was talking to a wartime padre who was now vicar of a parish in the north of the county. His encouragement and friendly advice cheered me up a great deal, and when I went in to bat my inner hurt had almost disappeared and I was able to make some valuable runs which helped the Regimental side to win the match.

Next morning in the office, I was a little apprehensive as I waited for the Colonel to arrive. I kept on telling myself that I mustn't react if I was provoked again, but in the event nothing happened as the Colonel was in a good mood for a change and seemed to have completely forgotten his unseemly outburst the day before. In fact the incident was never mentioned again, and life went on much as before during the few weeks that followed as the battalion prepared for annual camp.

That year, however, due to international tensions, the Government had decided to call up large numbers of Z reservists for two weeks' training and I had to make all the arrangements to cope with an influx of over 1000 men in addition to our own Territorials. It was a mammoth job and required very careful planning in every department. Peter Crofts, the 2 i/c, was responsible for the training, and my staff had to deal with the administration of some 1500 officers and men. Since the reservists came from all parts of the country one of the priorities was to prepare travel warrants to their home towns for every one of them. Then every officer and soldier had to be paid, and such items as marriage allowance and TA 'bounties' had to be added on where appropriate. It was a nightmare, and at the end of the first week I was driven to the bank to draw out over £7500 – in those days no one thought an armed escort was necessary.

During the second week, Monty visited the camp to see how the Z reservists were shaping up, and the whole battalion was paraded for him to inspect the men and speak to some of us. Bobby Armitstead was at his smoothest as he escorted Monty across the parade ground to meet the officers. After introducing Peter Crofts to him, he started to introduce me to the great man, but as soon as Monty saw me he interrupted the colonel, "Yes, yes, I know him well", shaking me warmly by the hand to the complete discomfiture of the Colonel! It was definitely one up to me and I took great delight in the incident, which of course was not mentioned after Monty had left.

I burned a lot of midnight oil adding up endless columns of figures, and on the last Friday when I went to the bank I drew out a little less than £25 000 – a huge sum for which, together with the previous week's pay, I was solely responsible. My TA staff gave me tremendous help, and we were all satisfied that we had got it right. It had not been simply a matter of getting the figures correct, for we had to check each man's entitlement to the various allowances. If we had been given wrong information, no doubt the Command Paymaster would soon pick it up, but I knew that by then I would be on the other side of the world.

# Chapter 19

## AN UNDESIRABLE INJURY

In September, I took a week's leave before going to the School of Infantry in Warminster to do the Company Commander's course. I spent four weeks there, and greatly enjoyed something more like real soldiering rather than the holiday attitude I encountered in the TA. My main occupation when not involved with the very full programme of instruction was to whip-in to the School of Infantry Beagles, and on one very wet and windy day we had met at Larkhill. Conditions had become so bad that by lunchtime everyone had had enough. I had scratched my hand rather nastily on some barbed wire, and I was quite glad when Major Scott, the Master, called it a day and blew for home.

A small group of friends and I decided to go to Bournemouth and spend the rest of the day there. We went to the Norfolk Royal Hotel and were sprucing ourselves up a bit in the cloakroom when I put my scratched hand into warm, soapy water. The resulting sting was agonising and I took my hands out of the water, lifted them above my head and brought them sharply down, turning about as I did so. Unfortunately a man of diminutive stature was walking past me to go to the 'heads' just as I brought my hands down, and I hit the poor man right on top of his bald pate. "Oh, you cad, sir," was the witty retort. It was Arthur Askey, one of the best-known actor/comedians of the time who was appearing in a play in the town and had just enjoyed a good lunch in the hotel with some of the cast. I apologised profusely but Mr Askey saw the funny side and invited us all to join him for a drink in the lounge, where we enjoyed an hour of hilarious chit-chat.

The Chief Instructor at the School was Brigadier Barclay DSO MC, who had done extremely well during the war. He was commonly known as 'Blood and Guts Barclay', a term of esteem for his well-known exploits, one of which was to cheer his men into an attack blowing his hunting horn. Barclay was a much-liked officer who endeared himself to all ranks. That did not mean he was not a strict disciplinarian. When he was off parade, he always had time to talk to the soldiers under his command, and we knew well that once we were on parade again, his word was law. I respected the Brigadier and adopted him as my role model.

*School of Infantry Beagles, Warminster, 1951*

On one occasion, when both the Company and Platoon Commanders courses were to attend a lecture by the Brigadier in the School theatre, the Company Commanders were kept a few minutes late by our instructor, Major Dickie Rasch, Grenadier Guards. When he realised the time, he dismissed the class and told us to get over to the theatre as quickly as we could. I was first in, and as I entered the auditorium I saw rows of young officers sitting stiffly to attention, waiting for the explosion which they thought was inevitable. I saluted smartly, and with his cane the Brigadier indicated the empty seats in front of the Platoon Commanders. I sat down and relaxed as I watched Brigadier Barclay display considerable annoyance by slapping his leg continuously with his cane as the rest of the Company Commanders came in, saluted and sat down. Finally Major Rasch, an unusually small man to be an officer in the Brigade of Guards, arrived and as a deathly hush descended he was heard to say, "Company Commanders' Division all present and correct, Sir. I am sorry we're late, Sir".

The Brigadier said, "Thank you, Major Rasch, please sit down." No doubt the rocket would follow out of earshot of the student officers, but the calm broke as Brigadier Barclay said in a quiet but deliberate voice, "Gentlemen, I fully appreciate that procrastination is the thief of time, but (*rising to a crescendo*) unpunctuality is just (*fortissimo*) bloody bad manners – and don't any of you ever forget it". It was perhaps one lesson that I didn't need to hear, for I had always been a very punctual person; nevertheless the incident was etched into my memory forever.

After the course, I reported to the depot where I was greeted with the news that the battalion in Hong Kong was under orders to move to Korea to replace the Gloucesters after their epic battle on the River Imjin. This was exciting news and I was delighted that what I had learned during the last four weeks would soon be put into practice. I was told to go on leave for a fortnight, and then report back to pick up a draft of reinforcements for the battalion. I had expected at least a month in which to say my goodbyes, but only two weeks left me very little time to visit everyone I wanted to. Inevitably I managed to spend a couple of days with Anne, and when I left I felt that things had cooled off quite considerably and that as far as I was concerned, I was glad that I was, so to speak, off the hook. In any case Anne was young and had many suitors, and as I expected to be away for at least 18 months I really couldn't expect her to wait for me. I saw it as a merciful release from what might have become an acute embarrassment when I would eventually have to tell Sir Richard and Lady Lettice that I was really almost penniless apart from my army pay. I drove away from Garnons with a feeling of relief and expectancy, looking forward to what I was sure would be serious soldiering in Korea. The rest of my leave sped by and once again I had to say farewell to my parents, just as when I sailed for India ten years before.

The draft was ready to move down to Southampton, where we were to embark in the troopship *Empire Fowey*, and to my surprise I was told that I was to be the ship's adjutant. That meant I would have my own cabin and generally enjoy many privileges for the next few weeks. The following morning the party was lorried to the station where we found two coaches and a goods van reserved for us. The train moved off on time and after an uneventful journey we arrived in Southampton where the train drew up on the dockside. I told one of the junior officers in the draft to get the men aboard the troopship, and I went in search of the Officer Commanding troops. I eventually found him in his cabin, with a half consumed bottle of Scotch and three or four glasses on the table. I introduced myself to Lt. Colonel Galbraith, Royal Scots (retired), who immediately invited me to have a 'wee dram'. I didn't like drinking during the day, and anyway I had a lot to do. I suggested that I should go and find my cabin and get myself sorted out first. OC troops agreed and asked me to join him later.

There were a number of reinforcement drafts on board and also several officers and their families on their way to take up duties in Singapore and Hong Kong. A number of unaccompanied wives included Jane McRobert, whose husband was already in Hong Kong. As the journey progressed and the heat became more oppressive, I found her becoming something of a menace. I had already experienced several hot summers during the war, and I was well aware of the effect it had on one's libido. Jane wouldn't leave me alone! Apart from this difficulty, the passage as far as Singapore was uneventful. I joined my draft for morning PT and I spent an hour or two each day walking smartly round and round the upper decks to keep reasonably fit.

At Singapore we had a 24-hour stop for watering and re-victualling the ship, so in the evening I and the three other officers in the draft took a taxi and went to the Airport Hotel in Changi. After a splendid dinner, we took another taxi to return to the ship, and found ourselves passing the famous Raffles Hotel. We decided to go inside for one more drink, and while I paid off the driver the other three went ahead. I followed them in, and as I ran up the marble steps into the foyer, my left foot slipped off the front edge of a step and wrenched my big toe. After some temporary but very acute pain, I thought no more about it, and inside the main lounge I found my colleagues already sitting with some planters and their wives, who asked us to join them for a drink. It developed into a most enjoyable party, and after being cooped up on the *Empire Fowey* for so long, it was a wonderful relief to be able to talk to other people and enjoy dancing. Soon it was time to go, and as we went on board I heard the sound of music coming from one of the ship's officer's cabins. I looked in to find another party in full swing, and as I was already well primed, I didn't take much persuading to join in the fun.

However, I soon felt my toe beginning to throb. To start with it was uncomfortable, but very quickly it became extremely painful and I quietly went outside into the cool night air, took off my shoe and stood leaning against the ships rail. But I got no relief and the pain had by now become agonising. I looked at my watch and was amazed to find it was already 4:00 am. I limped down to my cabin, but after half an hour I telephoned for one of the ship's nursing sisters to come and see me. Presently both the nurses entered my cabin, but they were utterly flummoxed by my very swollen big toe joint. It was tense and looked extremely angry, and the best they could do was to put an opium-soaked dressing on it. I got some slight relief from that, but it did not last for long and by breakfast time I asked the nursing sisters to come back, and also arrange for some breakfast to be sent to my cabin. Eventually the ship's doctor was called, and he declared that I had dislocated my toe. There was a young RAMC orthopaedic surgeon on board, and the ship's doctor asked him to have a look at the toe. He confirmed the first diagnosis, and promptly set about trying to get the toe back into its normal position. The agony this caused made me cry out, for it was far worse than the pain I had suffered so far, and the orthopaedic surgeon was clearly disconcerted. He stopped at once and advised me to rest and keep the foot propped up. The opium dressings were also to continue for a couple of days.

It was all a great embarrassment, and for the next few days I stayed in my cabin where I was given first class service, and, I suspected, rather better meals than I would have got in the restaurant. I was never lonely as many of my friends came to visit me, and we even had a poker school going. Of course, Jane McRobert didn't miss a chance to come and sit on my bed and I had to exercise considerable self-restraint. The nearer we got to Hong Kong, where Jane would be re-joining her husband, the more persistent she became. I had never before experienced being stalked by a not-unattractive woman, and I realised that I was able to keep her at bay only because so many of my friends kept dropping in unexpectedly. With hindsight, as I grew older and more worldly-wise, I realised that the moral standards of the world I was living in were not quite what my father had led me to expect.

By the time we arrived in Hong Kong, I was able to wear a gym shoe and walk without too much discomfort. The *Empire Fowey* was tied up alongside for 48 hours, and we were all allowed to go ashore to stretch our legs. A young 2ⁿᵈ Lieutenant called Angus Critchley-Waring who was taking a draft to the Vth Royal Inniskilling Dragoon Guards in Korea, invited me to go with him to visit some friends who were living in Kowloon. As I wouldn't be able to do much sight-seeing because of my foot, I thought it a good chance to go across the harbour and see a bit more of the place, especially as Angus told me that we would take a taxi to the ferry, and his friends would have a car to meet us on the other side. Angus, needless to say, was a wealthy young man and I imagined that his friends would generously entertain us, as was the case. Sometime in the early hours of the next morning the two of us made a somewhat unsteady return to the ship. The foot did not react to the large amounts of liquor I had consumed, and after lying abed until around 10:00 am, I decided to telephone an old war-time friend from the Guides named Micky Keyes, who I knew was working in Hong Kong with Jardine Matheson & Co. Micky was delighted to hear from me, and invited me to lunch at the Sports Club where we reminisced about our times together in Persia and Iraq. After lunch Micky had to get back to his office, and I took a taxi ride round the territory up to Repulse Bay before returning to the ship. Later that evening I joined a small group of friends and dined at the Parisienne Grill where I tucked into a huge T-bone steak. "Who knows," I thought, "it may be the last time for many months that I shall enjoy a meal like this, so I might as well enjoy it."

Early the following morning the gangways were removed and the *Empire Fowey* sailed from Hong Kong *en route* for Kure in Japan.

# Chapter 20

## "SHOOT ME"

———

As we headed for Japan, there was an aura of expectation and excitement as we drew closer to our destination. Two days before we reached Japan, a cruiser came close alongside at speed and signalled, "Good Luck". The officers on the bridge of the troopship made a similar signal to the Navy. Recognizable, waving from the bridge of the cruiser, was Captain Plunkett RN, who had been aboard the *Empire Fowey* as far as Hong Kong. He was clearly enjoying his new command but it was a brief and rather nostalgic meeting as he sped on his way to join the Royal Navy ships operating with the US Navy off Inchon, the seaport for Seoul.

The winter was all but over when we landed in Japan, and in the warm sunshine the flowers were breaking into bloom everywhere. It was all very peaceful and easy to forget the reason for being in Japan at all – to travel across that last bit of ocean and join battle with the communists who still posed a serious threat to the South Koreans and United Nations forces who had gone to their aid. After a few days in the transit camp just outside Kure in the southwest of Japan, during which I took my men on daily route marches to get us back into shape after our long sea journey and also to test out my toe, we were flown to Seoul in a couple of Royal Australian Air Force Dakotas. The crew were typical extrovert Aussies, full of fun and banter, and their farewell remark summed them up pretty accurately: "Rather you than me, matey. Mind you keep your heads down".

We were taken from the airport to the staging camp where we were to spend our first night in Korea, and were allowed to go into the city before our evening meal, after which a curfew was in force until daylight next morning. The city's war wounds were already showing signs of healing, and there was little to show that quite recently, within the space of only a few months, Seoul had changed hands twice. The North Korean and Chinese armies had swept southwards to the gates of the bustling port of Pusan, only to be slowly but relentlessly driven back by the hastily assembled United Nations forces and what remained of the South Korean army, to our present line along the 38th parallel some forty miles north of Seoul.

*The officers of the 1st Battalion, KSLI, June 1952*

The following morning we loaded our gear into 3-ton lorries, and the draft were embussed in open Chevrolet lorries with hard benches down each side. I had the advantage of an upholstered seat next to a chatty young Canadian driver. The soldier didn't look much older than a schoolboy but he had the self-assurance of a seasoned veteran. He drove his vehicle as fast as the bumpy road would allow, regardless of the discomfort he inflicted on those sitting in the back, for whom it was a back-breaking and liver-shaking journey. Throughout the two-hour drive, lorries and jeeps each trailing its own streamer of khaki-coloured dust passed us. They slowly headed south-wards towards Seoul either with personnel who were going on a few days leave in Japan or to pick up stores or troops waiting to rejoin their front-line units. The road picked its way through an intricate pattern of valleys with here and there burnt-out farms and villages, signalling that war had passed this way not very long ago. The landscape had become untidy and shaggy from neglect, and there were no civilians to be seen. For them this territory was off-limits and only soldiers lived and worked here. There was rusting barbed wire lying in the fields with fading notices advertising old mine-fields, and every now and then the dull, lazy crump of an exploding shell came from behind a nearby hill to remind us that this barren countryside was still at the heart of a war.

As the journey neared its end, the traffic was halted to allow a New Zealand artillery battery, deployed beside the road, to fire a salvo at some distant unseen target and we realised for certain that we had arrived and our travels halfway round the world were over. After a little while, as minor roads branched off where proud signboards pointed the way to the units which made up the Commonwealth Division, the south-bound traffic lessened and the crumps of incoming shells grew much sharper and closer. A notice bearing a code number and the words "B Echelon" indicated that the administration area of the KSLI was hidden away in the re-entrant behind it. Suddenly, round a bend, the lorry pulled up in front of a white pole slung across the road where a regimental policeman, looking as smart as he would have done back home in the training centre, saluted. He showed me where the officers' mess was, and then directed the Canadian driver to the parking area. This was battalion rear HQ, all makeshift and created out of anything that came to hand, but neat and tidy – a reflection on the morale and pride of this famous county regiment.

We then debussed and went over to the baggage lorry to collect our gear, and the duty corporal directed the drivers to the cookhouse where they could get themselves a cup of tea and something to eat. The regimental sergeant major appeared, seemingly from nowhere, to take charge of the draft. The firm set of his jaw had long ago earned him the nickname Rocky, and like so many others of his rank throughout the British Army, he had the ability to instantly impress any lesser bodies who came in contact with him. Tall, upright and immaculately turned out, he strode across, gave me a punctilious salute, and asked permission to "take command of the draft, Sir!"

I returned the salute and replied, "Yes, please, carry on RSM".

"Thank you, Sir," and another tremendous salute terminated the exchange. RSM Knight turned about to face the draft and cast a disparaging eye over them.

"What a shower", he was clearly thinking, as he put them through one or two 'attention' and 'stand at ease' drill movements.

The duty corporal, who had been standing nearby, then asked me to accompany him and handed me over to the driver of the adjutant's jeep, who took me forward to main battalion headquarters. Here we left the jeep and walked over to the adjutant's office, dug into the hillside, where Bob Garnett was already aware that we had arrived. It was nearly lunchtime and after a few enquiries about the journey, Bob took me over to the makeshift Mess where Lieutenant Colonel Bill Barlow DSO, known affectionately throughout the Brigade as Colonel Bill, was already enjoying a can of beer.

"Hullo, Bob," he greeted me, "nice to see you again. Had a good trip out, I hope?" We knew each other well from TA days when the Colonel had been commanding our 4th battalion. After lunch I went over to the command post with Colonel Bill who told me I would be commanding C Company which had had a bit of a hammering during the advance but had achieved all their objectives in spite of pretty severe casualties. "They were a damned good outfit", he said, "and sadly, as you know, poor old Hartley Gahan was wounded only a day before we reached the Imjin". He went on to say that he was confident that they were getting themselves together again, but what they needed was a good enthusiastic company commander. "I think you're the man for the job," he said. He gave me a run down on the other C Company officers. There was my second-in-command, located back at B Echelon, and the three platoon commanders. "I expect you've heard about the Peter Marsden affair, haven't you?" asked the colonel, and although I replied that I had, he still gave me a detailed account of the incident.

"Young Richard Maxwell, who is one of your platoon commanders, and Peter were very close friends. At school together, and then through the RMA you know. Richard took it very badly, but I'm sure he's come to terms with it now." We chatted for a while about our time together in the TA Brigade, and how this war was eventually going to be won by the United Nations. Colonel Bill then took me to the Adjutant's office and handed me over to Bob Garnet to take me forward to join my new company. He promised to visit me there next day after I had settled in. My gear was already loaded in the Adjutant's jeep, and Bob told his driver that he would drive and he must make himself comfortable in the back. I jumped in beside Bob and we were on our way.

It was only a short drive from battalion HQ to the front line, not more than a thousand yards as the crow flies, and the track was in a very bad condition. It had become a watercourse during the rainy season, but the hot sun had dried it out leaving it uneven and strewn with stones. After rounding the spur of a hill, it ran through a tunnel of camouflage nets without which it would have been in full view of the watchful Chinese, and after winding its way up a narrow valley the road turned abruptly up a steep rutted hillside and came to a dead-end just below the skyline. This was C Company HQ. I looked around and saw that the reverse slope, where bunkers had been dug into the hillside, was bare; no grass or the otherwise ubiquitous azalea grew here any more. Dark holes marked the entrances to the bunkers where the men lived, and yet even here, only a few hundred yards across the Sami-ch'on valley from the enemy, the soldiers had made an obvious effort to match the neatness of battalion headquarters a thousand yards further back.

There was little movement, and everything seemed quiet and peaceful. Men who had been out on patrol for most of the night were still asleep in what they affectionately called their gonkers (in gonk meant being asleep). Others, who had been on sentry duty within the company perimeter, were beginning to busy themselves washing or shaving, improving their dugouts perhaps, or sitting in the sun writing letters home. "Dear Mum, I hope this finds you in the pink, as I am," but they weren't pink. Stripped to the waist they were all burnt by the sun and were a dark mahogany colour.

As I got out of the jeep, Company Sergeant Major Bailey came over to welcome me. He saluted smartly, and I noticed at once that he had lost the two middle fingers of his right hand; he had been hit by shrapnel soon after D-Day just outside Caen, but had recovered in time to rejoin the regiment well before the end of the war. I had not met him before and I was duly impressed. Captain Bernard Houghton-Berry, who had been acting Company Commander pending my arrival, came over to meet me. After formally handing over command to me, he said goodbye to CSM Bailey and the few soldiers who were nearby, and Bob Garnet then drove him back to battalion HQ.

CSM Bailey first of all introduced me to the soldiers who happened to be within reach, and then took me to my newly prepared bunker where he introduced private Gordon Shiell whom he had selected to be my batman. Shiell had been with the company since Hong Kong days. He was a young National Service soldier and had done well in the fighting and proved himself steady and reliable under fire. Bailey felt that he would be a solid right-hand man for the company commander, and I asked the CSM to give me a few minutes to show Shiell what kit I had with me, and to discuss one or two things such as any particular likes and dislikes I might have; it was important that a batman should know of any foibles straight away so that misunderstandings would be avoided. Having placed my well-being in Gordon Shiel's hands, I walked over to the CSM's bunker to have a chat with him, and to be shown round the company position so that I could put myself fully in the picture, meet my platoon commanders, and make myself known to as many of my men as I could. Inside the bunker Bailey had a brew going – a 2 lb jam tin sitting on a home-made petrol stove with boiling water gently bubbling up through a layer of tea leaves.

"You will get used to good strong tea like this," he said. "What about a mug now, Sir?" I did not need a second bidding, and it was as good as it looked. "There's only one better drink than this," the CSM went on, "and that is what you see here with your rum ration added to it. Major Gahan and I used to put our rum into our early morning tea, and I hope you will join me in this enjoyable routine when we stand down at first light."

*KSLI soldiers bathing in the River Imjin*

*Air OP Auster plane flying along the River Imjin*

"Sounds a great idea to me, Sergeant Major," I replied, rather looking forward to the next morning's stand-down.

There was a great deal to talk about, and I kept up a barrage of questions about the battalion and C Company so that I quickly began to feel that I was already a part of it. Afterwards CSM Bailey led me to the entrance of a deep communication trench that ran from the warren which was company HQ, up through the crest of the hill, along a broad ridge and down to an area where the dark entrances of more bunkers facing away from the enemy lines were clearly visible. This was number 7 platoon area, and somewhere down there was Richard Maxwell, living amongst the soldiers he commanded.

As we moved forward along the trench, the CSM pointed out the positions of numbers 8 and 9 platoons over to the right, 9 laid back slightly so that they could quickly have reinforced either of the other platoons if they became too hard-pressed by a mass Chinese assault. Similar deep trenches connected each of those two platoons with company HQ, and wire and minefields had been put down in a continuous belt along the forward edge of the company perimeter linking with D Company on the left, and a company of 1st Royal Australian Regiment on the right.

As we moved forward along the main communication trench, we turned left along a spur of the system, through two sharp bends which had been dug to absorb the blast from shells exploding in the trench, and found ourselves in a well revetted slit trench just forward of the skyline above company HQ.

"This is your OP, Sir" said Bailey. "You and I share this for evening and morning stand-to, which as you know lasts for an hour at dusk and again for an hour before dawn. These are the dangerous times for the gooks to creep up and launch a surprise attack, but I usually leave just before stand-down in the morning to get that brew going."

The remark seemed to me more like a statement than a suggestion, i.e. that it was a well-tried practice and surely there was no question of discontinuing it. But I thought it was an excellent idea and furthermore that it would not be very diplomatic to argue about it.

"I think we'll carry on with that arrangement, Sergeant Major, unless you have any other ideas you'd like to try?"

Bailey's smile said all that had to be said, and I was thankful that it looked as though my CSM and I were going to see eye to eye. There is nothing more disruptive to the efficiency and morale of a fighting unit than a clash of personalities at the top, indeed at any level as I had found out during my time as TA Adjutant. The OP was like a pulpit, high above the surrounding battlefield. I stood for a while so that I could get a clear picture in my mind of the whole defensive position as well as the ground to the north where the Chinese were dug in, living out the same monotonous daily routine as we were. I looked down across the wide flat valley, lying calm in the afternoon sun, to where the craggy hills reared up in a series of sharp ridges, one behind the other into the far distance. Here and there trenches ran like veins up the spurs, protected by steely blue lines of barbed wire, a mirror image of the defence positions on our side of that latter-day no man's land. Between the forward hills there were deep re-entrants going back two or three hundred yards, and occasional straw-roofed huts still stood just inside them having escaped the burning and I wondered if the Chinese were using them at night as listening posts.

The sergeant-major broke the silence. "It looks so serene and tranquil down there, doesn't it, Sir? But almost every night somewhere or other along the valley vicious little fire-fights break out between our patrols and the gooks, and the toll of killed and wounded is steadily mounting. I expect you heard about Mr Maxwell's friend Lieutenant Marsden?"

I paused and decided to let my CSM talk about it. "Yes, I did, Sergeant-Major," I said.

"Yes, Sir," Bailey continued, "Mr Maxwell has taken it very badly."

I noted the use of the present, rather than the past, tense. After all, it had happened at least three months previous, and the implication was that Richard was still grieving and worrying about the loss of his friend. We left the OP and went down to No. 7 platoon. Richard was sitting in the sun outside his dugout, writing a letter, and he hadn't seen the CSM and me approaching.

"Hullo, Richard, how nice to see you again," I greeted him. We had met before, shortly before he had left home to join the battalion, and I had known Colonel Maxwell, Richard's father, during my two years as TA Adjutant. CSM Bailey diplomatically disappeared to have a word with the platoon sergeant, which gave us the chance to have a short talk about things in general. "Sorry to hear about Peter", I said sympathetically. "I gather there's still no news in spite of efforts by the Red Cross. Trouble is, the gooks only recognise that organisation when it suits them, and there's no other way we can try to find out what's happened to Peter."

"Yes, I know, Sir. Peter was such a great guy and his one burning ambition was to get an MC as a subaltern. It certainly misfired, didn't it?"

I quickly changed the subject as it was clear that Richard was still emotional about Peter's unexplained disappearance after the fire-fight with the enemy patrol. It was known that when his patrol had run into an ambush, Peter ordered his men to withdraw as best they could, every man for himself, and that he continued to fire his Sten gun at the Chinese until either he ran out of ammunition or he was hit. No one ever knew the answer and no trace of him whatsoever was found at the scene of the ambush. By now Richard should have come to terms with what had happened. I felt that the CSM was not too happy about his performance as platoon commander, and I wondered what effect it was having on his morale when he was down there in the valley carrying out the same sort of patrols himself.

"Well, we'd better have a quick look round your area, Richard," I said. "Is this your dugout?" Richard showed me inside the small dark hole in the ground with a shelf of solid ground on one side that served as a bed. Richard's bedding-roll was spread out on the shelf, and there were photographs of his parents and his girlfriend Liz by the bedside. We then went round the platoon position, and Richard introduced me to his NCOs and some of the soldiers, after which CSM Bailey led me to the other two platoon areas. I was glad of a few minutes in the OP to think things over.

The next afternoon Colonel Bill came up to the OP as promised and spent an hour discussing a whole variety of things with me. He was obviously very proud of the way his battalion had conducted itself, especially throughout the attack phase that had ended when we reached the 38th parallel. The important thing now was to maintain morale at its present high level, which the colonel admitted was not going to be easy with the possibility that the so-called peace talks at Panmunjon might end in failure. There was nothing to show that the Chinese were anxious to stop the fighting, and every time the two sides seemed to be on the verge of reaching an agreement, the inscrutable Chinese found some way of thwarting the United Nations negotiators.

As far as the UN soldiers were concerned, the time when the killing and maiming would end could not come soon enough. Every delay, therefore, tended to sap the soldier's morale a little bit more, and it certainly did nothing to help when a new American Corps commander, fresh from a home-based command, sent out a message almost as soon as his feet had touched the ground that "I gotta get me a prisoner". To achieve his aim, he demanded that patrol activity must be intensified, and all company commanders were to inspect their wire and minefields personally as there seemed to be no accurate records of those vital defensive areas.

It was going to call for leadership of the highest order, and Colonel Bill was confident that his officers would rise to the challenge although I felt that my company were already doing all the patrolling we could reasonably be asked to do. For example, to ease the pressure on the two forward companies, each of the two companies in reserve provided patrols every fourth day. The patrol commander was briefed by the forward company commander he was assigned to, and he was de-briefed by him when the patrol returned on completion of the assignment. A Company would be providing the patrol the following day, and Colonel Bill suggested a few possible tasks that I might ask the patrol commander to do. Before he left he casually asked, "Have you had a talk with young Richard yet, Bob?" Sensing what the colonel was getting at, I said that I had. Although Richard still seemed to be emotional about the incident, I was confident that with his background he was going to pull himself together. It would be one of my priorities to do everything possible to help him to recover his self-confidence.

Two weeks before I took command of C Company, Lieutenant Tony Pack, who commanded a platoon of A Company which was in reserve, was detailed to carry out a special patrol from C Company position. He had spent much of the afternoon the day before the patrol with Lieutenant Anthony Millen, 5th Royal Inniskilling Dragoon Guards, who commanded a troop of Centurion tanks, one of which was in a dug-out position overlooking the valley in front of C Company. Together they planned the patrol in detail including the fire plan, selecting targets for the extremely accurate guns of the Centurion. The precise range and bearing of each target was recorded and given a code name so that on whispered messages on Tony Pack's radio, Anthony could bring down immediate and precise defensive fire. C Company commander was of course involved in the plan and the following night Anthony and I monitored Tony's progress as he worked his way across the valley.

The patrol had gone according to plan, was a complete success and Tony was awarded an immediate Military Cross for this very dangerous patrol which he richly deserved.

Some two weeks after I had assumed command of C Company, Tony Pack MC was sent to my company to do another patrol down in the valley. When he arrived for his briefing I took him up to the OP and explained that I wanted him to find out whether a hut at the mouth of the re-entrant directly opposite No. 7 platoon's position was being occupied by the enemy during the hours of darkness. The patrol had to feel its way forward, noting obstacles such as wire and minefields.

If the answer was affirmative I intended to attack and destroy it; and I had it in my mind to send Richard Maxwell out to do it. Tony was to return to C Company position as soon as he was satisfied that he had obtained the information I wanted and having been out in the valley before, he knew that the Chinese were quite active in that sector.

On this patrol there was to be no supporting fire from Anthony's tanks, so having studied the ground carefully he worked out his plan, and asked me if he could stay with me until his patrol arrived for their briefing in an hour's time. I agreed, and we had a long chat to while away the time. Tony showed me exactly where he planned to go, avoiding one particular spot where he had heard some gooks chattering the last time he was out there, as he thought it was a likely ambush position. The corporal and four men, including a radio operator, arrived for Tony's briefing right on time, after which Tony crowded them into his Jeep and drove them back to their company position for their evening meal. Shortly before stand-to, they came back to C Company and as the light faded they had a last look at the ground they would soon be crossing. The corporal made a final check of his four men to make sure that they had all necessary equipment with them, asked if there were any questions, and reported to Tony that the patrol was ready and correct. I had made a note of the route out and back, and the various timings Tony had worked out, and if all went according to plan they should be back inside the company perimeter by 2:30 am.

As soon as the company had stood down, Tony said *au revoir* to CSM Bailey and me, and led his small group down to No. 7 platoon position where he spent about half an hour talking to Richard. Then he took the patrol down the crawl trench to the path through the minefield and wire, and they were out in no man's land. Meanwhile I stayed in the OP, listening and getting accustomed to the noises of the night: the frogs and cicadas, the sounds of intermittent distant artillery, mortar and small arms fire. My policy was that I would always stay on listening watch until every patrol which had gone out through my perimeter was safely back inside the protective wire and mines, in spite of the fact that it would mean long, tiring watches almost every night of the week. Gordon Shiell always rose to the occasion with frequent mugs of tea that were greatly appreciated, and sometimes CSM Bailey and one or other of my platoon commanders would pop in for a chat. It all helped me to keep awake during the small hours, and there was often some interesting radio traffic to listen to.

As the minutes ticked away, I thought back to one recent occasion when I had switched my radio channel after I had heard some explosions nearby from the direction of B Company, and I heard a platoon commander whose voice I immediately recognised, calling his company commander for help. It was John Yeoward whose father I had known quite well when I was in Hereford. Apparently a patrol from his platoon had walked into an anti-personnel minefield and had suffered casualties. There had been no marker wire in front of the minefield as the ground had softened and the supporting pickets had toppled over. John had gone out himself with a small party including a medical orderly to contact the patrol, administer First Aid to the wounded, and try to get them all safely out. But communications with his company commander had broken down and there was no answer from him; the only reply John could get was from the company radio operator. By the time Major Bancroft had been alerted to what was going on, it was too late for him to intervene except to call for illumination star shells from the gunners. By the Grace of God, the young lieutenant managed to reverse his men out of their situation without fouling another trip wire, and he decided to stay where they were until after stand-down when they could see the path through the minefield. It had been a close-run thing; by any yardstick it was a brave if not foolhardy thing to do, and in my estimation it was fully deserving of at least an MC. But in the circumstances, as far as John knew not a word of what he had done reached the ears of anyone apart from Colonel Bill and members of his own company. It convinced me that the policy I stuck to must be the right one, and should be adopted by every company commander in fairness to the men they sent out on patrol. It also had an uplifting effect on the morale of the soldiers out there to know that their company commander was awake and ready to respond immediately to a cry for help.

It was just past midnight when all hell was let loose. The staccato bursts of automatic fire punctuated by the sharp crack of exploding grenades shattered the tranquility of the valley, and tiny stabs of orange from half way across the low ground marked the spot where the fire-fight was taking place. It was all over in a couple of minutes and I waited anxiously for a radio message from Tony, but none came and my concern grew. In the meantime Richard had heard the vicious fire-fight and walked up to the OP to see if any message had come through. "I think you had better get back to your own OP, Richard," I told him. "If they're in trouble they may need some help to get back through the mines. Let me know the moment you hear anything. It doesn't look good at the moment, does it?"

Two hours later three survivors of the fight, the corporal and two men, found their way into No. 7 platoon area, and Richard brought them straight up to my OP. Their story was brief. They were making good progress towards their objective on the other side of the valley when they walked straight into an ambush. The Chinese had let them get into the middle of their position before opening fire, and Tony's patrol had no chance. It seemed clear that the radio operator was killed instantly, and Tony Pack had 'hosed' his Sten gun at the stabs of orange, at the same time yelling to the corporal and the two rear-markers to run like hell. They didn't need a second bidding, and somehow managed to get away unscathed. When the firing stopped as suddenly as it had started, the three men listened to the Chinese chattering like monkeys amongst themselves as they grabbed Tony's watch, compass and Sten gun before withdrawing to their own positions, their ambush successfully sprung. After a while the corporal and his two companions crept back and found Tony Pack and his signaller lying dead where they fell, and between them they had managed to drag their bodies back to the edge of the minefield where they had left them until daylight. Shiell brought hot drinks to the OP for the three survivors, and I looked for Richard, but he had already slipped away to his bunker to be alone with his sorrow for yet another of his colleagues now lying dead in the valley.

Immediately after morning stand-down, I spoke to the adjutant on the field telephone and gave him the full details of Tony Pack's death. A stretcher party from A Company was sent forward to recover the bodies, and Donald Cordon, the company commander, deeply saddened by the loss of such a gallant young officer and his radio operator, drank a cup of strong hot tea well laced with rum, as he and I discussed the night's events. After catching up on my lost sleep, I went down to see Richard. He had pulled himself together and after a good chat, my fears that this almost mirror-image of the ambush in which Peter had been killed might prove too much for him, were to some extent allayed; only time would tell, however.

For the next four weeks, nightly patrolling continued with Richard seeming to be in a much better frame of mind. In fact he seemed to enjoy going out on patrol, and gave me the impression that he was bent on exacting revenge on the enemy, to the extent that I had to tell him not to do anything silly. A week before the battalion was due to go into reserve for a month, word came through that we were going to build two complete battalion defensive positions between the 38th parallel and Seoul, and Colonel Bill called a special 'O' group to brief all the officers about this sudden change in plan. Intelligence reports were suggesting that while the peace talks at Panmunjon were bogged down, the Chinese might try to steal a march on the United Nations forces by launching a major offensive with the capture of Seoul as the main objective.

Most of the officers had already arrived in the Mess when word came through that Arthur Tait, D Company commander, had been trying to retrieve what appeared to be a written message from the wire in front of his company position, and as he reached forward over the wire he triggered an anti-personnel device. It was a typical ruse of the Chinese to creep up to the wire by night, lay AP mines or booby traps, and at the same time place a decoy to incite the unwary to investigate! Poor Arthur took the blast of the bomb in his groin and he was completely emasculated. There was little that could be done for him, and he died in terrible agony within half an hour. The effect of this dreadful tragedy on the rest of the officers was profound. I noticed one of the senior company commanders who had been a very close friend of Arthur, actually weeping as Colonel Bill went ahead with his briefing. "So even the toughest men can cry", I thought. "All this stiff upper lip stuff might have its place, but surely it is better not to try to suppress one's sadness too much."

That same evening I spotted unusual enemy activity on the ridge opposite No. 7 platoon. I watched it for a time but could not fathom out exactly what the gooks were up to. I kept it under surveillance for two days, and having put Colonel Bill in the picture I asked for an air strike to destroy whatever the Chinese were building up there. The colonel came up to my OP to have a look and agreed that there was something important going on. I thought it might well be the exit of a tunnel system through which possibly a field gun or small tank could be brought up to fire over open sights directly into our positions. He supported my request for an air strike, which was dealt with very quickly, and it was scheduled for soon after dawn the following day. Colonel Bill and Bob Garnet arrived just before the attack was due to go in to find that the OP had been taken over by four Americans who were bustling about, setting up the strike.

Dear Editor

The Summer 99 edition of The Silver Bugle came to my notice recently and in it I saw the photograph of Lt AG Pack's grave in Pusan. My memory at once went back 50 years to the time in Korea, on Point 159, a wretched hill protruding into Chinese territory, when, with my troop of 3 Centurion tanks, I supported Tony Pack's patrol, by night, into no-man's land. Tony and I spent the previous afternoon selecting targets for my very accurate 20 pounder guns and recording the precise range and direction of each one on the tank's instruments. Each target was given a name and a number so that, on whispered instructions on the VHF radio, I could bring down immediate and precise HE fire. Our joint plan, supervised by the company commander, Major Bob Maslen-Jones, seemed to be a complete success so that Tony's very dangerous patrol achieved total success. Tony was awarded a well deserved Military Cross.

His courage and skill on such a patrol led to his tragic death a very short time later. I remember Tony Pack with great affection and respect; he served the KSLI with great distinction. Bob Maslen-Jones and I have remained firm friends over the half century that has passed since that exciting time.

Yours sincerely

*Anthony Millen*

Brigadier ATP Millen

late 5th Royal Inniskilling Dragoon Guards

Soon the sound of aircraft engines could be heard high up in an apparently empty blue sky, followed by the scream of shells flying over just above our heads. They burst precisely on the target area leaving a cloud of bright orange smoke as a marker for the pilots. Several soldiers had emerged from their bunkers to watch the air strike and I noticed Richard standing with a group of his men on the open hillside at the end of No. 7 platoon ridge. The planes which were now circling overhead, peeled off in succession and with their engines screaming, dive-bombed the enemy position, each plane releasing two 500-pound bombs. From the other side of the valley came the sound of automatic small-arms fire as the unseen Chinese tried to fight off the planes, and as the third aircraft swooped down it suddenly swung away from the target. The pilot released his bombs but they whistled down into the valley and exploded harmlessly less than half way between C Company and the Chinese-held positions. Back in the OP the Americans uttered some rich expletives as they realised the plane had been hit, and the pilot made for home trailing an ominous ribbon of black smoke. Some of those watching from the end of No. 7 platoon ridge thought the two bombs were coming too close for comfort, and three of them hit the deck as an act of self-preservation. One of them was Richard and as soon as he realised that the bombs had fallen well away from him he got rather sheepishly to his feet and tried to laugh the incident off. To the Colonel and Bob Garnet, and indeed to me, Richard's instinctive action seemed to underline a certain lack of moral fibre.

The fourth plane then came in and finished the air strike with two direct hits. The hill had disappeared from view behind a dense cloud of reddish dust as the bombs struck home, filling the valley with the reverberating crumps which echoed and re-echoed between the hills on either side of it. The Americans packed up their equipment and after Colonel Bill and I had thanked them enthusiastically, they sped away in their jeeps leaving still more brown dust over everything in the vicinity.

As the cloud of dust over the target area settled, the result of the air strike could be seen. At least half the bombs had hit the target or been very close to it, but it was still not clear what the earthwork the Chinese had been so busy preparing actually was. "Keep an eye on it, Bob, and if you're not happy I will see if we can get the Centurion up here to blast it from a hull-down position." Having said that the Colonel and Adjutant left me to my own devices, and some time later I went down to see Richard. I mentioned the air strike and asked how far away the two stray bombs from the stricken aircraft had fallen. Richard was able to point out exactly where they had exploded, and I could see the craters about three hundred yards in front of the perimeter wire.

"Were you one of those I saw hit the deck?" I asked him.

"Yes, I was actually," answered Richard. "I thought they were coming straight for us. I don't see any point in standing up asking to be hit by shrapnel, do you, Sir?"

"Well, I suppose not," I replied, and thinking that there was not much point in arguing about a hypothetical question, I changed the subject and we talked about the tasks we had been set for our time in reserve.

It was just three days to go before relief, when we would be leaving this position for good, and it was Richard's turn to go out on patrol. I briefed him as usual in the OP, and mindful that so close to going into reserve survival was now uppermost in everyone's minds, I had deliberately and carefully planned 'safe' patrols for the last few days in the line, and had selected a number of places not too far out into the valley where it would be relatively easy to ambush an enemy patrol approaching C Company perimeter. Richard seemed to be in good heart, and before he left I reminded him that I would be on listening watch in the OP until he let me know he was safely back inside the wire. "Then come up to my bunker for de-briefing," I added, "and I'll have a cup of cocoa ready". Richard saluted and went back to his platoon to prepare for another long night out in the damp and chilly valley.

The night passed slowly with very little activity anywhere along the front, and the frogs and cicadas were loud in their appreciation of the unusual quietness. At 3:00 am precisely, Richard called me on the radio to say that he was withdrawing from his ambush position, and not long afterwards he reported that he had re-entered the perimeter. He dismissed his men, telling them to get some sleep in their respective gonkers, and after spending a few moments in his own dugout he made his way up the trench to report to me.

My dugout was well lit by a Petromax lamp, and it was warm compared to the chill night air outside. Shiell had made hot well-sugared cocoa for Richard and me, and had then excused himself to go and get some sleep. I heard Richard come through the narrow entrance of the dugout, and as I turned to greet him, I saw something glint in his outstretched hand...his revolver.

"What the hell –" I began, and then I paused as I realised that it was the butt and not the muzzle pointing at me.

"Here, Sir, you'd better take this and shoot me. I'm a coward, shot to ribbons, and every time I go out on patrol I just can't get Peter out of my mind," Richard interrupted. The young officer was shaking and sobbing.

I put a hand on his shoulder to calm him down and said quietly, "Go on Richard, tell me all about it."

Richard went on, "I haven't done any of the patrols you sent me out on, and all the reports I have given you have been lies. I always took the same three men with me and all we did was to stay in a position just outside the perimeter wire until it was time to come back in. We never went further out, and the others believed we were sent out as a listening patrol on this side of the valley. I haven't got the guts and I'm a disgrace to my family, especially my father who will never forgive me. Please take my revolver and finish it all."

I was only ten years older than Richard, but I was shattered. Then I took the revolver and placed it on the bunk behind me and began talking. "Your family do not have to know about this, Richard. You have gone through some very distressing traumas recently, and you will eventually learn to live with what has happened. We must give it time, for as you know, time is a great healer."

Richard listened and I went on talking to him until it was time for stand-to. By then I felt I was beginning to win his mind, and with a month in reserve I was fairly confident I could restore his self-confidence without anyone ever knowing what he had admitted to me. So far this was a secret shared only by Richard and myself, and although the thought had gone through my mind that perhaps I was playing with fire, I felt that if at the end of the reserve period Richard hadn't responded, then I could decide what to do about him. But the main priority at the moment was to try to save his career, and the alternative to my quickly worked out plan was to report the whole thing to Colonel Bill. Richard's career would then certainly be in tatters and his shame complete.

"Take your revolver with you, Richard. We'll have another talk later today." I told him to go back to his platoon for stand-to, "and don't say a word of this to anyone. As far as I am concerned, this never happened. OK?"

"OK Sir, and thank you" said Richard, as he left the dugout.

When we met later in the day, it was as though our early morning talk had been a dream, and it was now up to Richard to respond to the encouragement I had given him.

# Chapter 21

## DEFENDING HILL 159

––––

The battalion came out of the line without further incident. Our relief by the Royal Norfolks took place during the hours of darkness, and by dawn we were well on our way to the new defensive location we would be constructing. Having set up our own battalion camp under canvas, the company commanders were given the exact locations of our respective assignments. We were told to plan the layout of the new positions, and to await the commanding officer's approval before ordering our men to start digging. It was clearly going to be a mammoth task to have the two positions ready for occupation within the time laid down, especially as there were many in the battalion who were already overdue for R and R leave in Japan (Rest and Recuperation – a misnomer if ever there was one!) and Colonel Bill had insisted with the Brigade Commander that these men must go. It had been agreed, but as a result it was going to be an even more difficult job to meet the challenge presented to the company commanders. I preferred to command my company by leading from the front, and I saw no difference between actually leading my men into battle and taking my shirt off and digging trenches with them. It was a matter of showing them that I was prepared to share whatever danger or hard graft they might have to face, and it enhanced their respect for me.

It so happened that C Company's first position was nearest to the battalion camp and the other companies had to march past us to get to their respective digging areas. Not all the other company commanders shared my enthusiasm for wielding a pick and shovel, and every day at lunch time when C Company men were resting and enjoying a can of beer, which I insisted was to be brought out to the site with our rations, they were to be seen strutting out, smartly dressed, to see how their men were getting on. Some derisive remarks invariably passed the lips of the C Company men, but they were harmless, and I knew that most of the company commanders, regardless of their particular methods of dealing with their men, were excellent officers. In any case they had been tried in battle and had all done extremely well. In fact I was the only one who had not been in the battalion during the advance to the 38th parallel, and I would be on dangerous ground if I dared to criticise one of my proven colleagues. I was vain enough to feel that I myself was probably the pick of the bunch, and I would prove it by doing my damnedest to complete both the positions we had been ordered to construct.

I continued my confidence-building exercise with Richard whenever I had the opportunity, hoping that by the time we went back into the line he would have recovered sufficiently to carry out his patrols as ordered and not just sit down outside the perimeter. I gave a lot of thought to how I could reintroduce him to active patrolling and in view of what had happened, it was obviously going to be a traumatic experience for any young officer. My idea was that when we were back in the line in our new position, I would plan three progressively more difficult tasks for Richard to carry out, and I would monitor the patrol's progress by means of a code of signals on the radio. This was done by tapping the microphone with a fingernail, rather than speaking into it.

The digging went on unabated, and it became very monotonous to say the least. The men deserved better than that after their achievements of the previous few months, but morale remained remarkably high considering all things. Tempers now and then became a bit short-fused, and on one occasion I had to issue a red card to one of my platoon sergeants who showed dissent in front of some of his men when I had to scrap three half-dug trenches. It was not my fault, as a visit by the Brigade commander resulted in him suggesting that from the particular trenches there was insufficient field-of-fire. Together we had decided on new positions, and Colonel Bill and I both agreed that they were marginally better. When the Brigadier and Colonel had gone, I called Richard and Sergeant Brayshaw over to explain what was required, and the sergeant did not take kindly to it at all. He threw his shovel on the ground, and muttered, "Why the bloody hell don't they make up their bloody minds?" I was on to him like a shot. "One more word of dissent from you, Sergeant Brayshaw, and I'll have you out of this battalion just like that", and I clicked my thumb and middle finger to illustrate what I meant.

There was one more incident which I was to remember some years later, when the Divisional Commander, General 'Gentleman Jim' Cassells, came round to see how the two positions were progressing. With him were the CRA Major-General Pike, the Brigade Commander, Colonel Bill, and several lesser lights. There had been no warning that this party would be visiting the battalion, and as usual I was shirtless and beavering away in the bottom of a trench when I heard Colonel Bill ask: "Where's the company commander?"

"He's down there," I heard someone reply. The next moment I looked up and saw, as though through a fish-eye lens, a bevy of peering faces, topped with red-banded caps, looking down at me. I jumped out of the trench and came to attention with a somewhat sheepish grin on my dust-caked face.

"Sorry, Sir," I said to the Divisional Commander, "Good morning, Sir."

"Nothing to be sorry for", came the reply. "I'm glad to see you setting such a splendid example to your men. How are things going?"

I told him that we were doing everything we could to complete the positions on time, and so far we were on schedule. The General asked about the morale of my soldiers, to which I said 'fine' and asked him to have a word with one or two of them. The general did so, and as he turned to go, General Pike said, "Good show, Maslen-Jones. Keep it up." I felt elated that doing a bit of digging myself had certainly done no harm.

It was now August, and the summer had become almost unbearably hot which made the daily digging a morale sapping exercise. The men were almost longing to get back into the line so that we did not have to sweat our guts out all and every day. Soon the rains came, just as the tasks we had been set were almost completed and it was time to take a short rest before going back to the 38$^{th}$ parallel. This was just as well, for the rains that summer were so heavy that as soon as a trench was half dug, it was full of rainwater. It was torrential, and gently flowing streams suddenly became turbulent rivers of muddy, almost tepid, water. It was a losing battle to keep weapons clean and free of gritty soil. Further north where the famous Imjin River meandered across the countryside, things were even worse. In one night its level had risen by seventeen feet, and all the bridges were swept away. Those units to the north were temporarily cut off and could only be supplied by helicopter. But it was relatively short-lived, and the rains began to ease off within a couple of weeks. By early autumn the devastation was just a nasty dream, and for a while the weather was more like springtime, reminding us the onset of winter was not too far away as the evenings and nights became ever more chilly.

By the time our period in reserve was over, C Company had completed both its allotted tasks. We were the only company in the battalion to do so, and we went back into the front line with a feeling of a job well done, a special pat on our collective backs from Colonel Bill, and our morale as high as it had ever been. The position we took over from a battalion of the *Vingt-Deux* Canadian regiment was on the south side of the valley of the River Sami-ch'on, and was a good deal further west from the one we had handed over to the Norfolks nearly six weeks before. The bunkers and trenches were very strongly made, but because they had been lived-in for a considerable time, every bunker had its own family of brown rats. They used to come out of hiding and creep along the wooden joists of the shell-proof roofs, constructed of heavy timber beams with at least four feet of soil and rock on the top. I soon got used to this unwarranted intrusion into my private life, and in fact became quite attached to one particular rat that I called one-eyed Pete. How this creature lost one of its eyes, I never knew.

The Sami-ch'on valley was a little bit wider than our previous position, about a mile across at its widest point, but the hills on either side were more prominent, and the re-entrants deeper and longer. The valley turned forty-five degrees sharply to the southeast at the eastern end of the battalion sector, and there was one particularly dominant feature right at the turning point: Hill 159. This hill had a clear field of fire down the valley both to the west and to the southeast, and it was to be C Company's forward platoon position. I seized the opportunity to give Richard the responsibility for defending this feature, and I told Colonel Bill that I planned to site Anthony Millen's Centurion tank dug-in almost on the skyline so that it could dominate no man's land on both sides of the feature. After visiting Hill 159 himself, the Brigadier had no hesitation in agreeing with the idea, and the tank duly came up in support as soon as a big enough hole had been dug for it.

Further back on the right of No. 7 platoon, there was another feature that overlooked the southeast leg of the valley until it turned abruptly northeast in front of a battalion of Fusiliers, occupied by No. 8 platoon. Both No. 8 platoon and No. 9 platoon hills were smaller than Hill 159; Hill 159 was the lynch pin of the company defence. If No. 7 platoon were driven off, both the other platoon areas would be directly dominated by it, and would probably become untenable. The importance of holding Hill 159 was not lost on Richard, who seemed to grow in stature in the knowledge that I had entrusted him with a pretty awesome responsibility.

Patrolling began immediately after the battalion had completed the takeover, and Richard had already done both his first two assignments according to plan. I had given him a detailed and careful briefing and had been able to follow his progress to various points in the valley by means of the tap code. I had insisted that Richard's patrols should be stronger than those he had taken out the last time we were in the line, and that an experienced corporal or even his platoon sergeant should be included as his second-in-command. The success of each of these patrols was demonstrated by Richard's obvious satisfaction with his own performance, and his general demeanour was much brighter than it had been before we went into reserve.

The time for the third patrol, which in my plan was to be the ultimate test of his moral fibre, drew near and I decided that the objective would be to blow up a house just inside a large re-entrant across the valley. It was a complex briefing as the task would involve carrying explosives and equipment into the re-entrant and running out cable to the detonating plunger that was to be left halfway across, on the far bank of the river. At the last moment I decided to bring Colonel Bill into the picture, and I told him the whole background to the particular task Richard was about to undertake. I was not certain what the Colonel's reaction would be, and I was rather surprised when he applauded what I had done.

"I would have liked you to have told me about the problem sooner, Bob," the Colonel said, "but I can quite understand that you had made a decision to try to deal with it on your own, and the fewer people who knew about it the better. Yes, well done, and I would like to come up and see the whole show through with you in the OP." I just hoped and prayed that Richard would give it his best, and not make a hash of the job in any way.

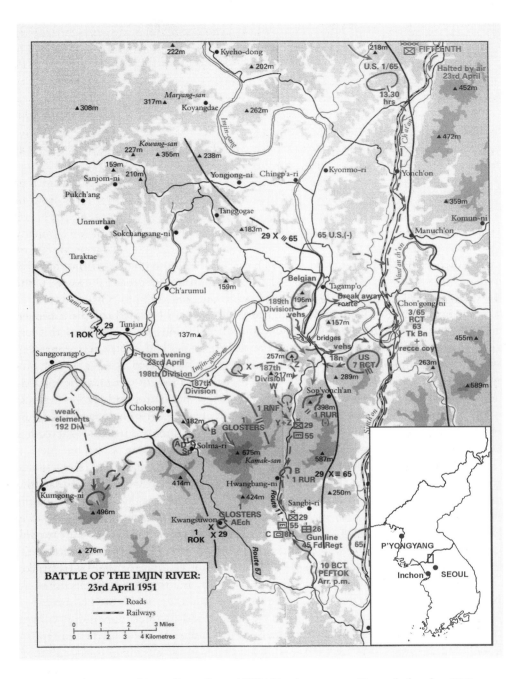

*Map of area around Sami-ch'on valley and Hill 159, where we spent 18 months from late 1951.*
*Courtesy of General Sir A Farrar-Hockley*

*Panorama of Samichon valley*

When Richard came to the OP to have a last minute chat with me, he was surprised to see Colonel Bill there. But the Colonel did not let on that he knew what was going on; he just told him he was on a quick visit, and asked him what his patrol task was for that night. Colonel Bill listened while Richard outlined the plan, and at the end of it he simply said, "Intriguing, and an ambitious ploy". I butted in that there was a good reason for choosing that target; gooks had been spotted nearby during the day, and it seemed pretty certain that it was being used as some sort of OP by the Chinese. "Good luck, Richard," the Colonel and I said in unison as he left the OP, and Richard grinned as he walked off to collect his patrol and start the great event. As Richard made his way across to the river, always a bit of a danger spot, and onwards towards the hut, he kept the OP informed of his progress using the tap code, and we were able to know the location of the patrol the whole time he was out there.

It was about 02:00 hours when a signal told us in the OP that the explosives had been placed round the hut, and half an hour later another signal indicated that the cable had been run out and connected. An OK from me meant that the patrol could fire the charge and make their escape back to the comparative safety of the company perimeter. All was ready; the OK signal was given and suddenly the whole valley was lit up as the straw-roofed hut was enveloped in flames. In the OP there were muttered words of congratulations and relief, but the job was not yet over. As the flames began to die down Richard decided that it was time to move, and the patrol, still mindful of the dangers down there in the valley, made its way cautiously towards the perimeter.

When they were safely back inside, Richard stood his men down after telling them what a "bloody good show" they had put up, and came up to the OP to report to me. He was surprised to see Colonel Bill still there, and it was obvious to us all that he was over the moon with his successful effort. The colonel was as ecstatic as me, because we alone knew that at last Richard had regained his shattered self-confidence. Colonel Bill told Richard that it had been a well-planned operation, excellently carried out, and in his opinion it was a superb performance. All of which, of course, was part of the plan to get Richard back on his feet again. But apart from the importance of this rather special patrol, the colonel was well aware that it was a typical example of what C Company was capable of, and he told me that I was commanding a good, reliable company which had displayed the enthusiasm and professionalism that he had expected of it when he had chosen me to succeed Hartley Gahan.

During the next few weeks, the Chinese appeared to have built up their artillery capability, and for many days they targeted each forward position in turn, from many different gun positions well behind their lines. This was not restricted to our sector; they were doing it all along the front and there was speculation that it might mean they were planning a big offensive. There was good reason to think so, as earlier intelligence reports had indicated that such an attack was very likely, hence the construction of the two complete defensive positions to the north of Seoul. Furthermore, there were reports coming in from air reconnaissance and South Korean infiltrators behind the Chinese line that troops were concentrating immediately opposite C Company. It was not surprising therefore that over a couple of days, the ranging suddenly increased in intensity, the centre of the enemy attention being focussed on Hill 159. On the first day of the increased shelling, company HQ area was bracketed and as luck would have it, the ranging began just as the ration truck arrived to deliver the 'compo' for the next two days.

A cockney corporal, Huxter by name, had jumped out of the truck to unload the boxes when the first shell landed a few yards from him. He had no time to take shelter, and a piece of shrapnel hit him, making a deep gash right across his buttocks. Huxter clasped his bottom with both hands, screaming, "Oh shit, I've lost me trade, I've lost me trade", and he leapt about, not knowing where to go. I had been in my dugout and looked out to see a sight which, had it been a burlesque on the stage, would have been screamingly funny.

"Poor sod," I thought, and rushed out to help the wounded man. Shiell and I applied a shell dressing to the profusely bleeding wound, and luckily it turned out to be not as serious as it had first seemed. It was only a flesh wound, but nevertheless the Medical Officer sent Huxter back to the Casualty Clearing Station to have it stitched, and he was soon back in action.

During the second day the increased shelling activity reached a peak, and it was not until after 16:00 hours that it quite quickly decreased, and within half an hour had ceased altogether. Divisional and Brigade HQ had been monitoring what was going on and they had come to the same conclusion as I had – that C Company was to be the main target for an assault. Colonel Bill spoke to me over the field telephone and told me that warnings had been received from higher up, and the probability was that soon after dark the Chinese would launch their attack. What was not clear was on how wide a front, and with what ultimate objective the assault would take place. It was likely that it was to be a muscle-flexing exercise to probe our defences and test the mettle of the United Nations forces. As most of the artillery ranging had been concentrated on C Company, this was the most probable. Whatever the answer might be, all of us in C Company knew that we were in for a very nasty night. Colonel Bill had wished me the best of luck, and said that he knew he could rely on my company to put up a good show. There was not a great deal of time left before stand-to, and I wanted to get round to see my platoon commanders and check that they were all in good heart and ready for the night's events.

First I walked over to talk to Anthony Millen, my supporting tank commander. He had just finished checking his fire plan, and greeted me with the words, "Well, let the little buggers come. I've got every possible line of approach to this hill covered with the Browning and my main gun is trained on the entrance to our re-entrant down there where they must close up before spreading out again to come up the hill. If Richard lets me know when they are coming through there, I will blast them with everything I've got."

*Company platoon commanders: (from the left) Brian Goss, Chris Hope and John Hibbert*

"Great stuff, Tony, that's what I like to hear. The men in good heart?" I asked, but I didn't get a reply as I saw Richard coming up from my forward 7 platoon position. "Well, Richard, everything ready?" I asked, and I was glad to get the same confident assurance that I had just had from Anthony. I walked down to the platoon area with Richard, and I spoke to a few of the men who were busy making sure their weapons were clean, bright and slightly oiled. We were all a little apprehensive knowing that the enemy guns had us in their sights, and had got our range precisely. Those moments waiting for a battle to begin were always fraught, whether you were waiting to be attacked or you were about to 'go over the top' and launch an attack on the enemy. Tense, anxious minutes ticked by, and before leaving, I took Richard to one side to have a quiet, private talk.

"You know the dice is about to be thrown, Richard, and some of us may not be around when the night's over, may we". It was not a question, but a statement of fact, and Richard answered by nodding his head. "Maybe you or me, or even both of us, will be wounded or killed, and if it happens to be you, is there any message you'd like me to give your parents?"

"Please tell them that I was thinking about them." Richard paused, but said no more. I said, "OK, please do the same for me."

The same brief conversation took place with both No. 8 and 9 platoon commanders, and as the light began to fade I went back to my OP to have a last look at the whole position, soon to be the battle area. Shiell brought my evening meal to me in the OP, and I tucked into it as though it was my last supper. Stand-to came and went, and the whole front became eerily quiet, save for the chorus of the ubiquitous cicadas and frogs. No distant crumps of incoming shells disturbed the peaceful valley, and it was all very ominous.

*C Company just out of the firing line: time for kit check*

# Chapter 22

## THE BOYS BECOME MEN

———

CSM Bailey came up to the OP soon after nine o'clock, and for a while we exchanged pleasantries. But the disquiet we were both feeling deep down was palpable, and at length I said "You know, sergeant major, the foreboding you get just before launching an attack is quite different to this, isn't it? Then you know what you are aiming at, and the moment the whistle blows, every man is intent on carrying out his part of the drill and if you get knocked out, so be it. This situation though is something none of us has ever experienced before, and we don't really know what to expect other than what we have read in the battle reports in *Stars and Stripes*. All we can do is to keep our heads down and wait for the blitz to finish. Then we must shake ourselves and be ready to take on the gooks hand to hand if they get that far. What do you think?"

"That's about the long and short of it, Sir," replied Bailey, and then we fell silent, both wondering how many of our company would come out of it in one piece.

After a short while of brooding silence, I said, "Well, any minute now I suppose. It's usually about this time when they open up somewhere along the front. Better get back to your gonker, CSM, and I'll see you after it's all over". Bailey bade me goodnight, and added, "Look after yourself, Sir", as he went back to his battle position behind the hill in company HQ area.

It was about an hour later, nearly half past ten, when I saw the lights behind the Chinese as the entire enemy artillery opened up. I had time to shout a warning to anyone who hadn't seen the fireworks display to get their heads down, before the whine of shells passing just above the skyline confirmed that we were right in the target area. Simultaneously, the ground shook as hundreds of missiles landed across the company position, some of them it seemed, almost on top of my OP. There was absolutely nothing I or anyone else could do about it except to crouch in the bottom of the trench and wait as salvo after salvo came crashing into C Company. I prayed as I had never prayed before, not even when there was just a minute or so before going over the top. As the shelling went on and on, we all grew weary of the shattering noise, the body-shaking crumps of exploding shells, and the fear that by the law of averages my trench would get a direct hit before much longer. Several thousands of shells had landed in the company area and I lost all sense of time, but eventually the noise stopped and I looked at my watch. The shelling had lasted for just over twenty minutes.

As I tentatively got to my feet, down in the valley I heard, faintly, the expected sound of bugles blowing as the Chinese infantry launched their attack. I was aware that my ears were buzzing loudly, and I hoped that the noise would go away soon. As the attack began, the Chinese lit up the whole battlefield with flares, and from my OP I could see the masses of enemy troops driving forward towards us across the low ground. At the same time self-propelled guns, which had been brought forward right to the edge of the Chinese positions across the valley during the shelling phase, opened up blasting their shells into the forward slopes of the company position. I seized the mike from my radio operator, and called for defensive fire on the pre-arranged targets in front of us. The Divisional artillery, a long way back, but nevertheless the target for heavy shelling from the Chinese big guns in a counter-battery role, had responded to the lifting of the saturation shelling of the forward positions, and were already standing to their guns when my message came through. Their response was immediate, and did a great deal to raise the spirits of our shell-shocked soldiers, and especially those in Richard's 7 platoon right in the sharp end.

Anthony Millen and his tank crew were engaging the enemy with everything they'd got and almost immediately we heard the shouting and cheering of the attacking Chinese as they threw themselves onto the defensive wire or blew themselves up in the protective minefields.

Wave after wave of screaming drug-crazed Chinese troops hurled themselves on the young soldiers of the KSLI, driven forward by pistol-waving women officers who were seen in the light of the flares to shoot some of their own wounded. Those following the leading assault waves used the bodies of their fallen comrades as bridges as they trampled over them and carried on through the mines and wire to attack on No 7 platoon, whose response was intense and prolonged. Back in the OP area we all knew that Richard and his men were putting up a tremendous fight, but suddenly they themselves were under close attack as a party of the enemy appeared on our right flank, having by-passed 7 platoon and infiltrated up a shallow valley right to the heart of the position.

All hell had been let loose as every man fought hand to hand, one of them even throwing empty beer bottles when his Sten gun jammed. The tank crew were back inside with the hatch securely battened down, but they continued to fire on their fixed lines to try to stop more Chinese coming through the gap. To both right and left I could hear heavy small-arms fire and the artillery DF fire was still coming down onto the selected target areas in the valley below. By now it was complete confusion as the battle swayed to and fro, and there was absolutely nothing I could do to influence it in any way. Every man was fighting his own local battle hand-to-hand with the tough and wily enemy, and it was up to each little group of soldiers to take on the

Chinese wherever they found them. During the shelling, down in Richard's platoon area, one trench had received a direct hit that had killed two of his men and left one badly wounded, but the rest had miraculously got away with only a bad shaking and temporary deafness. After three and a half hours, maybe a bit more, the Chinese had been held and had failed to achieve their objective. I cheered as I heard another bugle call, as I realised that the Chinese were withdrawing, for the time being at any rate. The artillery fire lifted to other planned targets further back across the valley that caught the enemy in disarray and added further to his casualties. I spoke to my platoon commanders and Anthony on the radio, told them they had done well, but the chances were that as the night was yet young, the gooks would probably try again. "Reorganise as quickly as you can", I told them, "and when you're ready, report back to me. If you want stretcher-bearers, call for them. We must get all the wounded out of the area as quickly as we can and we can deal with the dead chinks in the morning."

I then called up Colonel Bill and gave him a short sitrep. There was not a great deal I could tell him at that stage as the platoons had still to count their casualties, and until they had reported I could not say whether I would need to be reinforced by the reserve company. At present I thought we could hold out until daylight, even if there was another attack like the last one. The colonel was delighted with the news, but he realised that C Company had taken a hammering and he immediately put D Company on stand-by to move forward.

Meantime back in C Company, CSM Bailey came up to the OP and I asked him what the reverse side of our skyline looked like. "A bit of a shambles as far as I can see, Sir," he replied. "But I think we got away with it pretty lightly as most of the shells fell just behind HQ and landed somewhere between us and 8 and 9 platoons. I think your bunker took a direct hit, but it is still in reasonable condition. Shiell just told me that everything is covered with dust and is in a mess, but no real damage. He said to tell you that he hopes the rats have been frightened off and he'll be up with a cuppa shortly."

"Great", was my succinct reply. What I couldn't do to a cup of strong tea at that moment! The CSM left to get on with reorganising the HQ area, and a few minutes later the inimitable Gordon Shiell arrived with the life-saving beverage. He hadn't forgotten my radio operator either.

There had been casualties in all three platoons, and within an hour all the wounded had been evacuated to the Regimental Aid Post. Apart from the two soldiers who had been killed outright in Richard's platoon when their slit trench suffered a direct hit, two more of his men had been killed and several others were in a poor way with bayonet wounds inflicted during the hand-to-hand fighting. On the other hand, the attackers took a tremendous beating, and those they did not manage to drag back to the valley were dead men. The other platoons had also been engaged in close combat, but the main thrust had been against 7 platoon and company HQ. If the gooks had been able to drive Richard's men off their position, company HQ would have gone as well, and the Chinese would then have burst through in great numbers, spread out and rolled up the other two platoons, driving on to take the whole battalion position. It was thanks to the tremendous fight put up by Richard's men, supported by the tank crew and the company HQ defenders, in dealing with those enemy who did manage to infiltrate that the battalion front had remained intact.

I spoke to Colonel Bill on the radio as the land lines had all been destroyed by the shelling, and gave him an updated sitrep, confirming that I had reorganised, and that I did not need reinforcements. If they could be kept in reserve ready to counter-attack if the enemy made another attempt, I felt that would be the best way to deal with the situation. The colonel agreed and said, with some emotion, that he couldn't have expected any company in the "whole bloody army" to have put up a better show. I was delighted at this praise for my company, particularly as the main plank in the successful outcome of the battle had been my *protégé* Richard. I looked forward to writing to his parents to tell them how well he had done; furthermore, I would suggest to the Colonel that he be recommended for some sort of decoration. But I doubted whether Colonel Bill would need such a prod. From what I had said on the radio, he must surely have it in mind already.

The Chinese did not launch another attack during the night, and as the darkness slowly merged into dawn, the tired but proud men of C Company took up their stand-to positions. I noticed how strangely quiet the valley and, in fact, the whole area had become, for even the cicadas and frogs had stopped their nightly chorus soon after the shelling had ceased. When CSM Bailey came into the OP, I could only just hear what he was saying, and for some minutes I was scared that I had been made deaf by the dreadful noise of exploding shells earlier in the night. But the fact that I could still hear Bailey and could make out what he was saying, albeit with some difficulty, gave me reassurance that eventually my hearing would recover. This was confirmed by the medical officer during the morning when he came up to the position to check over any soldiers who had sustained minor wounds.

Soon after stand-down, I had a quick walk round the three platoons. The whole company area looked like a desolate wilderness; the azaleas had been stripped of their foliage and flowers, and the ground was pockmarked with many hundreds of small craters made by the twenty minutes of intensive shelling twelve hours earlier. It was a sad sight, but it struck me how very lucky we had been to have got off so lightly with only one direct hit on an occupied trench, although there had been many near misses. By the law of averages I had expected a lot more casualties than we'd received, and I quietly thanked God for guiding us through the night.

When Colonel Bill and Bob Garnet came up to see the damage soon after breakfast, I quickly assured them that my company had by no means had enough! We were all in good heart, and having done what we had done once, we were in no doubt that we could do it again – and again. After talking with several of the men in all three platoons, the colonel was satisfied, and I asked Bob Garnet to arrange for replacements

Tokyo, Monday, April 7, 1952     (KOREA EDITI

# ALLIES BEAT OFF ATTACK BY CHINESE

*In a tremendous barrage, "Long Toms," eight-inch howitzers and other heavy Allied artillery fired nearly 8000 shells as Chinese troops swarmed across a no-man's-land valley on the western front early yesterday morning.*

The Chinese pressed through the exploding shells to reach the barbed wire defences of one Allied position, but retreated as infantrymen bombarded them with grenades and small arms fire.

The Chinese left dead bodies strung in the barbed wire.

The Chinese attacked two positions following heavy Communist shelling with artillery and self-propelled guns.

Outposts were warned of the attack by the Chinese firing flare lights, shouting orders and moving equipment before they rushed down a hill in bright moonlight.

The "Long Toms" laid down 800 shells between the Chinese and Allied positions.

At the height of the attack, an Allied interpreter officer heard a Chinese officer shouting a command over the wireless: "Ignore the shelling. Advance and win medals for your country."

to be sent up from B Echelon immediately. It was vital that C Company be made up to strength and that the new men knew their way about before evening stand-to.

I was grateful for Colonel Bill's confidence, but after he and Bob had left the area, I went to my bunker to deal with a task that I always found emotional and tear-jerking – writing to the next of kin of those of my soldiers who had been killed. I prided myself on knowing some details of my men's families, so that I could relate to that knowledge when I had to write personal letters of sympathy. I found that Shiell had done a superb job of cleaning up, and I hardly noticed that my bunker had been hit only a few hours earlier.

"Well done," I exclaimed as I went to get out my writing things. "You've done a great job, thank you." I never forgot those two little words, which in my vocabulary were probably the most important in the book, and I knew how much they were appreciated when used at the right time.

I chose my words carefully, picturing the soldier alive, and tried to build an image of him in words that would, I hoped, do a little to soften the grief of his next of kin. This was not something I had been taught at Sandhurst or The School of Infantry; it was part of my nature, which had in many other ways endeared me to my soldiers. At last the letters were finished, and after reading them through with great care, I sealed them in their envelopes, ready for collection when the post corporal came up to deliver the incoming mail. As usual Shiell timed everything to perfection, and came in with a mug of tea just as I was putting my writing material away.

"That's that sad job done, Shiell," I said. "I hate having to write letters like these, but I'm sure they are appreciated at the other end."

Shiell looked into his mug, took a good mouthful, and agreed. "I'd like you to write to my Mum if I cop it, Sir," he said, "She'd be grateful for it, I know."

"Of course I would, but it's not going to happen. Must think positively, you know."

The conversation ended with the sound of a jeep coming up the slope to company HQ, and as my hearing was already beginning to recover, I heard CSM Bailey greeting the driver. The post corporal was always one of the most popular visitors, and never more so than after the company had gone through a traumatic night under heavy attack. Somehow a letter from home took the men out of themselves, and reminded them of better things to come when our stint in Korea would finally come to an end.

"There's one for you, Sir," shouted the CSM, and Shiell ran across to collect it. He waited around until he knew there wasn't a letter for him, and then came back to the bunker to give me my letter.

"None for me, Sir," he said, "and yours doesn't look all that interesting, does it?"

I looked at the buff envelope Shiell had handed to me, saw it was franked from the 'Commanding Officer, 1ˢᵗ Battalion The Herefordshire LI (TA)' and as he left the bunker I tore open the envelope with a feeling of deep misgiving.

# Chapter 23

## HELICOPTER RESCUE

———

My foreboding was not without good reason. The letter was typewritten, but it started in Lieutenant Colonel Bobby Armitstead's own handwriting: "Dear Maslen-Jones". The letter referred to the TA camp in South Wales the previous summer when the battalion had to deal with a limited Z reserve call up. No doubt I would remember, Colonel Armitstead went on, that I had been responsible for administering not only the pay, allowances and bounties for the TA personnel, but also the pay and allowances for the reservists as well. Yes, I remembered only too well. I'd had just one TA Regimental Quartermaster Sergeant and a clerk to help me with that enormous task. I reckoned I had done a good job, and as far as I knew there had been no comebacks. It had all gone smoothly, although I received not one word of praise from my commanding officer. But then I hadn't expected any considering the clash of our two personalities. I read on. The Command Paymaster had now completed his audit of the regimental accounts for the camp, and found a discrepancy of £78.

"In the circumstances, as you were personally responsible for the money, I must ask you to let me have a cheque for that amount which I will forward to the Paymaster." I was dumbfounded.

"What a rotten bastard," I muttered to himself, as my gorge rose. There I was, stuck in a bunker in Korea, feeling anything but cheerful having just finished writing to grieving parents whose boys had been killed during the night, having been awake for the past thirty-six hours, and my *bête-noir* had sent me that demand. One thing was certain: I wasn't bloody well paying it.

I was utterly choked off, and decided to show the letter to Colonel Bill. I went into the signals bunker, and asked if the landline had been repaired yet. "Not all of it", I was told, "but we have comms with battalion HQ".

"Great", I replied, "put me through to the adjutant, please."

Bob picked up the phone, and I told him I wished to see the Colonel as soon as I could. "Hang on a sec, Bob, I'll find out when he can see you," he replied. Two minutes later I was ordering my jeep to come up from B Echelon to take me down to see Colonel Bill.

The Colonel's reaction was as vitriolic as mine had been. "What a dreadful letter," he said, "but then that's what I would have expected from that man. What on earth does he think his Commanding Officer's fund is for if not to deal with a situation like this. We'll fight this, Bob, and you mustn't pay anything. I'll inform the Brigade Commander straight away, as this clearly affects you personally and I will not accept this sort of treatment when the battalion is involved in this bloody war. Forget it, Bob, get back to your company now and get ready for whatever the coming night may have in store for us."

I was almost moved to tears. £78 was not a very big sum in the context of the £28 000 I'd had to pay out for so many different accounts, but to me it was a fair slice of my monthly pay cheque. "Thank God I've got a Commanding Officer like Colonel Bill. What a super chap he really is," I said to myself as I was driven back to my company HQ. "I reckon I'll go anywhere, do anything, as long as he's in command."

Before stand-to, I once again went round to see my platoon commanders and to chat to as many of my men as I could. I came back to company HQ greatly heartened and sat down to unburden some of my thoughts on CSM Bailey. I told him about the demand for payment of £78, and how Colonel Bill had promised to take up the cudgels on my behalf. Bailey had known the Colonel a lot longer than I had, and he just said, "But that's why this is such a bloody good battalion. The men think the world of him, Sir."

I told him how proud I was of my company. "I brought some of those young National Service men out to this Godforsaken place, and I wondered how we would shape up to the sort of ordeal by fire we were subjected to last night. I have to admit that I was shit-scared, Sergeant Major, but those kids performed miracles. Talking to us now, they don't seem to be the same boys I brought out here. Suddenly, in the space of a few hours of sheer hell, the boys have become men." It was true, and I was much more at peace with myself knowing now that I could ask my men to do almost impossible things, and they would not let me down. I had worked hard to create a good team in my company, and following our performance during the digging operation during the summer only a few weeks ago, our successful repulse of the massed assault last night proved that I had succeeded.

It was time for evening stand-to, but everything was very quiet and peaceful all along the Sami-ch'on valley, and nobody expected anything to happen. I sent out a few small listening patrols, but after a short time it became clear that the Chinese were nursing their wounds; from their side there was no patrol activity at all. Most of our soldiers were able to catch up on a lot of lost sleep from the previous night, and the following days were spent repairing bunkers. After their defeat at our hands, the Chinese showed no sign of preparing for another attempt to break through on this sector held by the Commonwealth division but further west, the American Marines were involved in some very tough fighting for a feature called The Hook. If the Chinese were going to achieve a breakthrough, it must be before the winter set in and froze everything solid. But the Marines were as good as their reputation, and the line held. Meantime at Panmunjon the peace talks were still meeting every go-slow tactic in the Chinese book, and whilst the negotiations dragged slowly on the fighting was reduced to routine patrolling by both sides on the ground and bombing and straffing of selected targets by the United Nations air forces.

It was then October, and the battalion was issued with special winter clothing. During the previous winter, when the United Nations troops had been pitched into Korea at very short notice, we had to make do with ordinary battle-dress uniform and great coats and any woollen jerseys and mufflers which people back in Britain provided for us. It had all been very ad hoc, and the ordinary issue boots were far from adequate to keep feet from freezing. The issue of new arctic clothing and boots (cold, wet and windy) was more than welcome. Long Johns with slits both back and front caused some amusement, but it was explained that the men would soon realise how essential the back slit was when squatting in an icy gale blowing in from Siberia. Such winds could freeze the bollocks off a brass monkey, let alone a human being! But the arctic winter was still some weeks away, and daytime temperatures were for the most part quite warm and pleasant.

It was on one such day that I was sitting in my OP studying the valley and Chinese positions to the north. A squadron of American fighter bombers from a US Navy aircraft carrier, on station off the port of Inchon in the Yellow Sea, flew over on one of their routine missions to take out some enemy position of armour or guns. The attack took place out of my sight and sound, but one of the planes soon came back, flying very low and trailing smoke. It was heading straight towards us, but was still way out across the valley over the Chinese lines. It was obvious that it was losing height so quickly that there was no chance of it even reaching the valley, and while I kept my binoculars on the plane, I picked up my field telephone and rang Bob Garnet to tell him what was happening but in the meantime the pilot ejected and the plane crashed into enemy territory. Bob said he would come up and 'watch the fun' but first he radioed Brigade HQ and gave them the map reference of where the pilot had landed.

In the meantime, another of the American planes had come on the scene and was circling above the crash area, monitoring what was happening on the ground. I saw the pilot of the crashed aircraft land on the forward slope of the enemy position, and as he released himself from his parachute harness, two armed Chinese soldiers appeared from a trench and made towards him. He had the sense not to take on two men armed with rifles when all he had was a pistol, and was taken prisoner. His captors, prodding him with their bayonets, led him to the trench they had emerged from. I could see that for some reason the three men did not move once they were in the trench, and what in fact the gooks were doing was disarming and then stripping the American of anything of value such as his pen and watch. Another American plane now joined the first, but the Chinese soldiers kept jabbing the unfortunate pilot to prevent him jumping up and waving to them to show that he was alive.

Back in the OP, Bob arrived ten minutes or so after I had last spoken to him, and together we watched the drama developing. Bob kept in radio contact with Brigade HQ and was told that the Americans were sending in a helicopter to try to rescue the captured pilot. Surprisingly the Chinese made no effort to take their captive further away from the front line, and they were still in the same position in the trench when I heard the rescue helicopter flying directly towards us. As it dropped down almost to ground level, the co-pilot fired a few shots in the direction of the trench, and the Chinese could be seen jabbering to each other, momentarily forgetting to keep an eye on their prisoner. They had started to walk crouched down along the trench, and the captive pilot, seeing his chance, ran in the opposite direction and then jumped out of the trench. He raced down the slope towards the valley, and the helicopter pilot, seeing what was happening, flew down to hover only a few feet above the escaping pilot. Meantime the Chinese had realised that they had lost their man, and started after him, firing their rifles from the hip as they ran down the slope. The helicopter crew fired at them again, which gave just enough time for the escaping pilot to grab one of the bars used to support exterior stretchers, and we watched him swing one leg up and just manage to get his foot on one of the cabin steps. The helicopter pilot whirled the aircraft up and away from the hill with the crashed pilot hanging on with his hands and one foot! They flew across the valley and landed by my HQ area, got the chap inside the cabin, thanked us for passing on the information so quickly, shook hands all round, and flew off to deliver the lucky man back on board the aircraft carrier. It had been an exciting interlude in what was becoming a rather humdrum existence.

# Copter Tears Flyer From Communist Grasp

**Capt William Smart is back in Japan for a rest after a thrilling hour and a half behind Communist lines that ended when he grabbed hold of a hovering helicopter and was whisked out of Chinese hands to safety.**

The adventure began when he was shot down and immediately captured by two Communist soldiers while on an operation flight from the Navy escort carrier, USS Bairoko. He parachuted on to a hillside where he jumped into one of a number of trenches.

"Then a Communist soldier with a rifle slipped up behind me," said Capt Smart. "He called out something in his language and a second soldier approached. This one was a mean-looking fellow. His rifle had a bayonet on it, too, and he walked over to disarm me, threatening me with his weapon and a hand-grenade. He jabbed me with his bayonet as he took my weapon, watches and the rest of my personal belongings.

"The first enemy soldier stood with his rifle pointed at me. These two seemed quite perturbed when they found only one fountain pen but they were happy when they found two watches!"

American planes continued to circle overhead but Capt Smart was well jabbed with bayonets to keep him from getting up and waving to them.

"I was alone with the Communists for about 45 minutes when a helicopter appeared. As it came lower, someone in the machine fired a few shots in our direction. The Communist soldiers started jabbering and motioned to me to stay where I was.

"I knew it was the right moment when the soldiers turned their backs on me and started walking in a crouch down the trench. I went off in the opposite direction and then jumped out. Waving to the helicopter to follow me, I ran down the crest of the hill. Someone in the helicopter fired again at the Communists.

"The helicopter was low enough for me to grab a bar, which is used to support exterior litters, and I swung one foot up on a step. Then the pilot whirled the helicopter up and away from the hill with me hanging on with one hand and a foot. When we were a safe distance away, I put a sling around me and then they pulled me into the machine."
—AP.

# Chapter 24

## UNDER FRIENDLY FIRE

As the battalion settled down for the winter, everything became more organised and every man in the company had a hot shower, courtesy of the mobile bath unit, and a clean change of clothes every week. This did much to maintain morale, and was a pleasure we all looked forward to. Another development was the building of a semi dug-in church with a straw roof back in the battalion HQ area, where the padre held services every Sunday. For those so inclined it was a much-needed refuge, and was greatly appreciated. I attended service regularly and I was pleased to note that Richard usually accompanied me. Whether it was the force of example by their officers, or the fact that many of the soldiers began to realise they had so much to be thankful for, the numbers attending service steadily increased as the winter dragged on.

## FOXHOLE CHURCH ON KOREA FRONT

### BRITONS' HANDIWORK

WITH THE COMMONWEALTH DIVISION, KOREA, Wednesday.

Men of the King's Shropshire Light Infantry have built themselves an underground church in a snow-covered Korean hill-side. Straw packing from the beer rations has been used to thatch part of the roof above ground, and the windows are old celluloid map covers.

The church bell, which will sound through valleys where gunfire often echoes, is a captured Chinese action alarm bell. The pews are of logs and sand bags, set on the mud floor.

Capt. R. O. Wood, Church of England padre, said to-day he would celebrate Holy Communion in the church for the first time next Sunday. During the week soldiers could use it as a reading and writing room.

"We have had 10 churches, but this is the first time we have built, or rather dug, a foxhole church. We are proud of it."—Reuter.

*St Chad's church, a much-needed refuge behind the frontline in Sami-ch'on*

Inevitably, people living so closely together under such conditions tended to get on each other's nerves. I tried to keep out of arguments with my platoon commanders as much as I could, but one of them in particular, John Ballenden, seemed to relish stirring it up, and would argue vehemently just for the hell of it. One especially lively argument took place one day when an American plane, which had been crippled by anti-aircraft fire before the pilot had released his bombs, was limping back to his carrier off the port of Inchon aware that he was going to have to jettison his bombs before attempting to land. Unfortunately, he chose to pull the stick perilously close to John's platoon area, and the exploding bombs straddled the dugouts in which his men were resting. No one was harmed in any way, other than shock, but Lieutenant John Ballenden came storming up to me, cursing the Americans and using abusive language usually associated with the gutter, and it called for the greatest restraint on my part not to get too involved. I thought that the pilot had probably been wounded when his plane had been hit, and that he really did not know where he was when he ditched his bombs. I could not calm John, but I was as attentive as possible since after all he had very nearly lost his platoon.

"So what are you going to do about it?" John challenged me.

"I will report the incident and at least find out why the bombs were dropped on our company area. What else do you suggest I should do? Calm down, John", I told him.

A short time later, armed with the information I needed, I went over to see John, and was able to tell him that the American pilot had managed to land his aircraft safely on the carrier, but that he had, as I suspected, been so badly wounded that he had no idea he was over friendly territory when he jettisoned his bombs. But worst of all, the pilot had been bleeding badly from a shattered foot and it was a miracle that he was still alive. John had the grace to apologise for his outburst, and I took the chance to remind him that we were fighting a war, and things like this were to be expected now and then in the heat of battle. Such incidents soon came to be known as 'friendly fire'. The lesson sunk in, for John never again tried to cross swords with me.

The Chinese were adept at using loudspeakers for propaganda purposes, and they frequently broadcast intimidating messages to the United Nations troops who attempted to ignore them. Occasionally one of their messages got a humorous answer. For example, the 'lady' announcer warned us, in perfect English, "We're coming over to get you". Quickly as a flash came the reply from Private Bagley, in a loud cockney accent, "If you do, bring your own bottle!" It is doubtful if the Chinese heard the reply, but it caused great amusement in the battalion, and the 'party' was brought to an abrupt end by salvoes of mortar bombs aimed at the loudspeaker that had been spotted by one of my sentries.

By Christmas, Korea was firmly in the grip of winter, and the troops were feeling the benefit of our special kit. There was very little serious activity anywhere, but it was

## Bottle Party

A repeat performance by the Chinese propagandists in front of the Commonwealth Division happened last week.

Through a megaphone in perfect English came the warning: "We're coming over to get you."

Quickly came the reply in a loud Cockney voice: "If you do, bring your own bottle."

Rapid mortar and shell fire brought the performance to an end.

essential to maintain dominance over the Sami-ch'on valley and although Colonel Bill decided not to rotate the company positions, each company took it in turns to do the necessary patrols. That way the men were sometimes able to get a full night's sleep and after our exertions during the summer this was more than welcome. There could be no great celebration at Christmas, and it had to be limited to some beer and a good turkey dinner by arrangement with the American Marines, which happened to be on their menu almost every day! For a few days before Christmas, the Chinese loudspeakers started up again and constantly played seasonal music and carols. Whether they thought this would make the British soldiers homesick and undermine their morale remained a mystery, but in fact it had exactly the opposite effect and the men thoroughly enjoyed it. This time though, no mortars were fired at the speakers.

Sometime during the night in the small hours of Christmas Day, when the patrol in front of C Company had been provided by D Company, a Chinese patrol crept up to our perimeter and threw Christmas cards over the wire. The card was a small white one, with a simple message.

"Devious people these Chinese," I had commented to CSM Bailey, "But if my company's patrols had been out there last night, I'd want to know how the hell the Chinks were allowed to get so close to us". I didn't want to stir anything up, but made a note to mention my concern to D Company commander. He didn't take it too kindly!

*Greetings*
*from*
*The Chinese People's*
*Volunteers*

KOREA 1951

*Christmas card from the enemy*

# Chapter 25

## THE FINAL PATROL

———

For some weeks rumours had been getting round that the battalion was soon going to be relieved and sent home, and it was the best news we could have had when the official 'warning order' was received. The date for handing over to the incoming battalion was to be 14th September and naturally there was a feeling of great anticipation. Colonel Bill held an early 'O' group when he laid down an outline plan to prepare for the move, but the one thing he stressed above all else was that there must be no slackening off and that the battalion must continue patrolling at the same high standard until the last patrol on the last night was back inside its company perimeter. This message was impressed on all ranks, and I knew that as far as C Company was concerned my men would do just that.

With a little less than a month to go, there would be a risk that the men might relax, and both CSM Bailey and I were fully aware of that and the danger involved if it were to happen. I kept up my routine of staying awake as long as a patrol was still out, but the nights had begun to drag and with such desperately low temperatures prevailing it was difficult to keep even reasonably warm during the small hours. Shiell as always rose to the occasion and kept me well supplied with a hot brew, and often he would sit with me and have a mugful himself. We talked about home and what we intended to do on our well earned leave. As far as I was concerned, once we were on the ship at Pusan, I would get out my books and cram like hell for the Staff College exam which I was expecting to sit in the spring. It would be my last chance to get to Camberley as the following year I would be over the age limit. Shiell for the first time told me about his family and how much he admired and loved his mother who had brought him and his elder brother up on a shoestring and had sometimes gone without herself so that she could give the boys something they badly needed. He was an all-round sportsman, but I had realised that from his superb physique.

During one of these long night vigils soon after the news of our relief had broken, Shiell asked me if he could go out on a patrol. He'd had to put up with some snide remarks about his cushy billet as the company commander's batman, amongst which was the suggestion that he was chicken.

"It will only be for one night, Sir", Shiell had pleaded, and although I hated my routine being disrupted, I saw how much he wanted to go.

"OK", I said, "but you must arrange for someone to bring me my tea during the night while you are out there freezing to death!"

We laughed together, but he was clearly delighted and thanked me for agreeing. CSM Bailey arranged for Shiell to do his patrol at the end of the following week, and in the meantime routine patrolling went on as usual.

The weather got colder still and an extremely bitter spell set in, making it increasingly difficult for the men to lie on ground that was deep frozen, without moving about to keep the circulation going. If they did so, they could easily give their position away to an enemy patrol that might be nearby. A few nights before Shiell was due to go out, a radio message from Corporal Prescott who was in an ambush position some way out in the valley, simply asked permission to return to the company perimeter as "we are freezing to the ground". I could well believe it; I was cold enough inside my bunker, and I knew it must be sheer hell out there. "If you really can't stick it any longer, come back. But take care, and report to me as soon as you get in." There was a reason for this; I wanted to see the evidence of his complaint. I had no real doubt, as Corporal Prescott was a good and reliable NCO, but Colonel Bill or Bob Garnet might ask me why I had allowed the patrol to come in early, and I wanted a ready answer. When the corporal came into the bunker Shiell had the tea ready and the shivering man soon started to warm up a bit. I immediately saw what I wanted: pieces of grass and rushes frozen to his Parka jacket that had been torn from the ground when he got up from his ambush position. "Well, was it really bad out there tonight, corporal?" I asked.

"Yes, sir", replied Prescott. "It was so cold that we lost all feeling in our hands, and if we'd needed to fire our weapons, we just couldn't have done it. Apart from that, the deep cold was penetrating right inside us and I was afraid that maybe one or other of us might not be able to get up again."

"You did the right thing, corporal," I said. "No point in staying out there in those conditions, but you must realise that these patrols are not of my volition. We must continue, otherwise the Chinks will seize the initiative and all we have done for the past weeks will be lost. There are only a few patrols left now, so go and get some sleep if you can. All your men all right are they?"

"Yes sir, they all turned in before I came to report, sir."

"OK. Good night corporal Prescott."

When he had gone, Shiell laughingly said that he wished he hadn't volunteered to do a patrol after all, but as Corporal Prescott was going to be his commander on that night, he now felt more confident in his leadership. "You'll be all right with him, Shiell, have no fear about that," I told him, and we both turned in to our freezing bedding rolls.

When Corporal Prescott reported to me for his patrol briefing, I told him that I didn't want him to do anything unduly risky, but there was always an element of chance every time a patrol stepped outside the perimeter defences. There was only a week to go before our relief, and I particularly wanted Gordon Shiell to do his patrol safely and be able to hold his head up amongst his peers. The biting wind had eased off somewhat during the last couple of days, and it was nothing like as cold as it had been on Corporal Prescott's last patrol. But nevertheless I had decided that static ambush patrols were out as far as I was concerned, and it would be better to keep the patrols moving stealthily round a given route. The briefing over, I wished the corporal good luck, but as I watched them go I had an uneasy premonition. However, I usually got that worried feeling and it was never until the last patrols were in that I felt at ease with myself.

The patrol was to be out in the valley for about four hours, and at various reporting locations the corporal was told to send a tap signal, and also to tap twice every fifteen minutes. After the last reporting point it would take some twenty minutes for the patrol to reach the perimeter, and right on schedule the final fifteen-minute reporting tap came through on the radio. I called my stand-in batman to start getting the tea ready and, as I waited, I heard an explosion somewhere fairly close in. "Probably a mortar shell or someone letting off a grenade," I thought, but deep down I suddenly felt a chill as though there was a presence in my bunker. "Pull yourself together, man", I said to myself, and then the field telephone rang.

"Richard here, Sir," he began, and as I listened he told me there seemed to have been some sort of mine explosion just in front of his position. I asked him if there was any sign of the patrol yet, but Richard had no news of it.

"OK, leave it for a few minutes," I said, "maybe they've already come back inside the position", but secretly I didn't think they had. "Richard, you'd better wait fifteen minutes, then go and have a careful look but don't go outside the wire. Its maybe a trap; just do what you can and let me know." Richard 'wilcoed' the instruction and I sat back to wait with my thoughts and fears, alone and anxious.

Some twenty minutes later Richard was on the line again. "Very bad news," he began, "I can't say exactly what happened, but literally only a few feet outside the wire some sort of jumping jack anti-personnel mine seems to have gone off and I'm afraid the three men in the patrol are all dead. The corporal is in complete shock, and I can't get any sense out of him. He has no injuries himself, and there seem to be no shrapnel or other wounds on the three men. Must have been a blast bomb". I was hardly listening, but I thanked Richard and told him not to do anything more until after stand-down which would be in an hour and a half. I then went over to tell CSM Bailey the devastating news.

So near to our relief, and one of the dead was my own batman who needn't have been there anyway. It all seemed so unlucky. Bailey knew how I was feeling. He knew that Shiell and I had been a good team and had complete empathy with each other, and as far as I was concerned I would be lost without my right-hand man. He didn't try to say anything sympathetic for he realised that words are pretty meaningless at a time like that.

"I'll arrange to get the bodies back here as soon as there's enough light, sir," he said.

"Yes, Sergeant Major, please do that. I'll let them know at battalion HQ, and we can arrange for evacuation. I'll also want the MO up here as soon as possible to see to Corporal Prescott. I'll go and do that now."

We parted company and still not believing what had happened, I went to my bunker and for some minutes buried my head in my pillow. Soon CSM Bailey came into the bunker to tell me it was stand-to time, and conscious that the show had to go on, I put on my parka and went out into the cold of another Asian dawn. "God, how I hate this bloody place," I said as I went up to the OP. It was a bleak and unhappy hour and neither I nor Bailey said more than a few perfunctory words to each other. Both knew that we might break down, and it was better for the time being to keep our thoughts to ourselves. As usual, shortly before stand-down, Bailey said he would go and get the brew going. "Put in plenty of grog", I said.

At that time of the day, the human spirit is usually at its nadir, and I prepared myself for the horrors that I knew were soon to be unfolded. The first act was when Corporal Prescott was brought back to company HQ. As soon as Richard had told me that he was leaving 7 platoon position, I called the MO, who came straight up from the RAP to see what could be done with him. Captain Hooper, RAMC, and CSM Bailey came into the bunker with the corporal, and the MO asked him if he could say what had happened. By now Prescott had a good grip, and although he was still finding it difficult to control himself, he told us that the first man had already entered the gap in the wire, followed by the other two, and he was bringing up the rear. As far as he could make out, the first man must have tripped over a wire and triggered a jumping jack that had been planted just to one side of the track. It exploded at head height just as the second man was level with it, and all three of them took the full blast on the right side of their heads. They were killed instantly. The corporal himself had been a few feet behind, keeping a careful watch to the rear of the patrol in case they had been followed, and apart from the shock wave from the blast-bomb, he suffered no damage other than temporary deafness that was easing off.

"I think that the gooks must have seen us go out, and then crept in to lay the device so that we would trigger it off as we returned at the end of the patrol", said Prescott. "It certainly couldn't have been there when we went out, could it?"

"No, it couldn't", I agreed, "and it would be well nigh impossible to spot the trip wire in the dark. You just have to give it them, it was a hideously clever ambush, very skilfully carried out, and I cannot blame you or any of the others for what has happened."

Captain Hooper, the MO, took Prescott away with him to keep him under observation for a while, though by then Prescott protested that he was OK and wanted to stay with his section – or what was left of it. I told CSM Bailey to let me know when the bodies of the three men had been recovered, and in the meantime I told Bob Garnet what had happened. Colonel Bill came on the line in due course and told me that in his view no blame could be attached to anyone. It was just "bloody bad luck". Then came the worst part of the whole business, when Bailey came in to say that the three bodies were ready to be taken back to battalion HQ. I swallowed, said "Oh my God," and followed my CSM out of the bunker. There, lying side by side were my three young soldiers, with one or two of our colleagues standing round in complete silence, shattered by this appalling tragedy. I looked at each one in turn, remembering some little thing about them, but when I came to Gordon Shiell, I knew that I wouldn't be able to contain my grief much longer. "These three young men look so peaceful, I'm sure they are just asleep", I thought to myself. But as I looked at each of their faces in turn, I could see that they had been ever so slightly blasted out of shape – the only physical sign of any injury. They had been cut down in the prime of their lives, and before very long their families would all be devastated when the news reached them from the War Office. "Thank you, Sergeant Major", I said. "Carry on, please. I have some letters to write." I bowed my head as I walked away to my bunker, and the tears began to course down my puckering face.

In the quiet of my bunker I wept a little. I knew from past experience that trying to bottle up one's emotions was not a good thing, and it was much better to let it out. After a while I got out my writing things, and started to write the usual letters of sympathy to the families. Only one of them, private Jim Smiles who was nicknamed Smiler, was married, and as far as I knew he had no children. Privates Walker and Gordon Shiell were both unmarried, and I dealt with them first, telling their parents what excellent soldiers they had been and that I was proud to have had them in my company. Writing to a young widow was a bit more difficult, but eventually I was satisfied that I had written the right sort of letters to both parents and to the widow. I hoped they would believe what I was telling them, as in every respect I was telling the truth and not trying to ease their pain with half-truths or exaggerations. I also wondered if my letters would help to ease the inevitable grief the parents would feel when they arrived through their letterboxes.

The letters written, I called for my jeep and went down to see Colonel Bill in the Mess. A drink – a good stiff pink gin – was what I needed now, so that I would be better able to take the sympathetic remarks of my brother officers. I handed the three letters to the Mess Sergeant and asked him to make sure they were in the outgoing mail that day. Time was all-important if the letters were to achieve their full purpose.

I managed to get through lunch, but my world had temporarily fallen apart, and I was hardly aware of what I was eating. My thoughts were elsewhere for the moment, but I knew that I would soon snap out of it, and although that night my company was not providing the patrols, I felt that I must be seen to be back in command of events when I returned to my company HQ. I left battalion HQ soon after lunch, and after dismissing my jeep driver, I walked down to speak to Richard and my other two platoon commanders, in a sense to 'show the flag'. I was happy to see that Richard seemed to be less affected by the previous night's events than I might have expected. The other two were in reasonably good heart, but John as usual couldn't avoid expressing his views about the patrolling policy under such diabolical conditions. I was not to be drawn, and merely reminded him that there were only three more nights' patrolling for C Company and we must sweat it out and not slip up at the last hurdle.

I then went to talk with the CSM, and brought up the question of a replacement batman. I felt it would be a waste of time to take on a National Serviceman that would only be a short-term measure, and if possible I would like a time serving soldier who would be with me during the next year when the battalion would be in 11$^{th}$ Armoured Division in Germany. I wanted a reliable man so that together we could lead the company through what I imagined would be an intensive period of training from Battalion to Divisional level. Bailey had already given some thought to this during the day, and he thought that Private Roden would be ideal if he would accept the job. "Please ask him, Sergeant Major, and if he says yes, I'll have a talk with him." The following day CSM Bailey told me that Roden had immediately accepted the position and he had him outside if I would like to interview him. "That was quick work. Yes, I'd like to see what he expects from the job," I said. "Please bring him in, Sergeant Major."

I knew the man, but only as a soldier who was always smart and well turned out, and who kept a clean sheet. He had never done anything particularly noteworthy, but on the other hand he was a good steady chap. The two of us talked for a while and I learned that Charlie Roden came from Church Eaton, near Stafford, was not married, but had a girlfriend whose parents did not approve of him because his father was a council road sweeper. Surprisingly he wanted me to know that he supported the Tories, and back in England he read the Daily Telegraph. I must have shown some surprise, and Roden quickly added that he wanted to better himself and that was the best way to do it.

"Well, Roden," I said, "I'm interested in what you've told me, and I think we should get on well together. But don't expect me to get involved in arguing politics, will you?" Roden laughed quietly and promised that he wouldn't do that unless I started it.

"Well, we'll give it a go, and I'd like you to start tomorrow morning, if that's all right with you, Sergeant Major?"

"Yes, sir", said Bailey, thankful that that job was satisfactorily dealt with. "Will you tell Mr Ballenden or shall I?"

"I think I should tell him, Sergeant Major. No officers like losing their better men, do they?" I left Roden in no doubt that I expected much of him. And so it was all arranged that we started as officer and batman the next morning.

# Chapter 26

## WELCOME HOME

———

From now on it was all bustle as the battalion prepared to hand over the position to the 1ˢᵗ Battalion Durham Light Infantry and move out. Remembering how filthy the position was when we took it over, I ordered my men to leave it as clean as we could, and before handing over to the relieving company I personally inspected every dugout and trench, and was delighted with the response to my bidding. Cleanliness might be next to Godliness as my mother used to tell me, but it was also the outward and visible sign of a well-disciplined unit, and nothing but the best would be good enough for another Light Infantry battalion

The handover went without a hitch; I showed the new company commander round the position, and explained the geography of the valley and Chinese positions to the north. I also briefed him about the patrolling policy and as he had no experience of this kind of warfare I asked him if he would like me to tell him a bit about the habits of the Chinks. He was anxious to get all the background information he could, as he had already heard how well C Company had done throughout the year and a half we had been there. I told CSM Bailey to send the men down to battalion HQ and I spent an extra half hour in the OP until CSM Bailey reminded me the company was embussed and waiting at battalion HQ to leave. The Major and I wished each other the best of luck, and I took one last brief look around my company position, especially at the path through the wire where only a few days earlier Gordon Shiell and the two other young soldiers had been so tragically killed, turned towards my jeep, now being driven by the new company commander's driver, and for the last time I was driven down the slope to battalion HQ.

It was a tremendous relief knowing that I would never again be returning to that place with its evil memories, and I was filled with the sadness I would always feel when I thought of the many weeks we had spent facing everything the Chinese and dreadful weather could throw at us, of the men who had been wounded and of those who wouldn't be going home with the rest of the company. And as I was driven along the rutted track, I was mindful not least that my God, in whom I believed devoutly, had brought me through my ordeal in one piece, and I was thankful. As soon as I arrived at the lorries, the RSM reported that the convoy was ready to move off, and asked "Permission to leave, Sir?" I was the last company commander to leave, and I replied, "Yes, please, Regimental Sergeant Major, let's get going." The drive to the railhead in Seoul was uneventful, and as soon as the convoy arrived, the company embarked in the troop train for the overnight journey to Pusan where we arrived in time for breakfast.

Before being lorried to the quayside where our troopship was ready for the battalion to embark, we were taken to the United Nations Military Cemetery just outside Pusan to bid farewell to 56 officers and men of the battalion who had been killed or were missing in action during our long stay in Korea. The cemetery was carefully tended and at the entrance the flags of all the United Nations that had sent troops to take part in the war against the Communists flapped limply in a light breeze. Inside the gates there were serried rows of neat white gravestones bearing the details of each soldier buried underneath. Between the graves there was well-mown lawn, truly a peaceful place to be laid to rest. Not far away, to the north, rugged hills formed a protective background in keeping with the countryside where the men had fought and died.

The battalion was marched in and formed up for the farewell service that was to be conducted by the senior Padre of the Commonwealth Division. Caps were removed, and the service began with that most emotional of Remembrance hymns,

"O valiant hearts, who to your glory came, Through dust and conflict and through battle flame, Tranquil you lie, your knightly virtue proved, Your memory hallowed in the land you loved."

The lesson was read by Colonel Bill and the Last Post was sounded by the battalion buglers, the final notes appearing to be echoing back from the surrounding hills. Complete quiet fell upon the cemetery while the thoughts of everyone present dwelt on our comrades who lay buried in front of us, or whose resting places were still unknown. After two minutes, the buglers sounded Reveille, which brought minds back to the scene in front of us. Colonel Bill laid the first wreath at the base of the Union Jack flagpole, followed by RSM Rocky Knight and private Davidson, A Company, who had been with the battalion since it had arrived in Korea. The final hymn was one of my favourites and gave everyone the opportunity to lift their heads and sing lustily. It was of course,

"Guide me, O Thou great Redeemer, Pilgrim through this barren land ..."

Some were still too choked to sing, but I managed to get through it all and I felt the better for it. After the service had ended, the battalion was allowed half an hour to walk round the gravestones to pay their respects to the fallen, and I took the opportunity to photograph the stones of the men who had been killed during my time commanding C Company. I would make sure, when I got back to the UK, that a copy would be sent to the next of kin of each of them.

The battalion was then taken to the transit camp near the docks where we were given lunch, after which we embarked on the *Empire Trooper*, a troopship run by P&O. Soon afterwards we were on our way home with the Regimental band, recently employed in the line as stretcher-bearers, playing us out of Pusan. Other troopships and cargo vessels blew their sirens in a cacophony of sound until the *Empire Trooper* was clear of the harbour.

It was an uneventful and calm journey home, during which I spent most of my time reading up for the Staff College Entrance exam which I anticipated sitting, as far as I knew, about the middle of March. As the *Empire Trooper* passed through the Straits of Gibraltar, it suddenly seemed that it had all been a bad dream, and we were about to wake up at home. Only two days to go, and the whole battalion was a mass of smiling faces. The excitement was tangible, and grew by the hour until at last we were tied up in Southampton. The Colonel of the Regiment, Major General John Grover, and other dignitaries were there to meet the battalion, and whilst we were waiting to be disembarked into a troop train standing on the quayside, the General spoke to us over the tannoy system, welcoming us home and thanking us all for enhancing the already proud record of the Regiment. He then met the officers in the ship's lounge, and chatted informally with us all. The actual home-coming was almost over, and when the officers had joined the rest of the battalion, the troop train slowly pulled out of the docks and steamed away to Lichfield, from where we were lorried to Whittington Barracks, a short distance outside the town.

As soon as we had settled in, Colonel Bill called an O group to tell company commanders the plans for the next two days. Firstly he announced that as soon as they had been fed, the men would be allowed to go into town, but he warned that any unseemly behaviour would be dealt with very severely indeed. Secondly, as had been expected, two days later the battalion would be feted by the County of Shropshire and following a service in Saint Chad's Church in Shrewsbury we would march past the Lord Lieutenant. The following day the battalion would be taken to Hereford in buses, and following a service in the Cathedral we would march past the Lord Lieutenant of Herefordshire *en route* for the Shirehall where the whole battalion would be given a sit-down meal. On our return to Whittington Barracks, the men due for leave would be free to go.

Immediately after the O group, I told CSM Bailey to parade the whole company so that I could speak to them collectively, probably for the last time before we all went on leave. Some of the National Service men were due for 'demob' and they would be civilians again before the rest returned from their month's leave. I briefed the company about the plans for the next two days, and passed on Colonel Bill's warning about drunken behaviour if the men went on the town that night. I then thanked them all for their performance during the time I had commanded C Company, and told them that I hoped we would do even better during the coming year in Germany. The parade was dismissed.

I went to the Mess to telephone my parents. They already knew about the Welcome Home parades but couldn't be there to watch them as Dad had a full list in the theatre and Mum, being so short, knew she wouldn't be able to cope with the crowds and would probably not even get a glimpse of me. It was arranged that Dad would drive over to the barracks after the Hereford parade at about 5:00 pm and bring me home for a celebration dinner with family and friends. I had dinner in the Mess and having decided not to go out I enjoyed a few drams with some of the others before turning in for an early night. The next day every man spent most of the time cleaning his equipment and making sure that he would be properly turned out for the march past the Lord Lieutenant in Shrewsbury. The day passed slowly as the men were anxious to start their leave that would last over Christmas, and get home to see their families and girlfriends. At last it was evening and we all knew that in 48 hours we would be in our own homes. Human nature being what it is, some would not want to talk about their experiences, while others would tell their stories with gusto, especially in the pubs – a ploy that always produced plenty of free pints and often resulted in the soldier drinking too much.

The day of the Shrewsbury Welcome Home celebration broke fine and warm for the time of year. It was all very exciting and moving and once again I thanked God for bringing us all home safely, and prayed for those left behind. The next day the weather was still fine, and on arrival in Hereford, the battalion marched to the Cathedral for the Thanksgiving Service after which we marched past the Lord Lieutenant of Herefordshire, Sir Richard Cotterel, whom I had known quite well during my time as TA adjutant. As I shouted my command "Eyes right!" to C Company I found myself looking straight into the eyes of Anne, my erstwhile girlfriend who was standing just behind her father, Sir Richard. She smiled, but I had other things to think about, and in a few more steps I shouted, "C Company, eyes front".

Soon afterwards we were all inside the Shire Hall enjoying a pre-lunch drink. The other ranks were all given beer courtesy of local breweries, and the sergeants and officers each had their drinks in separate rooms. Many retired members of the regiment came to enjoy the fun and to talk to the officers, and I was soon in animated conversation with someone whom I had never met before. One of the other company commanders, a pre-war regular officer for whom I had little time, joined in and the retired officer was asking many questions about the motivation of the men and so forth.

"Tell me," he said, "how did you explain to your chaps what they were fighting for?"

*Welcome home parades in Hereford, 1953*

I was just about to tell him I did it by talking to small groups of my men when the opportunity provided, when the other Major puckered his moustache and bombastically replied, "We never tried. Just told them what to do and to get on with it."

I blanched with anger. No wonder, I thought, that when one of his patrols wanted help after blundering into a minefield, he was asleep and unable to do anything about it. But I bit my tongue and turned away. As I did so, a uniformed porter approached me.

"Major Maslen-Jones?" he asked.

"Yes, that's me", I replied. "What is it?"

"There's a young chap at the entrance who wants to see you." I looked at my watch; there were still ten minutes before we would be going into the main hall for lunch.

"OK, lead me to him, please." I said and putting down my glass of sherry I followed the messenger to the front of the building where there were still many people chatting in small groups. At the bottom of the steps there was a young man standing alone, and when he saw the messenger and me coming towards him he walked up to us. I thanked the messenger who went back inside the Shirehall, and I then looked at what I thought was a ghost. I must have gone quite white as I looked at the mirror image of Gordon Shiell.

"Major Maslen-Jones?" said the young man, his voice so like my old batman's.
"Yes, that's me", I replied.

"I'm Bill Shiell, Gordon's elder brother. Mum wanted to meet you, so I've driven her over from Leicester to see the parade. She's sitting over there on that bench".

Bill and I went across to speak to her, and the lady got up, her hand outstretched. I shook it, and did not let go. I felt the warmth of that grieving mother and it was an experience I had never had before. I looked at her, and saw her exactly as Gordon had described. She showed the unmistakeable signs of having worked hard all her life, but she also showed that she was a very proud woman. Her coat, I noticed, was some sort of fur that had seen better days, but I knew at once that it was her best. She wore a hat that was sadly outdated, but she held her head high.

"I had to come to thank you for your lovely letter about Gordon," she said. "He was such a good boy, and he was so proud to be your batman, and a member of the regiment too," she went on. "I know you must have other things to do in there, so I won't keep you, but now I've seen you and said thank you, I can go home."

All the bad memories of that hellhole where we spent a year and a half came flooding back, choking me. I hugged her, for a moment or two unable to find any words. At last I said, "Yes, Gordon was a splendid young man, and I was proud to have had him as my batman. So often the best men are the ones who get killed, and that was certainly so with Gordon. You have paid me a great compliment by coming all this way to see me, and I will never forget it".

Mrs Shiell and Bill said they must be going as they had to get home in time to get Dad's tea. I shook hands with both of them, and we turned to go our separate ways. I was still emotional after such an unexpected meeting when I went back to join the other officers, and I struggled to show a cheerful face. I couldn't help thinking that in Mrs Shiell I had just met someone who was the true backbone of the British nation.

The lunch was a success, and thankfully the speeches by the Lord Lieutenant, welcoming the battalion home, and Colonel Bill's reply, were short and to the point. After returning to Whittington barracks to pick up their kit and travel warrants, the men going on leave were taken to the station to wait for their various trains. Having seen my men off, I had gone up to my room to collect my gear while Roden went down to fetch his travel warrant from the orderly room. There were still a few men around when Dad drove into the barracks and he didn't know who to ask where to find me. He saw a young soldier walking across the barrack square, and got out of the car to ask him. Dad was very impressed that the one man he should ask knew exactly where Major Maslen-Jones was, and even offered to take him to me! "My boy must be popular", he thought, but before they got to my room, the soldier had admitted that he was my new batman. Roden loaded the kit into the car, and I wished him a very enjoyable leave, adding, "Don't do anything I wouldn't". As Dad drove me out of the barracks, Roden saluted, to which I returned a somewhat perfunctory one from the passenger seat. As the miles sped by on the way home I did most of the talking and Dad felt eternally grateful that his boy had come safely through it all once again. It was the end of another chapter; I had climbed another ladder, but on this one, apart from my late commanding officer in the 1st Battalion Herefordshire Light Infantry TA, who had still tried to knock me down from halfway across the world, the only snakes I had come up against had been lethal yellow ones. I had come through it all unscathed and wondered what the future had in store for me.

# Chapter 27

## THE LIMITS OF TOLERANCE

———

As Dad drove me home, he gave me an update on what had been happening locally during the 18 months I had been away. Uppermost in my mind, however, was the fact that I had only one more chance to take the Staff College Entrance exam and get the coveted 'PSC' tag. I had already sat the exam once, but missed my second and third chances (on the first occasion because of illness, and the previous year because I was fighting in Korea). In May I would reach the upper age limit, and I was well aware that unless I passed the exam in March and was given a vacancy at the college, there would be very little hope of reaching the higher echelons of command. I made up my mind that until mid-March I would make the Staff College exam my top priority and although I fancied living it up a bit after so long away from home, I decided to limit myself to enjoying just one or two parties with my special friends before getting my head down. I had already booked myself on the pre-Staff College course at Saighton Camp in Chester, after which there would be just two weeks left to revise before the exam at the beginning of March.

On 12th February, the battalion was sent on embarkation leave to reassemble at Whittington Barracks early in March. When I returned to the barracks after my leave, I was told that a senior and somewhat pear-shaped major, who had conveniently been posted to a cushy staff job before the battalion had sailed for Hong Kong, had taken over command of my company. I had been demoted to Intelligence Officer pending the arrival of the new Commanding Officer after the battalion had settled into its new location in BAOR.

The battalion was going to be stationed in Göttingen, a small university town near Hildersheim. It was located close to the border with East Germany, commonly known as the Iron Curtain. There was a requirement for a Secret Room, permanently under guard, in which were held the necessary maps and orders for the evacuation of all BAOR service and civilian personnel if the Russians were to launch an attack on the West. An officer was to be in sole charge of the Secret Room, and Colonel Bill planned that I should have this job as a sort of 'super' Intelligence Officer. The course in Chester had been extremely useful to me, and when I sat the exam I found that most of the questions fell neatly into the subjects I had covered most thoroughly. I felt that I had probably passed reasonably well, and I must now wait until the results were published in mid-summer.

Colonel Bill included me in the advance party, with Major Guy Thorneycroft in command, and we were to prepare to take over from the Royal Irish Fusiliers on 19th March. After a long weekend leave, we left Whittington Barracks by train on 15th March. The journey was uneventful, the ferry crossing from Harwich to Flushing quite calm, and we arrived in Göttingen late afternoon on 16th March. After a good meal in the Mess, Major Guy and I turned in early, and were awoken the following morning by the pipe band of the Fusiliers marching round the barracks to celebrate St Patricks Day!

There were no problems preparing for the arrival of the battalion, and it was after dark on 19th March when the local British Resident, Brigadier Kenchington, and Brigadier Peddie came to welcome the battalion. A few days later it was time for Colonel Bill to hand over to Lt Colonel C James, whom I had been warned about by Captain Barnes, Adjutant of Oundle School OTC, when I met him at an old boys' reunion soon after the end of the war.

Barnes had asked me if I had met C James yet, and when I said no, he simply said, "He was at school here you know, in your house actually, and he must have been the most unpopular boy who ever set foot in the place". He had been much more explicit and I had pondered about this conversation during the intervening years, but as no one ever mentioned his name I had come to the conclusion that he must have left the Army. Now he had surfaced out of the blue and stories began to spread through the Officers' Mess about his past. I chose to ignore most of what I heard about him, but I certainly had misgivings about a 'new broom' whom it seemed had not served with troops for a number of years but who on the other hand had a reputation of being a good staff officer.

The moment I was introduced to my new Commanding Officer, I took an instant dislike to him. This was out of character for me, but there was something I didn't like about the man and I remembered all too clearly what Captain Barnes had told me. As was my way, I would make every effort to get on well with Colonel James, who accepted Colonel Bill's plan for me to be the 'super IO'. The Secret Room job did not take up very much of my time, and Colonel James decided to dispense with a second IO. What he didn't appear to have realised, however, was that a major part of the super IO's responsibilities would be to liaise closely with units on either side of the battalion. These included the South Wales Borderers, on the left, and an American regiment on the right. Before long I was arranging joint patrols along the Iron Curtain with the US 14th Armoured Cavalry. Each patrol had its Regimental Band to boost the morale of the local inhabitants in a big public relations exercise, with a joint concert in the border town of Duderstadt. My American colleagues and I soon became very friendly and I frequently flew along the frontier in an L19 light aircraft or a two-seater 'bubble' helicopter, piloted by Major Ike Strange, to see what the Russians were up to on the other side of the border. It was part of the fun to see rifles being aimed at us, but sometimes not so funny to realise that we were actually being fired at.

*KSLI border patrol commanded by Lieutenant John Ogden presenting arms*
*to motorised patrol from US 14th Armoured Cavalry*

*14th Armoured Cavalry patrol returning the salute*

*"How d'ya start this goddam machine?"*

*Waiting patiently for the helicopter to start: (from the left) Captain Crick Grundy,
Major Keith Heard, myself and Brigadier Curtis*

Unfortunately Colonel James soon expressed his dislike of all this fraternisation; for some reason he had a manic dislike, hatred almost, of the Americans, and I mentioned this to Keith Heard, the senior major in the Mess one night and learned quite a lot about the colonel's service career. He told me it was eight years since he had actually served with troops, having been removed from command of a battalion in the Burma campaign because of nervous exhaustion. The American General Patton had another word for that! But whether what I had been told was true or not, the long summer of training from battalion to Army exercises would certainly put him to the test.

Although it did not bode well for our future relationship, I had no intention whatsoever of compromising on the border patrols. I never discussed the colonel's previous service with him on what were to become quite frequent excursions and exercises together during the summer, and I chose not to believe everything I heard. Stories of that sort very soon became grossly exaggerated and I felt that it was a pity that all the senior married pre-war officers were living in quarters and seldom appeared in the Mess. They had all known James since before the war, and would have been able to put the record straight in a number of ways, but whether it was to show him a degree of respect and support they usually referred to him by his first name. As time went on, I began to find this pseudo-affectionate form of address increasingly offensive to me as I felt our relationship becoming steadily more and more tense.

I soon realised that one of the reasons for the growing rift between Colonel James and his officers was his insane jealousy that he had not been in Korea. It was anathema to him to hear his officers discussing their time in action in Korea but not be able to join in himself. He found it unbearable to be in command of an infantry battalion that had been in Korea for longer than any other in the British Army and which had covered itself with glory, thereby enhancing the already fine record of the Shropshires. There was justifiably much concern in the Mess about this, and before long there was an almost universal growing dislike of Colonel James' huge chip on his shoulder. He clearly felt out of place and was determined to rebuild the battalion as he remembered it before the war, "to lick it into shape" with sport, especially polo, hockey (in which he excelled) and shooting. This unhappy situation was greatly resented by those officers who had fought in Korea and soon became apparent to the soldiers. I watched from the sidelines as what had been a self-confident, happy, highly-tuned and very professional fighting battalion slipped into a below-average one. As Colonel James's right-hand man during the training period I knew that my job was to listen to what was going on, but not to get involved (although it later transpired that the Colonel suspected me of doing so anyway). As the second senior officer living in the Mess, I could not escape my responsibility to show respect and complete loyalty to my commanding officer, the way I had been brought up by my father.

For the first few weeks of our time in Germany, the battalion was occupied mainly in basic training at platoon and company level. Battalion exercises were to begin in June, and thereafter Brigade and Divisional exercises would follow, leading ultimately in late summer to The Big One – the Army manoeuvres – which would last for two weeks. In between these exercises, I carried on with my border patrol programme, but I was becoming increasingly troubled by what I observed happening amongst some of the junior officers. It all came to light when a young second-lieutenant named Jason Atkins asked if he could see me privately as he had a personal problem and needed advice. I was somewhat mystified why this young officer should choose me rather than the senior major or his own company commander to discuss his problems. I felt that I'd enough on my plate trying to get on with the Colonel, but I agreed to hear what he had to say. He told me he had been persuaded to play Bridge and as time went on the stakes were getting higher and higher and although all winnings and losses by individual officers were supposed to be entered in the Bridge Book, Jason said that the sums were frequently falsified downwards. I asked him how much he was losing and he replied that it was far too much and more than he could possibly afford.

"More than your monthly pay?" I asked.

"Yes sir, and I'm running into heavy debt which I just cannot pay".

As he told his story, Jason became more and more embarrassed and it was clear that there was something more he wanted to tell me, but he couldn't bring himself to do so. It was obvious to me that he was in deeper trouble than he had revealed, and I was left to work things out for myself. Jason had mentioned the name of the officer, Captain Crowe, who was insisting that Jason paid his debts in full. This officer had an extremely unenviable reputation and I asked Jason if he had been compromised by him in any way. It was a long shot, but it hit home and Jason broke down and cried a little. I didn't press the question and he went on, "I'm not that sort of person. It's all so filthy, and he has got me into a situation I just cannot escape from". I felt incensed that an officer in my Regiment could stoop so low, and I was genuinely very sorry for Jason, although in my opinion he had been stupid and weak to have let things get so out of hand.

I thought through the options open to him, but one thing was clear; it had to stop at once otherwise the cancer would spread through the Mess and possibly even through the battalion. Jason would inevitably have to leave the battalion; his position would be untenable as news of what had happened would very quickly become known amongst the soldiers who, through snide remarks and obviously directed body language, would make his life a misery. The fewer people who knew what was going on the better, and I offered to discuss the matter with the senior major Keith Heard. Jason was not sure that he wanted me to do that, and I told him to think about it very seriously and to let me know if he wanted me to take the matter further for him. I never knew what he finally decided to do, although when the other officer concerned was questioned, he admitted amongst other things he had been expelled from a large public school in the Home Counties. It also became known that he had run up huge debts with a local bookmaker in Shrewsbury from which the regiment was in no position to bail him out, and he was invited to resign his commission.

It was not long before the battalion exercises began and as his Intelligence Officer I found myself constantly at Colonel James's side. Having quite recently done the Company Commanders course at the School of Infantry in Warminster, and then commanded C Company in action in Korea, it was not surprising that the colonel frequently asked me if I agreed with his plans. Unless I could see a very good reason why I didn't like his plan, I would tacitly agree, and we managed to get through the early exercises with comparatively little trouble. However, deep within me I soon detected a lack of confidence in the colonel that I put down to a lack of regimental soldiering during the last few years. I therefore did my best to help where and when I thought he would accept it. In the end the battalion did remarkably well in those large scale exercises and Colonel James came out of it all with considerable kudos.

*2nd Lieutenant Chris Ballenden and I in Duderstadt*

Before the first exercise, I had been invited to join the Independence Day celebrations in Wiesbaden where the 14th Armoured Cavalry was stationed. The commanding officer of the cavalry, Brigadier Tim Roberts, whom I had met on more than one occasion during the border patrol programme, asked me to invite Colonel James to come along as well, and although at first he refused to have anything to do with the Americans, I eventually persuaded him that he really ought to come with me. We went down to the American base in the Colonel's staff car, and it was a journey that I was not to forget. From the moment we left Göttingen, Colonel James appeared very ill at ease and he sat on the forward edge of the rear seat with his cane gripped in both hands between his knees, nervously twisting it round and round. To make conversation possible, I had to sit right forward as well, which I found excruciatingly uncomfortable. Instead of being able to have a sensible conversation on the two-hour journey, the Colonel constantly asked me what Brigadier Roberts was like, how he should address him, and what he should say. He seemed to be a bundle of nerves and it became clearer than ever that there must have been good reason for the rumours that he had been removed from command of troops towards the end of the war.

We were warmly welcomed by my American friends, and I introduced the Colonel to all of those I knew well. Throughout the evening I kept an eye on him and made sure that he was not left on his own, frequently coming back to introduce him to some other Americans. Why on earth, I wondered, would any one want to talk to such a dreary person whose body-language made it abundantly clear that he was not enjoying himself one little bit? At last the party was over, and the Colonel and I started our return journey to Göttingen. He had made no attempt to find Brigadier Roberts to thank him and say goodbye, and he couldn't get back into the car quickly enough. The journey was frigid, and I realised that my hopes of some sort of improvement in our relationship had come to nought.

Brigade exercises had now begun, and as Intelligence Officer, I was once again Colonel James' right-hand man. All went well as we prepared our operational plan and the Brigadier declared that it was quite first class and that the KSLI had secured their objective well ahead of the flank battalions; this would have greatly assisted them in gaining their own respective objectives as well. Lt Colonel C James positively beamed with delight. His position was secure, but in his mind there was a small nugget of fear that I had rumbled him and knew his weakness, and I wondered how far I could now trust him. But until the end of the Army manoeuvres, I could not risk falling out with him, or my position might well be compromised.

Divisional and Army exercises all went much the same way and on our return to barracks, I found a signal from the Brigadier congratulating me on passing the Staff College Entrance Exam. There was one other officer in the Brigade who had taken the exam, a Staff Captain in Brigade HQ. I had never met him, but I found out that he had been an ADC to a senior General, and that he was some three years younger than me, and could, therefore, still have three more attempts to pass the exam if he failed this time. A few days later I was told that my name was close to the top of the list and the young captain's name was well below. On the strength of this a few of us went out to celebrate at the Officers' club as it seemed pretty certain that I would be given a vacancy. I celebrated too well, and was very sick.

In between the various exercises, I had to liaise with the senior Frontier Constabulary officer in Duderstadt and my visits normally involved the two of us enjoying supper together in the local Gasthaus with large T-bone steaks, washed down with excellent German beer while we planned the programme for the morale-boosting patrols and band concerts for the next few weeks. Shortly before the Brigade exercise, I had made one of those visits, and on that occasion I decided to go alone in a Volkswagon Beetle driven by an employed German civilian driver. On the way back, I dozed in the back of the little saloon, but something made me sense that we were no longer on the route back to the barracks. I became immediately alert, quietly took my loaded Smith and Wesson pistol out of its holster, and watched very carefully to see where I was being driven. It wasn't long before we passed the sign of a village that I knew led straight over the border, and where, at the far end of the village, there was a Russian checkpoint. I did not hesitate, and pressed the muzzle of my revolver into the back of the driver's neck and ordered him to stop and turn around. The German had no option, and not until we were safely back at the battalion Guard Room in Göttingen did I relax. I told the guard commander to make a note of all relevant details about the man and then let him go home. The next morning I reported the incident to the agent in charge of all civilian employees, who said that the man concerned would be sacked immediately. But he was nowhere to be seen, and he never turned up for work at the barracks again. I was convinced that this man, seeing me dozing on the back seat, decided to go for some easy money by taking me to the check point and handing me over to the Russians. It was a lucky escape, and I learned to take the Cold War more seriously.

Before the Army manoeuvres were due to begin, Colonel James told me that the Brigade rifle meeting was going to take place soon after the end of the exercise. As I had shot in the Army team at Bisley and for Great Britain in the 'Free Rifle' event in the 1948 Olympic Games, he wanted me to captain the battalion team. I had little idea who were the best shots in the battalion, and in the short time we had available to practise, I could only rely on the company sergeant-majors to provide me with some names. As it happened there were only two free days for me to take some twenty men on the range and put them through their paces. Of those who seemed to be the most promising shots I selected a team of eight with two reserves, but it would be pot luck how they would perform individually on the day, and I was particularly concerned about the falling-plate competition. This involved two teams, each of eight men with ten rounds, running side-by-side 200 yards down the range, adopting the prone position and firing rapidly at eight steel plates lodged in the sand in front of the butts. The team to knock down the most plates within a given time would be the winner. I had taken part in this competition many times before and had firm ideas about how the team should carry it out. Some experts would say that we should sprint flat-out over the 200 yards, while others preferred to run down at a steady pace so that they would not be completely out of breath when they reached the firing point. I had always preferred the latter and I instructed the team to do it that way.

In the meantime I saw very little of the Colonel, but as our relationship seemed to be deteriorating somewhat after working so closely during a long and arduous summer, it had become obvious to me that I would have to leave the battalion sooner rather than later. My expectation that I would be going to Camberley in a month or so filled me with hope that I could put up with the Colonel until then, but I could never have believed what was about to happen. My father had, when we were out walking together once, warned me about what he called life's game of snakes and ladders. Every ladder was a stage in one's life: at school, university, and at every stage of one's career. Starting at the bottom, each ladder had to be climbed and on reaching the top there was another ladder waiting. But on every ladder there would be snakes lying in wait to throw you back to the bottom and one had to start all over again. Never did I think that his words of wisdom might apply to me, but how wrong I was.

It all started at the Brigade rifle meeting, which was quite a social event with officers and soldiers with their families all mingling together and enjoying the festive atmosphere of a school sports day. On the 600 yards firing point the Brigade staff manned the statistics office, and it was around the large score boards that the supporters of the competing units gathered.

My team had acquitted itself well enough in the individual practices and were well up with the leaders. Everything now depended on the Falling Plate competition that was the last event in the programme. In the first round we were drawn against a Cavalry regiment which sprinted down the range, leaving my team several yards behind them. The Cavalry knocked their last plate down a split second ahead of us, and this effectively knocked us out of the competition. As we picked up our empty cartridge cases, I told my team not to worry too much, they had carried out the competition as we had practised it but it had not worked on this occasion. We turned to go back to join the party round the score boards, only to see our Commanding Officer storming down the range towards us. As he approached, I could see that under his peaked Service Dress cap, his face was as black as thunder and his anger was apparent by his body language and the way he was hitting his leg with his cane.

"Oh, oh, here comes trouble," I said, "Let me handle this". I saluted as Colonel James stopped in front of us, but I did not get a response, just a shower of abuse.

"You are all an absolute bloody disgrace to the Regiment," he screeched, "All bloody idle, every one of you. How dare you let a Cavalry regiment see the Light Infantry off the range".

"Permission to speak, please Sir?" I asked.

"Go on then", he shouted back at me.

"I take full responsibility for the way we carried out the practice, Colonel," I said. "The men did exactly as I told them to, and that is the way I have always been trained to do it myself. We were beaten, but these men did their best with the absolute minimum of training time."

The Colonel screeched again. "You are the most disloyal officer I've ever had to serve with and you'll hear more about this, Maslen-Jones. The best thing you can do is to get this bloody shower back to barracks and out of my sight."

"Is that all, Colonel?" I said, and saluted as I sensed that this paranoid and obscene little man was about to turn away. Once again he did not return my salute and after waiting until he had walked half way back to the crowd at the other end of the range, I broke the dismal silence by saying, "Well, you heard all that. I take the blame, but don't let it get to you. He's just like that; it's a personal thing between him and me." I felt entitled to say just that and no more, and we walked silently back to get our kit together before going back to barracks.

I was absolutely furious and felt utterly humiliated that Colonel James had made such a damning accusation of disloyalty against me, a commissioned officer, in front of men under my command. It was unforgivable and as we approached the officers' tent I began to understand more clearly what Captain Barnes had meant when he asked me if I had yet met Patrick James when we met in Oundle soon after the war had ended. The adrenalin was pouring through my body as I entered the officers' tent. It was a 180 lb tent, open at one end, and I went to the far end to take off my equipment. In sheer frustration I threw it on the ground, muttering the 'f' word. Right at that moment, the Colonel walked past the open end of the tent. Unfortunately, he had seen my gesture that was not meant to be seen by *anyone*, least of all by him, but the damage had been done and I feared the worst. It was not long in coming.

I had by now lost all interest in the Brigade Rifle meeting and how our team had fared. I knew that we had done well in individual events, but I'd had high hopes of winning the whole competition. A few minutes later, just as I was leaving to go back to barracks, Neil Fletcher came into the tent.

"Bob", he said, "what on earth has happened? The Colonel is almost out of control with anger and wants to see you by the scoreboards immediately."

I told the adjutant exactly what had happened, tidied myself up as best I could and followed Neil to see the Colonel. I came to attention, saluted smartly, and said, "I believe you want to see me, Sir".

I realised at that moment that Colonel James had deliberately set me up so that he could publicly humiliate me in front of as large a number of people as possible. Regardless of the fact that we were surrounded by the throng of spectators, Colonel James shouted his reply, intending the whole world to hear what he had to say. "I saw your insolent gesture in the tent just now, and I will not tolerate that sort of insubordination. You are the most disloyal officer I have ever had under my command, and if there is any repetition I will have you out of the Regiment before you know what has hit you. Is that understood?" I was aware that I had flushed from my neck upwards, and that every one within earshot had fallen silent to listen to that dreadful outburst. I had been given a severe dressing down in front of officers and other ranks and their families alike, and my humiliation was complete. I was as furious as the Colonel himself and only by exercising the utmost self control did I avoid actually fulminating and telling this damnable little man just what I and most of his officers thought of him.

For two pins I would have made matters worse by hitting him in the face, but my self-control was far better than his, and I merely asked, "Is that all Colonel?" There was no reply, just a look of intense hatred, so I turned about and walked away. Neil Fletcher followed me to the tent and told me that I had managed the incident in the only way possible, and he promised to try to pacify the Colonel. But I was beyond caring; as far as I was concerned my time would shortly be up anyway and very soon I would be off to the Staff College.

Three days later I was walking through Göttingen when I met the Brigade Intelligence Officer. He was a young French Lieutenant on an exchange posting, whom I quite liked.

"Hullo, Bob," he greeted me. "We're so glad you are coming to Brigade as Staff Captain."

I swallowed hard. "But I'm not," I replied. "I'm going to the Staff College next month so what's the point in going to Brigade HQ?"

Francois then told me "Haven't you heard? You didn't get a vacancy". I then asked him whether Captain Somerset had got a vacancy and he said he had, and that I was going to Brigade as his replacement. "I think your CO had something to do with it as we all understood that you were definitely going to the Staff College".

I was outraged. I said *au revoir* to Francois and went straight back to barracks to see the Adjutant. "I've just been told by someone in Brigade HQ that I am being posted there immediately, and that I haven't got a vacancy at Camberley. Is this true?" I asked.

"I'm afraid it is, but hasn't the Colonel told you?" Neil replied. "He told me he wanted to break the news to you himself."

"Neil, you know he wouldn't have the guts to do that, so why didn't you forewarn me? Anyway, I'm not going and that's that."

Neil then told me that it had all been arranged between the Colonel and the Brigade Commander, to which I replied I could not possibly work under the Brigadier any more than I could carry on under Colonel James. The situation had become totally untenable. The adjutant, wishing to draw this very unpleasant interview to a close, told me that whatever I said, I would be going to Brigade and that was the end of the matter. I said yet again that I would not go and swept out of the office. I was incandescent and crossed the Barrack Square beside myself with anger. I went to my room where I spent some time thinking of the implications of what had happened. The one thing I was certain of was that if he had not already done so, Colonel James would give me a severely adverse confidential report that would ultimately be filed away and held against me if I was ever to be considered for higher command. Therefore, to all intents and purposes my career in the Army was at an end; there would be no point in soldiering on and the sooner I got away from this dreadful scenario, the better. I took out a piece of notepaper and there and then wrote out my resignation as a commissioned officer. I returned to the Adjutant's office, threw the letter on the desk in front of Neil Fletcher, and said, "And that's bloody well why I refuse to go to Brigade. I also wish to apply for two weeks compassionate leave as from now".

My letter of resignation was a little white lie. I claimed that I was needed to run the family farm, whereas in reality the farm I had in mind belonged to my brother Ted, whose marriage was on the rocks. Only a week or two earlier he had written to tell me that he was planning to sell the farm and go into the commercial side of agriculture. It now seemed like a gift from Heaven, and while I realised I was stretching the truth somewhat, in reality the story was basically true. It was never questioned, but what I had never given a thought to was that if I served for only another six months, I would qualify for a pension, small though it was. In the event I would get an almost insulting gratuity of only £1350, but such was my state of mind at the time that nothing mattered except to get away from the only man I had ever actually hated.

I went on leave that afternoon, and when I returned to the battalion, I was posted to a rifle company while the company commander was away on a course. I suddenly found an immense amount of friendliness and sympathy from my brother officers in the Mess, who thought the way I had been treated was utterly despicable. Within two and a half weeks, my resignation had been accepted and I returned to the depot for final documentation before leaving the Army. During the last few days with the battalion, I had absolutely no contact with the Colonel who studiously avoided me, and on my final night in the Mess I was dined out by my brother officers. The Colonel did not attend, much to my relief, but my many friends made up for this barbed and spiteful insult and I was given a great send-off. It would be a lie to pretend that I was not deeply affected by it all.

At no time since that dreadful outburst at the Brigade Rifle meeting had Colonel James spoken to me, so that I did not have the opportunity to ask him what the Mess would like as a leaving present from me. It would have made me feel just a little bit smug to rise above the meanness and spite of the Colonel, but it was not to be like that. I had to wait until I arrived home, and then I wrote a courteous letter to Colonel James to which I received a very brusque reply suggesting that a decent copy of *A Shropshire Lad* would be welcome. I duly sent an expensive edition of the book to him, but it was never acknowledged, neither did it ever grace the shelves of the Mess library. On my way home, I thought back over what was undoubtedly the unhappiest period of my life. I already knew that I had been too precipitate in resigning my commission, but the die was cast and come what may I now had to face the hard world outside the close comradeship of the Regiment in which I had been so proud to serve. It was strange, I pondered, how in the Army one's whole life depended on having a fair-minded Commanding Officer. Clashing personalities were bound to happen in civilian life too, but I hoped dearly that they would not affect me as had those between myself and Colonels Armitstead and James, and I looked forward to having as my friends people like Bill Barlow and Ian Beddows.

My final visit to the regimental depot was quite short, and it was made clear that my decision to leave the Army was much regretted by all who knew me. I received a number of letters from erstwhile fellow officers all expressing their regrets in one form or another, and I also had a remarkably kind letter from the Colonel of the Regiment, Major General John Grover. While no one actually said as much, I was left in no doubt that Colonel James was the most disliked officer in the Regiment, and of course the story about his treatment of me at the Brigade Rifle meeting became common knowledge. No one believed that the reason for my resignation was because I was needed on the family farm, and a great deal of sympathy was expressed for the impossible position I had found myself in. I wished 'if only' as I drove away from the barracks for the last time. But it was not a time for regrets. I had made my bed and now I had to lie on it for better or worse, likewise for richer or poorer. The future lay in my own hands, and I was determined to prove that I had made the right decision even though at that moment I knew how much I would miss Army life. As I made my way homewards the old chapter came to an end and a totally new book was already beginning.